# UNDERSTANDING INFORMATION SYSTEMS

## What They Do and Why We Need Them

**LEE RATZAN**

AMERICAN LIBRARY ASSOCIATION

Chicago    2004

Composition and design by ALA Editions in Times New Roman and Optima, using QuarkXPress 5.0 on a PC platform

Printed on 50-pound white offset, a pH-neutral stock, and bound in 10-point coated cover stock by Victor Graphics

The paper used in this publication meets the minimum requirements of American National Standard for Information Sciences—Permanence of Paper for Printed Library Materials, ANSI Z39.48-1992.⊚

**Library of Congress Cataloging-in-Publication Data**

Ratzan, Lee.
    Understanding information systems : what they do and why we need them /
Lee Ratzan.
        p.   cm.
    Includes bibliographical references and index.
    ISBN 0-8389-0868-3 (alk. paper)
    1. Information science.  2. Information storage and retrieval systems.
3. Computer science—Popular works.  4. Mathematics—Popular works.
I. Title.
Z665.R366 2004
020—dc22                                            2003021878

Printed in the United States of America

08   07   06   05   04        5   4   3   2   1

This book is dedicated to my wife Karen,
my daughter Jill Sarah,
my son Aaron Wilford,
and all the members of my close
and extended family.
*Hazak. Baruch.*

# ▶ Contents

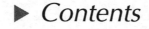

*Figures   ix*
*Tables   xi*
*Acknowledgments   xiii*
*Introduction   xv*

**1 ▶ Describing Information   *1***

What Is an Information System?   *1*
What Is a System?   *1*
What Is Information?   *2*
Working Definitions of Information   *3*
Information Distortion   *7*
Exercises and Research Questions   *11*

**2 ▶ Representing Information   *12***

The Cumbersome Decimal System   *12*
The Simple Binary System   *14*
Converting Binary to Decimal and Back Again   *15*
The Hexadecimal System   *18*
Number Humor   *20*
How Did the Romans Deal with Fractions?   *21*
Prefix and Postfix Representation   *22*
Exercises and Research Questions   *23*

**3  ▶ Organizing Information  25**

Fundamental Information Structures  *25*

Who Wants Short Sorts?  *33*

Exercises and Research Questions  *36*


**4  ▶ Retrieving Information  39**

The Nature of Information Retrieval  *39*

Boolean and Beyond  *42*

Vector Methods (Simplified)  *47*

Fuzzy Information Retrieval  *50*

Inverted Files  *54*

Exercises and Research Questions  *56*


**5  ▶ Networking Information  57**

Network Topologies  *57*

Bridges, Switches, Routers, and Gateways  *61*


**6  ▶ Securing Information  62**

Physical, Data, Server, Backup, and Network Security  *62*

First Line of Defense: The Lowly Password  *66*

Viruses, Worms, Trojan Horses, Logic Bombs, and Other Nasties  *68*

A Dangerous Script  *71*

Misdirection  *73*

Exercises and Research Questions  *75*


**7  ▶ Concealing Information  76**

Codes and Ciphers  *76*

Key Issues  *79*

The Unbreakable One-Time Pad  *80*

Symmetric (One-Key) Cryptography  *81*

Asymmetric (Two-Key) Cryptography  *82*

The Secret History of Public Key Cryptography  *86*

Other Cryptographic Systems  *87*

Steganography: Hiding Information in Plain Sight   *89*

Exercises and Research Questions   *90*

**8 ▶ Measuring Information   92**

Bibliometrics: Measuring the Printed Word   *92*

Sabermetrics: Measuring Baseball Information   *96*

Web Metrics   *101*

Exercises and Research Questions   *102*

**9 ▶ Counting Information   105**

Counting Tools   *105*

Counting Methods   *108*

Counting Things   *111*

Exercises and Research Questions   *133*

**10 ▶ Numbering Information   138**

Prime Cuts   *138*

The Intriguing Nature of Pi   *142*

Pascal's Triangle   *147*

Exercises and Research Questions   *149*

**11 ▶ Managing Information   150**

Characteristics of a Successful Information System   *150*

Building a Successful Information System   *152*

Why Things Go Wrong   *154*

Costs and Risks   *155*

**12 ▶ The Computer as an Information System   157**

How Big Is an Exabyte?   *157*

Data Compression: Reducing Redundancy   *158*

Information Issues in the Background   *160*

Exercises and Research Questions   *161*

**13 ▶ The Internet as an Information System   *163***

Basics of Internet Protocol Addressing   *163*

Addressing Schemes   *165*

The Internet Metaphor Project   *168*

Is Internet Access a Privilege or a Right?   *172*

Other Internet Issues   *175*

Exercises and Research Questions   *177*


**14 ▶ Music as an Information System   *179***

The Nature of Music and Sound   *179*

Tuning Information Systems   *181*

How Many Tones Belong in a Scale?   *184*

Making Cents of It All   *185*

Melody Machines   *186*

Fundamentals of Music Information Retrieval   *188*

Exercises and Research Questions   *195*


**15 ▶ Interpreting Information: Numbers as Meanings   *197***

Gematria   *197*

The Numerology of 666   *203*

Exercises and Research Questions   *206*


**16 ▶ Counterintuitive Information   *207***

Not Quite Paradoxes   *207*

The Trouble with Infinity   *214*

Exercises and Research Questions   *218*


*Appendixes*

**A**   Which Librarian Has the Server?   *219*

**B**   The Square Root of Two Is Irrational   *220*

**C**   Who's on First?   *222*

*Answers to Selected Exercises*   *229*

*References*   *237*

*Index*   *247*

# ▶ *Figures*

**3-1**    Linear (Sequential) Organization   *25*
**3-2**    Binary Tree Organization   *26*
**3-3**    Hierarchy Organization   *27*
**3-4**    Relational Organization   *29*

**5-1**    Bus Network Topology   *57*
**5-2**    Ring Network Topology   *58*
**5-3**    Mesh Network Topology   *59*
**5-4**    Star Network Topology   *59*
**5-5**    Star-Bus Hybrid Network Topology   *60*
**5-6**    Star-Ring Hybrid Network Topology   *60*

**9-1**    Tower of Hanoi Puzzle   *126*

# ▶ *Tables*

**1-1**    Approximations to the Square Root of Two  *8*

**2-1**    Binary and Decimal Comparisons  *14*
**2-2**    Binary Digit Count  *15*
**2-3**    Comparison of Binary, Decimal, and Hexadecimal
       Representation  *18*
**2-4**    Hexadecimal and Binary Analogues  *19*
**2-5**    Common Roman Fractions and Symbols  *21*
**2-6**    Egyptian Fractions  *22*
**2-7**    Prefix and Postfix Forms  *23*

**4-1**    Information Retrieval Effectiveness Experiment  *42*
**4-2**    Sample Document Vectors  *48*
**4-3**    Fuzzy Query Example  *53*
**4-4**    Word Indexing  *55*
**4-5**    Inverted File Indexing  *55*

**6-1**    Password Possibilities  *68*

**7-1**    Key Length and Cases  *79*
**7-2**    Navajo Code Talkers Dictionary  *88*

**8-1**    Classic Bibliometric Measures  *93*
**8-2**    Theoretical Application of Lotka's Law  *94*
**8-3**    Zipf's Law Applied to *Ulysses*  *94*
**8-4**    Sample Bradford Distribution  *95*
**8-5**    Some Standard Batter Metrics  *98*
**8-6**    Proposed Optimal Batting Lineup  *100*
**8-7**    Optimal Batting Lineup  *101*
**8-8**    Common Web Metrics  *102*

**9-1**    Chisenbop Finger Positions and Their Values  *111*
**9-2**    Grains per Chessboard Square  *113*

9-3    Moves and Chess Positions    *114*
9-4    Maximum Possible Moves by Chess Piece    *116*
9-5    Net Chess Moves    *116*
9-6    Counting English Words    *117*
9-7    Two- and Three-Letter Words Using the Same Letters    *118*
9-8    Surnames    *120*
9-9    Extinction of Family Names: Theoretical Distribution    *122*
9-10    Extinction of Family Names: Empirical Data    *122*
9-11    Floral Fibonacci Values    *124*
9-12    Day of the Week Frequency for the 13th Day of the
         Month    *125*
9-13    Tower of Hanoi Moves    *127*
9-14    Winning the Lottery: Pick-4 Game    *130*
9-15    Winning the Lottery: Pick-6 Game    *131*
9-16    Poker Hands    *132*

10-1    Types of Natural Numbers    *138*
10-2    Distribution of Digits in Pi    *146*
10-3    Binomial Expansions    *147*

11-1    Asking the Right Questions    *153*

12-1    Byte Sizes    *158*
12-2    A Simple Abbreviation Compression in the Bible    *159*

13-1    Internet Protocol Class Addresses    *165*
13-2    IP Addresses by Class    *165*
13-3    Metaphor Types    *169*
13-4    Internet Description by Level of Perceived Expertise    *171*

14-1    Typical Tunings    *180*
14-2    Pythagorean Tuning Scale    *181*
14-3    Galilei (Just) Tuning Scale    *182*
14-4    Comparison of Seven- and Twelve-Tone Equal-
         Tempered Scales    *184*
14-5    Tones, Ratios, and Cents    *186*

15-1    Gematria Letter Values: Ragil Method    *198*
15-2    Gematria Letter Values: Mispar Godol Method    *199*
15-3    Chinese Numerology Years    *203*

16-1    Probability of Two People Chosen at Random Sharing
         the Same Birthday    *213*

# ▶ *Acknowledgments*

The author gratefully acknowledges the following individuals who offered their guidance, insight, and advice during the production of this text. I thank you all for your support without which this work would not have been possible.

Professor Richard Bumby, Eve Burris, Jan Carrato, Connie Deymann, Martin Feuerman, John Hauman, Ann Hirschman, Dr. Joseph Katz, Professor Joseph Kedem, Melody Massa, Thomas Maugham, Professor Geoffrey McAuliffe, Kerry O'Rourke, Michael Ratzan, Professor Ronald Rice, Professor Allen Rippe, Mona Ratzan Rippe, Larry Royce, Swadesh Sharma, Adele Sommer, and Professor Nina Wacholder.

# ▶ Introduction

There are an enormous number of books dealing with information and its applications. This book differs from others in that it offers an innovative approach to information studies *not oriented to any specific application, time, or technology*. There is a compelling need for this type of book because too many others rapidly lose their relevance.

The text provides a unique overview of information by means of intriguing topics that supplement conventional texts and curricula. It is derived from a highly successful graduate-level course entitled Information Systems that the author has taught for many years at the School of Communication, Information and Library Studies of Rutgers University.

*Scope.* This book uses a mathematical perspective to discuss the description, representation, organization, retrieval, networking, security, concealment, measurement, and management of information. It discusses the computer, the Internet, and music as information systems. The foundations of these and other information systems are discussed and illustrated with examples. Alternative number systems and counterintuitive information round out the overview.

*Structure.* The text is intentionally organized as independent chapters. Each chapter discusses an important aspect of information. Examples, exercises, research questions, and humor emphasize salient points. The text may be used as course reference material, supplementary readings, homework exercises, or springboards for class discussions.

*Progression.* We must describe information before we can use it, for otherwise we do not know what we have. The act of describing information reveals that information depends on its representation. Different representations have different attributes. Represented information must be organized within a framework for effective and efficient retrieval. Retrieved information is often shared across computer networks. If information is shared then it must be secured, but private information must be concealed. Information has worth and so it should be measured, counted, and managed.

*Audience.* This book is intended for multiple audiences: library and information studies instructors seeking innovative and unusual (and fun) topics for intriguing and stimulating their students; library students seeking an overview of information topics and why things work; humanities students desiring a background on the elusive nature of information; computer science students wanting a broader perspective beyond computation; and the general public intrigued by the paradigm of information.

This book is suitable for both undergraduates and graduates. The text content is both qualitative and quantitative. It has been used in library informatics programs.

It is hoped that this book will give readers a deeper appreciation of both the simplicity and complexity of information. They will gain a perspective on relevant methods, assumptions, and limitations. Readers will not become instant computer scientists, reference librarians, database architects, or information managers. It is the goal of the author that readers receive a broad overview of the paradigm of information and one day perhaps make their own contribution to the field.

*Warning!* This text contains math. There is not much, and most of it is arithmetic. Unavoidably, some applications (IP addressing, counting, Boolean, binary, etc.) are better expressed in mathematical symbols than in words. Math-phobic readers may skip over those expressions, gaining meaning directly from the text.

LEE RATZAN
School of Communication, Information
and Library Studies
Rutgers University

## CHAPTER 1

▶ Describing Information

## WHAT IS AN INFORMATION SYSTEM?

An information system is a consistent, coordinated set of components acting together toward the production, distribution, or processing of information. This definition sacrifices precision for generality, but in doing so it applies to computer information systems, networked information systems, biological information systems, and a variety of other intriguing contexts. The terms "system" and "information" should be defined.

## WHAT IS A SYSTEM?

A consistent, coordinated set of components acting together as a single unit toward a common function or purpose constitutes a system. System components must work together. An inconsistent system works against itself.

Systems may have adaptive or nonadaptive characteristics. An adaptive system modifies itself to its environment. A nonadaptive system operates independently of its external environment. A car antilock braking system reacts to road conditions and is an adaptive system. In contrast, a car radio system remains oblivious to the mechanical world surrounding it. Some system models are amenable to mathematical analysis. Other systems are more amenable to visualization than to equations. An active library constitutes an enormously complex interactive adaptive system.

Most systems have boundaries. A boundary is the demarcation of what lies within and what resides beyond the system, what follows the system's rules and what does not. A computer domain defines the security boundary. A jurisdictional boundary defines the limit of the law. It seems self-evident that everything has an inside and an outside, and the two are easily distinguished. But neither of these statements is entirely true.

### Systems with No Obvious Boundaries

The state of being inside or outside is a surprisingly elusive topological concept. Take an ordinary belt, give it a half-twist, and close it at the buckle. Place your finger on any location, then follow the path of the belt in one direction without removing the finger from the belt. Your finger will emerge on the other side, having traveled *from inside to outside without crossing any obvious boundary.* (The effect is even more striking if the belt has different colors.) This construction is called a Möbius strip. It is not clear which is the inside or outside.

The inside of a system is not always self-evident. The criterion for inclusion is not entirely clear for closed curves, much less for complex political systems. Bergamini (1963, 186) cites the example of a Jordan curve whose interior is unclear and a vest that can be removed without ever removing the jacket above it (179).

Boundaries need *not* be linear, sharp, and crisp. A sharp boundary provides a clear, unambiguous demarcation of the inside versus outside. A boundary is the graphical representation of a rule; those objects satisfying the rule reside inside the system.

Suppose the rule of inclusion consists of all points within three inches of the center of a circle. A point located four inches from the center lies outside the circle. A point located two inches away lies within it.

Few things in life are so clear and unambiguous. When does a teenager become an adult? How old is a person who claims that they are "thirty-something"? What time is a meeting called for "around three o'clock"? If "nearly everyone" who reads this text receives an A in the course, then how many receive an A? The field called "fuzzy information retrieval" involves information systems with no sharp boundaries.

## WHAT IS INFORMATION?

Most people know what information is . . . or at least they think they do. Try this test: ask someone to define "information." They hesitate. They struggle to find the right words. A platitude may emerge. Defining "information" is a fiendishly difficult process.

Some people might define "information" as "data." Data are not information for two reasons. First, "data" are not intrinsically imbedded with meaning or significance, as is information. Data use symbols, numbers, or letters for the process of representing information. And second, the word "data" is a plural noun. Data *are* but a datum *is.* Let's avoid this common syntactical error.

Why define "information" at all? A definition (Latin *de finis,* "knowing the end, limits, or boundaries") restricts what information is and what it is not. Philosophers, theologians, academics, and fools have pondered the nature of information for a very long time. There is at least one eminently practical need for a satisfactory definition of "information." If we don't know what information is, then how can we expect computers to manipulate it for us?

### Properties of Information

Perhaps information can be defined in terms of its characteristics.

*Information is objective.* Mathematics and science champion the concept of objective information. This may be true in an abstract formalized setting. It is often not true in the real world.

*Information is subjective.* What is information for me may not be information for you. Who decides what is and what is not information?

*Information is temporal.* What was not information in the past might become information in the future. In contrast, what was information in the past might not be information in the future.

*Information is ephemeral.* Information might have value at one time and never again.

*Information is not fungible.* Information does not have identical interchangeable parts.

*Information is not reduced by giving it away.*

*Information is not always additive.* Twenty books on the same subject do not provide twenty times as much information.

*Information is both a process and a commodity.* At this moment your body is processing thermal, tactile, audio, and visual information about your environment. At this moment somewhere, information is also being bought and sold.

*Information is measurable. Information is not measurable.* Econometricians measure financial information. Sabermetricians measure baseball information. People measure information by its value or worth. In contrast, information may be entirely qualitative.

> "Information professionals fall into two camps.
>
> There are those who believe that information is *always* measurable.
>
> There arc those that believe information is *never* measurable."
>
> (Penniman 1988)

## WORKING DEFINITIONS OF INFORMATION

A variety of information attributes appear in the works of Buckland (1991), Machlup (1980, 1983), and Belkin (1978, 1987). The problem of explicitly defining "information" is easily avoided by limiting our attention to its practical applications. A working definition provides emphasis, utility, and direction. Working definitions of "information" exploit its salient characteristics within a specific context. They enhance the communication of information through symbols and words.

> "Words are all we have . . . " —Samuel Beckett

### Working definition 1

Information is *"the reduction of uncertainty . . . "* (Shannon and Weaver 1948).

This definition was developed within the context of telephone and signal-processing applications. The communication model is sender-message-receiver. The signal arrives intact, distorted, or not at all. Distortion and entropy (disorder) measure information content. A perfect transmission has zero distortion and total certainty. A noisy transmission has distortion and uncertainty.

The Shannon and Weaver definition emphasizes the distribution (or dissipation) of information *in terms of a signal.* Information is measurable in terms of uncertainty, and the definition does not address the *meaning* of the signal. The Shannon and Weaver definition has important engineering applications but is problematic when applied to human affairs.

### Working definition 2

Information is *"a difference that makes a difference . . . "* (Bateson 1979).

This definition of information involves a change of state, and the change must be significant. There is no information at equilibrium because there is no change. Data become information in conjunction with a threshold.

The Shannon and Weaver articulation expresses information in terms of delivery fidelity. The Bateson view expresses information in terms of meaning when crossing a threshold. An insignificant change induces no information.

Consider the message:

> "No!
>
> No!
>
> No!"

The first sentence indicates forceful renunciation. It produces a change of state. The word "No!" makes a difference. There is information, but note that the information is not measurable. The second and third sentences provide no further change. Repetition gives emphasis, but it does not tell us more. One may argue that only the first sentence provides information.

Consider the famous cry:

> "The British are coming!
>
> The British are coming!" —attributed to Paul Revere, April 18, 1775

The first sentence was a clarion call to the local villagers. It implied "Take arms!" or "Take flight!" The information made an impact on their current state. Once they were so informed by the first sentence, the second sentence did not tell them more.

### Working definition 3

Information is *"that which informs . . . "*

This is a circular definition. One form of the word defines another. The word "inform" derives from the Latin word *forma,* meaning "shape." That which informs changes the shape or form of our mental image and by extension *our cognitive perception of the world.* The act of being informed presupposes a commonality of meanings between speaker and receiver. Information is not a signal or a change of state, but a process of communication.

I may offer information *to* you, but it may not be information *for* you. It may be meaningless. For example, the Cauchy integral theorem produces a quick proof of

Liouville's theorem. This in turn provides an elegant six-line proof of the so-called fundamental theorem of arithmetic, which formerly required a 200-page doctoral dissertation. (Graduate math students now routinely do this problem as a homework exercise.)

Are you impressed? Probably not. Most readers are not mathematicians. There is no commonality of understanding, so what I have offered you contains no information.

### Working definition 4

Information is *"a coherent collection of data organized in a particular way that has meaning . . . "* (Ruben 1988).

Information involves structure, organization, and meaning. Information is not data. Information is *represented* by data. Data must be consistent. Inconsistent data produce no information. ("Walk! Don't walk!" is not information.)

Information requires an organizational structure, but this definition does not specify the nature of that structure. There can be and probably are many possible structures. The development of modern chemistry offers one example.

The organizational structure of the elements eluded chemists for a very long time. Dmitry Mendeleyev (1834–1907) developed an organizational scheme based on atomic number. This framework, now known as the periodic table, revealed relationships between elements with a clarity previously impossible. The early table of the elements contained gaps where elements would have been expected but no element was then known. Mendeleyev's organizational framework provided clues leading to the discovery of the missing elements (gallium, 1875; germanium, 1886; xenon, 1898; radium, 1898; rhenium, 1925; francium, 1931; technetium, 1937; astantine, 1940, etc.).

The Ruben definition mandates organization but does not specify the organization. It mandates the presence of meaning, but it does not specify what meaning, to whom, when, where, or how. The definition appears sufficiently vague as to be useless. On the contrary! Ambiguity provides interpretative freedom. The definition is well suited to contemporary information system design.

### Working definition 5

Information is *"the meaning that a human being assigns to data by means of the conventions applied to that data"* (Stallings 1988, 1).

Information is *meaning*. Organization is irrelevant unless it induces meaning. Computers have no sense of meaning, so computers always process data, not information. The nature of data structure or data organization is not addressed.

*Example 1.1* (information from syntactical structure)

Punctuation imposes grammatical structure. Using punctuation, make sense of (make information of) the phrase: That that is is is not that so

*Solution:* (Read backwards) ?os taht ton si, si, si taht tahT

*Example 1.2* (information from context)

Is the following sequence of numbers information? 4, 14, 34, 42, 59, 125

Yes, if you live in New York City. The numbers are subway stops for the A train, an express line along the West Side of Manhattan. The data values are organized in a particular way that has significant meaning to local commuters.

*Example 1.3* (unfamiliar representation obscures information)

Is the following sequence of letters information? O, T, T, F, F, S, S, E, N, T

Yes, if you recognize numbers written as initial letters (One, Two, Three, Four, Five, Six, Seven, Eight, Nine, Ten). Changing the representation obscures the meaning. Codes and ciphers operate on this principle.

*Example 1.4* (phonetic representation)

Two children pick flowers in a field. One points to a bee and says:
"D B S A B-Z B!" (Steig 1968)

Is this information?

Yes, once you realize that the words are represented phonetically ("The bee is a busy bee!").

*Example 1.5* (meaning derives from structure)

Is this information? 18009222233

Or this? 18,009,222,233 or 180.09.22.223.3 or 1-800-922-2233

The comma-delimited example suggests that the string is one single large number equaling eighteen billion nine million two hundred twenty-two thousand two hundred and thirty-three. It could be a bank balance (alas, not mine).

The dot-delimited structure suggests a science fiction star date or a set of coordinates in some frame of reference. The dash-delimited structure in a 1-3-3-4 grouping suggests a telephone number. The number must be important, because it has a toll-free area code. In fact, 1-800-922-2233 was the phone number of New Jersey NightLine, a free after-hours library reference service for state residents sponsored by the New Jersey State Library. From chaos, then order, then meaning (and value).

The next examples demonstrate different information meanings resulting from different structures.

*Example 1.6*

The following headline appeared in a local newspaper during the Falkland Islands War between Britain and Argentina in 1982:

"British Left Waffles in Falklands"

If two letters are changed from uppercase to lowercase, the sentence read:

"British left waffles in Falklands"

In the former case, a British political party vacillated on a foreign policy regarding the Falkland Islands. In the latter case, British soldiers neglected their breakfast before departing.

*Example 1.7*

Victor Borge (1909–2000) once observed that

"Am I an idiot?" poses a question.
"Am I an idiot!" removes any doubt.

*Example 1.8*

I'm sorry. It's not loaded.
I'm sorry it's not loaded.

The first sentence expresses regret for frightening the listener who mistakenly believed a gun contained ammunition. The speaker of the second sentence wished it had.

*Example 1.9*

The man, said the witness, was a thief.
The man said the witness was a thief.

The first sentence states the man is the thief. The second indicates the witness is the thief.

*Example 1.10*

A woman, without her man, is nothing.
A woman: without her, man is nothing.

This pair illustrates a gender power reversal.


## INFORMATION DISTORTION

Information is easily distorted in the process of communication. Human language is rich and also vague. The parlor game of "telephone" demonstrates how easily voice-based information becomes distorted. We have trouble communicating with each other, yet we insist our data be transmitted across large and complex networks with no loss of fidelity.

The Shannon and Weaver perspective on information shows how even simple signals can get lost or battered. Digital and analog representations of information are in fact controlled distortions of the original information.

Numerical information is not immune to distortion either. The ancient Greeks made the disturbing discovery that some numbers have precise geometric representations but imprecise numerical representations. Consider a common square floor tile one foot on each side. What is the length of the diagonal? The Pythagorean theorem states that the sum of the squares of the two sides equals the square of the diagonal. The length of the diagonal (in feet) is *exactly* the square root of two, but the decimal representation is *approximately* equal to 1.414213562.

Rational numbers are expressed as the ratio of two integers (hence the name). But the square root of two is irrational; that is, the square root of two can *never* be expressed exactly as the fraction X/Y for *any* positive integers X and Y. Some information will *always* be missing. The result will always be distorted. (See table 1-1.)

(A simple proof that the square root of two is irrational using a reductio ad absurdum principle appears in appendix B for the interested reader.)

Irrationality violates a rationalist conception of the universe. Early philosophers dismissed irrationality as an unwelcome artifact of the number system, but Georg Cantor (1845–1918) later proved that irrationals dominate the number line. As in the case of human affairs, the rational ones are in the minority.

**Table 1-1**
Approximations to the
Square Root of Two

| Value | Squared Value (exact value = 2) |
|---|---|
| 1.4 | 1.96 |
| 1.41 | 1.9881 |
| 1.414 | 1.9993 |

## Information Distortion by Translation

Language translation produces information distortion. A skilled translator takes into account the meaning, significance, and context of words. A literal translation is always fraught with peril. ("Out of sight, out of mind" becomes "Invisible idiot.") Idioms often do not translate well between languages. Some words have no counterparts between languages. Information becomes easily distorted in translation. The comedian Lord Buckley (1906–1960) performed a stage set translating classical oratory (Shakespeare, Lincoln, etc.) into contemporary slang.

## Information Distortion by Metaphor

Metaphors are figures of speech describing the unfamiliar in terms of the familiar. Metaphors embellish description through the use of implied meanings associated with the compared object. The vocabularies of information systems and the Internet are littered with metaphors by design (desktop, windows, recycling bin, trash can, Explorer, Navigator, electronic mail, etc.). Informational metaphors can distort meaning if they are extended too far or taken too literally.

"The New Jersey Turnpike is moving slowly this morning . . . "

"The Lincoln Tunnel to New York is especially heavy tonight . . . "

"The White House said no comment . . . "

"She is really into dance . . . "

"She was my English rose . . . " (Prince Charles referring to Princess Diana)

## Information Distortion by Overload

Inconsistency distorts information, noise distorts information, and truncation distorts information. Overload distorts information by excess. Most people have difficulty answering the following question because they approach the problem directly, trying to store too much relevant data simultaneously.

> *Problem:* You are dealt two cards from a standard deck of playing cards.
>
> Rule 1:    *Only one* of the Rules 2, 3, or 4 is true
>
> Rule 2:    You are dealt an ace, king, or both
>
> Rule 3:    You are dealt an ace, queen, or both
>
> Rule 4:    You are dealt a ten, jack, or both
>
> *Question:* Do you have an ace?
>
> (Brooks 2000; Johnson-Laird et al. 2000)

Many people answer yes. Wrong. You do *not* have an ace. A direct approach to the problem lists cases, but there are too many and too much information is lost. An indirect approach uses a contradiction argument and solves the problem in two steps as follows:

> Assume that you *do* have an ace.
>
> Then Rule 2 and Rule 3 are both true.
>
> This violates Rule 1.
>
> Contradiction!
>
> You cannot have an ace.

(This example also demonstrates the power of indirect methods to slice through myriad possibilities with unfettered ease. Arguments by contradiction are a powerful tool.)

## Information Distortion and Humor

Changing word meaning changes information content. Different contexts engender different meanings. Being "cool" is both thermal and social. Being "mean" refers to being bad and outrageous. If someone says that I play a mean saxophone, it might be praise or condemnation. A single word might even be the context of an entire conversation:

> Speaker 1: Dude.
>
> Speaker 2: Dude?
>
> Speaker 1: Dude!
>
> Speaker 2: Dude!!!!!
>
> Speaker 1: Well, if you put it that way . . . (Motion picture: *BASEketball,* 1998)

Linguistic information distortion (e.g., plays on words) is often used to generate humor:

> "Time flies like the wind. Fruit flies like the banana." —Groucho Marx

"You can lead a horse to water but a pencil must be lead." —Groucho Marx

"Outside of a book, a dog is man's best friend, but inside of a dog it is too dark to read." —Groucho Marx

Linguistic distortion also can occur in the misuse of pronunciation rules. George Bernard Shaw (1856–1950) noted that the English language is particularly fond of such aberrations. Consider the nonsense word "ghoti." Most people would pronounce the word as gi-ho-tee or gi-hot-i.

| | |
|---|---|
| The letters *gh* are pronounced as in cough  =  F | |
| The letter *o* is pronounced as in women  =  I | |
| The letters *ti* are pronounced as in nation  =  SH | |

Hence "ghoti" is pronounced as "fish."

Information distortion by grammatical misuse is not limited to nonsense words. Mixed references can promote chaos. Abbott and Costello's comedy routine "Who's on First?" provides a classic example of information distortion. The complete text appears in appendix C.

A *cryptogram* appears as nonsense. But with each guess of letters the description becomes more and more evident until the message reveals itself. Simple single-letter substitutions are amenable to the Shannon and Weaver definition of information as "the reduction of uncertainty," since there is total uncertainty at the outset but no uncertainty at the final resolution.

*Example 1.11* (cryptogram)

(Estimated solution time = 10 minutes)

ABCDEF  GHI  FIJKLN  MBGA  ABIO  FIIN,

FLQH  NCJP  NGFRQIHGKIF  GF  THIGN.

M. ECJUIHA        (B.N.F.  XCDGZLHI)

*Hints:*  (name of lyricist)     (famous British naval operetta)

*Clues*

The most common letter in English is E, so I becomes E.

The most common letter ending a word is S, so F becomes S.

Thus GF becomes IS or AS.

If G were I, then there would be a three-letter word beginning with I (unlikely), so G becomes A.

GF becomes AS. Then GHI becomes ARE and FIIN becomes SEEM.

Hence THIGN becomes CREAM and NGFRQIHGKJF becomes MASQUERADES.

Similarly, FIJKLN becomes SELDOM, NCJP becomes MILK, and
MBGA becomes WHAT.

Continue this way until the message appears.

Alternatively, one might guess that the operetta is H.M.S. PINAFORE,
revealing the name of the lyricist and providing a host of letters.

## EXERCISES AND RESEARCH QUESTIONS

(See "Answers to Selected Exercises" for answers to some of the following exercises.)

E1.1    Is a tree an information system? What information does it provide? Is a
museum an information system? What information does it provide?

E1.2    How is a person an information system? (A human information system contains approximately four billion parts, comes in two models, and currently one
version.)

E1.3     Does the Shannon and Weaver definition of information apply to the message
"Happy birthday!" or "I love you so much!"?

E1.4    The manner in which the following sentence is read makes all the difference in
describing its information content. Show that one word can be formed from
these letters: OEDONWR.

E1.5    How might the pronunciation of the word "ghoughpteighbteau" be described
as "potato"? Break up the letters as gh/ough/pt/eigh/bt/eau and examine the
words hiccough (pronounced hiccuP), thOUGH, PTomaine, nEIghbor, deBT,
burEAU.

*Research Question 1.6*

Political or religious systems that do not adapt generally do not survive.
Identify two such systems.

CHAPTER 2 ▶ Representing Information

How information is represented affects how it is perceived. How it is perceived affects how it is used. Indeed, all arithmetics are not created equal.

This chapter begins with a puzzle for those who skipped the exercise in the previous chapter. What is the next element in the sequence?

O, T, T, F, F

Here is a hint:

O, T, T, F, F, S, S

Here is the solution:

O, T, T, F, F, S, S, E

Otherwise known as One, Two, Three, Four, Five, Six, Seven, Eight.

Why do some people find this problem difficult? Because numbers are customarily represented by symbols, not by letters. The sequence of numbers did not change. The representation of them changed.

## THE CUMBERSOME DECIMAL SYSTEM

Decimal arithmetic seems natural. This is a subjective assessment because we are used to it. The decimal system is based on powers of ten. For example, the expression 1,234 is a shortcut for:

$$1,234 = (1 \times 1,000) + (2 \times 100) + (3 \times 10) + (4 \times 1)$$

The decimal system is not "natural" because nature does not always operate in powers of ten. We think of it as natural only because we have ten fingers and because it was imprinted into our heads by rote. There is nothing natural, holy, or sacrosanct about the decimal system.

The decimal system operation is traditionally unidirectional (vertical). Try the following simple horizontal arithmetic problem: 32 + 55 + 19 = ? Obtaining the answer by performing simple addition on this horizontal representation seems awkward. This is a cultural bias.

### The Decimal System Requires High Overhead

Elementary school education ingrains students with the multiplication and other tables. Learning this math was an endless drone of drill and practice. Arithmetic tables and rules are a sine qua non without which the decimal system ceases to function. The decimal system requires an enormous amount of cognitive overhead.

A ten-by-ten table of addition contains 100 entries. A nine-by-nine multiplication table contains 81 entries. The process of adding or multiplying small numbers requires immediate access to 181 isolated numerical facts. To appreciate the cognitive effort involved, try memorizing the first 181 digits of the number pi!

### The Decimal System Uses Complex Rules

Decimal addition involves operations performed from top to bottom and right to left. Subtraction involves boosting a value by "borrowing" from an adjacent column on the left. Multiplication and division mandate intermediate results placed into very specific positions. Try speaking aloud the following problem while you solve it:

$$
\begin{array}{r}
48 \\
+\ 77 \\
\hline
?? \\
\end{array}
$$

Did you say to yourself "put down the five and carry the one"? If so, this is an unconscious return to the drill of yore while transferring values from one column to another. The Harvard University mathematics instructor Tom Lehrer demonstrated the absurdity of a naive approach to such machinations in his humorous song "New Math" (Lehrer 1965).

### Decimal Representation Is Incomplete

Simple natural numbers engender simple, rational, geometric forms. The compass (generator of circles) and straightedge (generator of lines) were the primary tools of ancient rational geometric construction. Are the following possible using only a compass and straightedge?

> Construct a square whose area is that of a given circle (squaring the circle).
>
> Construct a cube with a volume exactly twice that of another cube (duplicating the cube).
>
> Divide an angle into three equal parts (trisecting the angle).

The answer to all three problems is no. All three tasks are impossible under the given constraints because the values involve irrational numbers. They do not have an exact decimal representation. The decimal system does not apply well to nonrational numbers. In this sense, the decimal representation is incomplete.

The decimal system is not natural, requires a high overhead, contains complex and unforgiving positional rules, and is incomplete. Why then is it used? It is used because it works reasonably well for practical problems in real life. Common values only need a few decimal places. An ordinary yardstick has a resolution of $\frac{1}{16}$-inch (an error of about six parts in a hundred). Six decimal digits suffice for the building of bridges and the launching of rockets. Eight decimal digits suffice for calculating trajectories to the Moon.

The decimal system has another advantage. Powers of ten grow rapidly (Morrison et al. 1982). The difference between the smallest and largest known objects in the universe spans an interval of less than fifty decimal places. The decimal system allows the same sets of symbols to apply to small and large numbers.

### Alternative Systems

The abacus is an ancient calculating tool with a positional notation akin to the decimal system. The decimal system requires column addition performed in a specific order (top to bottom and right to left). The abacus representation permits addition in any order.

The ancient Romans represented numbers with letters. It was as natural to them as the decimal system seems natural to us. Their system is not natural to us now. Try doing your tax return using Roman numerals!

## THE SIMPLE BINARY SYSTEM

The decimal representation of information uses ten symbols and a complex set of arithmetic rules. But any other consistent basis would be equally valid. The simplest such basis is the binary system. It involves only two symbols (0, 1) and three fundamental arithmetic rules.

A decimal digit (dit) assumes integer values from zero to nine. A binary digit (bit) only assumes values zero or one. A bit represents only two possible states: on/off, left/right, true/false, in/out, up/down, male/female, etc. Most of life is not binary.

A byte consists of eight bits grouped together as a single unit (byte size may vary for specialized computers). (Computer folklore claims that the word "byte" derives from "binary yoked transfer element.") A byte often represents a letter or a character. In this sense, a byte is a unit of digital information.

Every position in a decimal number represents a power of ten. Every position in a binary number represents a power of two.

**Table 2-1**
Binary and Decimal Comparisons

| Decimal Number | Corresponding Binary Number | Number of Decimal Digits | Number of Binary Digits |
|---|---|---|---|
| 9 | 1001 | 1 | 4 |
| 99 | 1100011 | 2 | 7 |
| 999 | 1111100111 | 3 | 10 |

Since two is smaller than ten, it should not be surprising that a binary representation of a number requires more digits than its decimal counterpart. (See table 2-1.)

Knowing the number of binary digits has practical applications because it has an impact on data storage requirements. How many binary digits does it take to represent a decimal number? The following is a simple estimate. (The math-phobic can ignore the formula and skip directly to table 2-2.)

Find Q such that 2 raised to the Q power is less than or equal to N, then add one.

> *Solution:*     1 + [logarithm(N) / logarithm(2)]       (*exact*)
>
>                1 + 3.332 logarithm(N)           (*approximate*)

(Add one, since counting begins with the units digit.)

The estimate is a reasonable approximation to the true value. Binary numbers are bulky!

**Table 2-2**
Binary Digit Count

| Decimal Number | Binary Form | Number of Binary Digits (true) | Number of Binary Digits (estimated) |
|:---:|:---:|:---:|:---:|
| 2 | 10 | 2 | 2 |
| 4 | 100 | 3 | 3 |
| 10 | 1010 | 4 | 4.3 |
| 25 | 11001 | 5 | 5.6 |

## *Binary Arithmetic*

Decimal addition has complex rules and multiple symbols. Binary arithmetic is simpler, with only three rules and only two symbols.

> Rule # 1       $0 + 0 = 0$
>
> Rule # 2       $0 + 1 = 1$
>
> Rule # 3       $1 + 1 = 10$ (pronounced "one-oh," not "ten")

(*Note:* An abacus mimics these rules by moving a bead up or to the next column.)

## CONVERTING BINARY TO DECIMAL AND BACK AGAIN

Computer processing moves data between its binary and decimal representations. The decimal number 123 represents:

$$123 = (1 \times 100) + (2 \times 10) + (3 \times 1)$$

By analogy, the binary number 111 represents:

$$111 = (1 \times 4) + (1 \times 2) + (1 \times 1) \; (= \text{a decimal value of 7})$$

The following values are often useful as reference.

| Power: | 6 | 5 | 4 | 3 | 2 | 1 | 0 |
|---|---|---|---|---|---|---|---|
| Ten powers: | 1,000,000 | 100,000 | 10,000 | 1,000 | 100 | 10 | 1 |
| Two powers: | 64 | 32 | 16 | 8 | 4 | 2 | 1 |

## Converting Binary to Decimal

The following method converts binary numbers to decimal numbers:

Write the binary number digit by digit under the appropriate column

Multiply the binary value by the corresponding power of two

Add

*Problem 2.1*

What is the decimal value of the binary number 10101?

*Solution:* Write the power of two table.

| Powers of two: | · | 16 | 8 | 4 | 2 | 1 |
|---|---|---|---|---|---|---|
| This binary number: | | 1 | 0 | 1 | 0 | 1 |

The decimal value corresponding to 10101 equals

$$(1 \times 16) + (0 \times 8) + (1 \times 4) + (0 \times 2) + (1 \times 1) = 21$$

*Problem 2.2*

On February 1, 1988, the science fiction program *Star Trek: The Next Generation* aired episode no. 116, entitled *1001001*. The plot involved alien life-forms called Binars who communicated only in binary. What was the decimal name of the episode?

| Powers of two: | 64 | 32 | 16 | 8 | 4 | 2 | 1 |
|---|---|---|---|---|---|---|---|
| This binary number: | 1 | 0 | 0 | 1 | 0 | 0 | 1 |

The decimal value equals

$$(1 \times 64) + (0 \times 32) + (0 \times 16) + (1 \times 8) + (0 \times 4) + (0 \times 2) + (1 \times 1) = 73$$

## Converting Decimal to Binary

The following method converts a decimal number to a binary number:

Determine the largest power of two that does not exceed the number

Place a one in the corresponding column (and zero elsewhere)

Subtract off the corresponding power of two

Repeat steps 1–3 using the remainder value

(The last entry will be zero if the original number was even and one if it was odd.)

*Problem 2.3*

Convert 73 to binary representation.

*Solution:* Write the power of two table.

64   32   16   8   4   2   1

The largest power of two that does not exceed 73 is the number 64.

Mark 1 in the 64 column. Subtract $73 - 64 = 9$

| 64 | 32 | 16 | 8 | 4 | 2 | 1 |
|----|----|----|---|---|---|---|
| 1  | 0  | 0  | 0 | 0 | 0 | 0 |

The largest power of two that does not exceed 9 is the number 8.

Mark 1 in the 8 column. Subtract $9 - 8 = 1$

| 64 | 32 | 16 | 8 | 4 | 2 | 1 |
|----|----|----|---|---|---|---|
| 1  | 0  | 0  | 1 | 0 | 0 | 1 |

Thus the decimal number 73 equals the binary number 1001001.

This method is recursive. Computer engineers love recursive algorithms. Develop the code once, optimize it, and use it over and over again.

## Why Don't Computers Do Decimal?

Decimal representation is cumbersome, and it requires ten symbols. Binary representation requires only two symbols. Decimal arithmetic is complex. Binary arithmetic has only three rules. Decimal circuits involve complex structures. Binary circuits involve only two states.

Decimal number manipulation involves three processes. The system must convert the decimal value to binary, perform arithmetic, and then convert the binary form back to decimal form. This is a triadic process, but electronic circuitry performs the conversion so rapidly that binary representation actually enhances computer performance.

"There are 10 kinds of people in the world.

Those who understand binary

And those who don't." —Unknown

This quote is really a joke. If you don't get it, note that 10 is the binary representation for the number two. It then reads as: "There are two kinds of people in the world. Those who understand binary and those who don't."

### Representing Binary by a Simple Circuit

A simple electronic circuit with a lamp and a switch mimics a binary representation. The lamp is on (= 1) or off (= 0) depending on whether the switch is closed or open. The rate at which the switch changes state controls the rate at which circuits represent zeros and ones. The speed and processing power of a computer ultimately depend on the number and speed of its switches. If information is represented by binary data, then the more bits, the more extensive the information representation. The quality of hardware and software processing is a function of the efficient and effective manipulation, storage, and movement of these zeros and ones. Good computer code does not waste bits. Fast computer code uses as few bits as possible.

## THE HEXADECIMAL SYSTEM

The decimal system is natural for people, but this is only by accident of biology. The binary system is natural for computers and this is by design. The hexadecimal system offers advantages over both the binary and decimal systems. Ah, the joy of hex.

### Recognizing the Hexadecimal Format

The decimal system uses digits from zero to nine. The binary system uses only two digits, zero and one. In contrast, the hexadecimal system uses a base-sixteen arithmetic with the digits 0 to 9 and A to F.

Letters are valid hexadecimal digits. The hex system requires 16 symbols, but there are only 10 decimal symbols, so others are taken from the alphabet. Hexadecimal representations employ powers of 16. The same symbols do not represent the same values in different systems! (See table 2-3.)

$$\begin{aligned} \text{The number 2153 (decimal)} \quad &= \quad 2 \times 1000 + 1 \times 100 + 5 \times 10 + 3 \\ &= \quad 2{,}153 \end{aligned}$$

$$\begin{aligned} \text{The number 2153 (hexadecimal)} \quad &= \quad 2 \times 4096 + 5 \times 256 + 1 \times 16 + 3 \\ &= \quad 4{,}275 \end{aligned}$$

*Note:* Henceforth we will avoid ambiguity by ending a hexadecimal number with the letter "h."

**Table 2-3**
Comparison of Binary, Decimal, and Hexadecimal Representation

| Symbol | Representation | Decimal Value | Reason |
|--------|----------------|---------------|--------|
| 111 | binary | seven | (4 + 2 + 1) |
| 111 | decimal | one hundred and eleven | (100 + 10 + 1) |
| 111 | hexadecimal | two hundred and seventy-three | (256 + 16 + 1) |

## The Advantages of Hexadecimal

Why use an information representation requiring more symbols, mixed symbols, and more complex calculations? Because the hex system is compact and convertible.

Hexadecimal representation is compact. Powers of two grow fast, but powers of sixteen grow faster:

The largest two-digit binary number: $\qquad 11 = (1 \times 2 + 1) = 3$

The largest two-digit decimal number: $\qquad 99 = (9 \times 10 + 9 \times 1) = 99$

The largest two-digit hexadecimal number: $\quad FF = (15 \times 16 + 15 \times 1) = 255$

The decimal number 99 has a value slightly less than 100. The hexadecimal number 99h has a value of 153 (about one and a half times as large).

Hexadecimal representation is convertible. Converting a binary representation to a decimal notation is a laborious process. Converting binary to hexadecimal is simple because sixteen is a power of two. The process relies on a conversion table. (See table 2-4.)

**Table 2-4**
Hexadecimal and Binary Analogues

| Hexadecimal | Binary | Hexadecimal | Binary |
|---|---|---|---|
| 0 | 0 | A | 1010 |
| 1 | 0001 | B | 1011 |
| 2 | 0010 | C | 1100 |
| 3 | 0011 | D | 1101 |
| 4 | 0100 | E | 1110 |
| 5 | 0101 | F | 1111 |
| 6 | 0110 | | |
| 7 | 0111 | | |
| 8 | 1000 | | |
| 9 | 1001 | | |

## Converting Binary to Hexadecimal

The following method converts binary numbers to hexadecimal numbers:

Pad the binary number with leading zeros on the left

Partition the number into blocks of four bits

Look up each block of four using the table

*Example 2.1*

Convert the binary number 0010111001 to hexadecimal:

The number contains ten digits. Add two leading zeroes, making it twelve.

Partition it into blocks of four: 0010111001 becomes 0000 1011 1001

The left is hex 0. The middle is hex B. The last component is hex 9.

The hex representation is 0B9 (or more properly 0B9h)

### Converting Hexadecimal to Binary

Look up each component in the table and substitute.

*Example 2.2*

Convert F23h from hexadecimal to binary:

F corresponds to 1111
2 corresponds to 0010
3 corresponds to 0011

The binary representation is thus:

1111 0010 0011 or 111100100011

Computers can rapidly transfer information from binary to hexadecimal and back.

## NUMBER HUMOR

Number humor often originates from word play. Don't drink and derive. Why was six afraid of seven? (Because seven eight [ate] nine.) Why does adding three trees make nine? (Because tree and tree and tree make nine.) The English language is fraught with auditory homonymic numerical references. (WONder, beFORE, decorATE.) A query for a date might ask RU/18? (Are you over eighteen?)

Victor Borge (1909–2000) was a multilingual world-class musician and entertainer with a trained ear for sound. He created an "inflationary language" based on the premise that if prices increase, then language should also. Numbers and words follow different rules. The use of inappropriate rules leads to humor.

Borge developed the following story in which numerical sounds are increased by the value of one. The result of applying number rules to language rules generates amusing nonsense. The words are difficult to read but fun to hear:

Twice upon a time there lived in sunny Califivenia a young man named Bob. He was a third lieutenant in the U.S. Air Fiveces. Bob had been fond of Anna, his one and a half sister. They were both proud that two of his fivefathers had been a crenineor of the U.S. Constithreetion. They were dining on the terrace. "Anna," he said as he took a bite of marinnined herring. "You look twonderful threenight. You have never looked that lovely befive."

"Yes," repeated Bob, "you do look twonderful threenight, but you have three of the saddest eyes I have ever seen."

They were now talking about Anna's husband from whom she was separnineded, while on the radio an Irish elevenor sang Tea Five Three. It was midnight. The clock in the distance struck thirteen. And suddenly there in the moonlight stood her husband Don Two, obviously intoxicnined. "Anna," he bawled, "Forgive me! I'm only young twice. And you are my two and only!"

Bob jumped to his feet. "Get out of here, you three-faced triplecrosser!"
Anna warned, "Watch out, Bob, he is an officer!"
"Yes, he is two but I'm two three!"
He then left and when he was one and a halfway through the revolving door he said, "I'll go back to Elevennessee and be double again."

> *"Farewell, Anna! Threedeloo, Threedeloo!"*

(Victor Borge, courtesy of Werner Knudsen, 2002)

## HOW DID THE ROMANS DEAL WITH FRACTIONS?

The Roman Empire made significant contributions to law, government, architecture, and civil engineering, but relatively few to pure science and mathematics. Why such a dichotomy? Was one of the most powerful civilizations on Earth limited by its inability to process abstract numerical information?

### Roman Fractions

The Romans built magnificent buildings, roads, and aqueducts. Engineering requires accurate measurement and numerical representation. But Roman numerals do not lend themselves easily to arithmetic. How did the Romans deal with fractions?

Several possible solutions have been proposed. Roman engineers might have merely copied Greek engineering principles without any substantive originality. They may have exploited the Greek sexagesimal (base sixty) system. The number 60 is significant because it is divisible by the first few whole numbers (2, 3, 4, 5, 6, 10, 12, and 15). *Many common fractional proportions work out evenly!*

The Romans may have *spelled out* their fractions. The value two-thirds was expressed as *tribus duas partes* ("with thirds two parts"). They may have used fractional *abbreviations*. Fractions may have been written *in terms of other fractions*. For example, the value $\frac{9}{16}$ could be represented as one-half plus one-sixteenth. (See table 2-5.)

Roman numerals were actively used for more than 1,000 years, suggesting that the system must have had some advantages. Three possible factors come to mind:

**Table 2-5**
Common Roman Fractions and Symbols

| Symbol | Numerical Value | Comments |
|---|---|---|
| S | ½ | semisque |
| T | ⅓ | sometimes notated as TK |
| F | ⅔ | sometimes notated as Z or FZ |
| C backwards | ¼ | scilius |

(Working examples appear in *De Architectura* by Vitruvius, Book 10.)

Six symbols sufficed for most users (I, V, X, L, C, M).

Most citizens did not need more than simple arithmetic skills.

Hash marks (I, II, III) were amenable for counting.

Some researchers (Dehaene 1997, 64) believe that the symbol V derived from a hieroglyphic image representing the open hand with five fingers, or possibly the reversal of an earlier Etruscan symbol. The numeral X originated as an artistic embellishment of two V symbols. The Greek letter theta $\theta$ originally represented 100 and later evolved to C (*centum*) in Roman usage. The Greek letter phi $\phi$ originally represented 1,000 and was later replaced by M (*mille*). Those who marched 1,000 steps at a time were the *miles* ("soldiers") from whence come the English words "military" and "mile."

Europeans used Roman numerals for bookkeeping and financial recording purposes well into the eighteenth century, despite the gradual domination of the decimal system. The Roman numeral form was actually more efficient than its decimal counterpart in cases where arithmetic worked out evenly (e.g., V + V = X or C + C = CC).

### Fractions in Other Ancient Civilizations

The ancient Egyptians developed the use of fractions to a greater extent than the Romans. The Rhind Papyrus (ca. 1650 B.C.E.) contains arithmetic problems and possibly puzzles. The name of the author-scribe is known (A'hmose or Aahmes), but the purpose of the document is not. Who was his audience?

The Egyptians manipulated complex fractions, but their format usually placed a one in the numerator. Complex fractions were constructed from the sums of simpler fractions. (See table 2-6.)

**Table 2-6**
Egyptian Fractions

| Value | Symbols Used | Evaluated as |
|-------|--------------|--------------|
| ¾ | (½, ¼) | (½) + (¼) |
| ⅗ | (⅓, ⅕, ¹⁄₁₅) | (⅓) + (⅕) + (¹⁄₁₅) |

(Newman 1956, 176)

## PREFIX AND POSTFIX REPRESENTATION

### The Problem of Precedence

Most people perform arithmetic pairwise, two numbers at a time. Mixing addition and subtraction together makes sense (e.g., 2 + 5 − 1 = 6). But mixing multiplication and addition is ambiguous.

Does 4 × 5 + 6 mean (4 × 5) + 6 = 26 or 4 × (5 + 6) = 44? The issue is important because misinterpretation produces entirely different answers. Which one is correct?

The problem occurs because arithmetic exhibits precedence. Multiplication and division have the same precedence to each other. Addition and subtraction have the same precedence to each other. Operations with the same precedence can be done in any order. But operations with different precedence must be done in a particular order.

Grouping usually clarifies the order of operations. For example, 2 + 3 × 4 is unclear, but (2 + 3) × 4 = 20 and 2 + (3 × 4) = 14. This representational notation is called *infix* notation. Most people (unconsciously) do infix arithmetic!

### Prefix and Postfix

Inserting parentheses into any computer operation adds additional computer processing. The computer must pause, recognize the grouping, store the components, perform separate operations, return the results, and then continue onward. This process wastes time.

Jan Lukasiewicz (1878–1956) developed a formal system of arithmetic that overcomes this problem. In *prefix* notation the operator (e.g., +, ×) appears before its argument. In *postfix* notation the operator appears after the argument. (See table 2-7.)

Prefix notation is also known as "Polish notation" in honor of its founder. Postfix notation is known as "reverse Polish notation" (RPN). *Most users are oblivious to the fact that many handheld calculators actually operate in RPN mode.* Both prefix and postfix representations appear weird at first exposure, but this is due to a cultural bias.

RPN makes arithmetic processing more efficient. There are no parentheses or any need for excessive intermediate storage space. Expressions are evaluated immediately as they are entered. Arithmetic is accelerated, and storage is conserved.

**Table 2-7**
Prefix and Postfix Forms

| Type | Example | Meaning |
|------|---------|---------|
| Infix notation | (2 + 3) × 4 | add 2 and 3, get 5, multiply by 4 |
| Prefix notation | × 4 + 2 <enter> 3 | store 4, multiply by the sum of 2 and 3 |
| Postfix notation | 2 <enter> 3 + 4 × | store 2, store 3, add them, store 4, multiply |

RPN is often implemented on computers using register stacks. In one Hewlett-Packard hand calculator model, there are four vertical stacks labeled (from bottom to top) X, Y, Z, and T. The display window always shows the contents of the bottom stack. This procedure permits arithmetic using minimal space and maximum efficiency.

## EXERCISES AND RESEARCH QUESTIONS

### Exercises: Representation

E2.1    (warm-up exercise): Find thirty or more words of four or more letters in the word INFORMATION.

E2.2    Verify that LXI + XXXIX = C.
        Now do it without converting the numbers to decimal form first.

E2.3a    Bud Abbott and Lou Costello developed much of their comedy based on the misrepresentation of information. The following examples were performed many times on stage and screen (*In The Navy*, 1941). What is the flaw in the following arguments that 13 × 7 = 28?

*Questionable Proof 1*

```
      13
   ×   7
   ─────
      21        (because 3 × 7 is 21)
       7        (because 7 × 1 is 7)
   ─────
      28        (because 21 + 7 is 28)
```

*Questionable Proof 2:* 13 times 7 means 13 added to itself 7 times. Add down the right-hand column (3, 6, 9, . . . 21). Carry that value over to the next column. Add the seven ones in the next column. The sum is 28.

E2.3b   The same words can represent different meanings at the same time in the same context. Act out "Who's on First?" (see appendix C). At what point does the representation become clear?

E2.4    Why does an even number always end with a final zero in its binary representation? Why does an odd number always end in one?

*Research Question 2.5*

Might an advanced extraterrestrial intelligent life-form with seven fingers consider base seven as natural? How might arithmetic be represented differently?

## Exercises: Hexadecimal

E2.6    (hexadecimal chess): Folklore says that the inventor of chess asked for one grain of wheat on square number one, two grains of wheat on square number two, with the number of grains doubling on each successive square of the 64-square chessboard. Suppose the inventor asked for increases by sixteen instead of two. How many squares are needed to exceed more than one million grains on a square?

## Exercises: Fractions

E2.7    Add ⅔ + ⅙ orally using the names "of three parts, two" and "of six parts, one."

E2.8    Add ⅔ + ⅙ orally using the standard decimal terms.

*Research Question 2.9*

Does the symbolic representation of numbers drive a culture or does the culture drive the representation of numbers? To what extent does the choice of number system discourage human imagination?

CHAPTER 3 ▶ Organizing Information

## FUNDAMENTAL INFORMATION STRUCTURES

Trees have of course been in existence since the third day of creation . . .

(Knuth 1973, 405)

The Ruben definition of information as "a coherent collection of data organized in a particular way that has meaning" places special emphasis on organized data. Organization provides a structure or framework for a collection of data. The nature of that structure affects the manipulation of the data and, by extension, both information management and retrieval. This discussion focuses on several fundamental models of data structure.

### Linear (Sequential) Model

The simplest data organizational model is arguably the linear (sequential) model. Data are appended one after another in a line, hence the name. Magnetic tapes, music cassette tapes, and index cards utilize this data structure. (See figure 3-1.)

People stand in line at a library circulation desk or supermarket cashier. *The first person in is the first person out.* This process describes the first-in-first-out (FIFO) linear model. By contrast, a person enters an elevator, walks to the back, and turns around. The next person enters, stands in front of the previous person, and turns around. *The first person in is the last person out.* This process describes the first-in-last-out (FILO) linear model.

**Figure 3-1**
Linear (Sequential) Organization

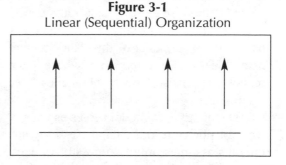

25

## Advantages

The linear model is simple because the metaphor is a simple line. Append new data to the end of the line. Delete old data by removing it from its place in line. The linear model is always effective because data can always be located given sufficient time.

Linear information media tend to have high storage capacity and low cost. Such media are generally stackable, itself a linear model! They are often used for system backups.

## Disadvantages

Linear retrieval may be effective, but it is not efficient. If the desired item is in position 100 and the reader is currently at position 1, then the process involves traversing 99 extraneous positions. If the item's location is not known beforehand, then finding it may require passage through the entire data set. In the best-case scenario, the desired value is only one position away from the current position. In the worst case, it is at the furthest extreme. Linear retrieval may be fast or slow as a function of position.

Suppose a linear data set contains 4,000,000 items in a row and the retrieval system processes 100,000 items per second. It could take as long as 4,000,000 items/100,000 items per second = 40 seconds to find the desired item.

The system deletes linearly organized data by removing it from its position in the line. This process is simple, but removing data leaves gaps. The number and size of such gaps degrade information system performance. Selectively copying the data set onto a new medium eliminates gaps but also requires time, effort, and expense.

By contrast, the process of merging linearly organized data is hard. Merging often involves pushing aside all other items further down the line. This process involves considerable computer processing time.

*Example 3.1* (music cassette tape)

It is easy to add a new song to the end of a tape. It is easy to delete a song from its current position. It is not easy to play songs in a different order or insert a new song between two existing songs.

## *Binary Tree Model*

Some information is intrinsically two-valued (true-false, on-off, male-female, yes-no, true-false, right-left, in-out, paid-not paid, etc.). The model of this data structure resembles an inverted tree where each branch has precisely two subbranches. (See figure 3-2.)

The binary tree model serves especially well for library or other databases in which the data assumes only two possible values.

**Figure 3-2**
Binary Tree Organization

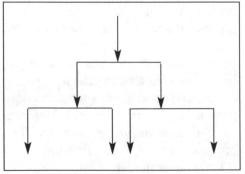

Typical examples include resources (present or absent), collection development (items ordered or not ordered), and staff (achieved levels of certification or not). The model is also efficient for a ranked path of two-valued choices; for example, Library Board of Trustees approval (yes/no), Director approval (yes/no), Ordered (yes/no), Delivered to patron (yes/no).

### Advantages

All data are located above or below other data. Their relative positions rank the data. Each branch represents a level of context. There is information in the data and in its position. *The data structure itself supplies information.*

Inserting data is simple (add a new branch). Block deletion is simple (remove a branch and it removes everything beneath it). Binary coordinates uniquely determine a specific position on a specific branch. These coordinates together constitute a path. If the path coordinates are known, then retrieving information involves following the path. *This process not only leads to the data directly but also avoids extraneous searching.* Contrast this with the linear model, where every element might need examining.

### Disadvantages

Life is not always binary. In many cases, a two-valued (coordinate) system is neither sufficient nor realistic. The binary model is not always sufficient because different data values may have different paths pointing in opposite directions, with no direct path between them. This structure complicates retrieval because the only way to travel between data requires backtracking up the tree.

### *Hierarchy Model*

The basic hierarchical model is an extension of the binary tree model. Any branch may have any number of subbranches accommodating multivalued data. The model retains all the other desirable binary tree properties. (See figure 3-3.)

The UNIX operating system uses this type of file system. The uppermost level is called the root (an amusing inversion of terminology, since a root is usually at the base of a tree). Each sublevel is called a directory and is denoted by slashes. The root is denoted by a single slash.

**Figure 3-3**
Hierarchy Organization

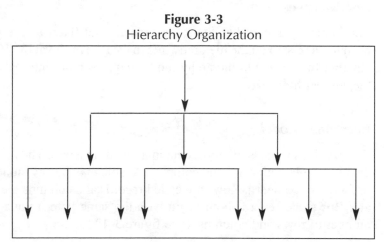

*Example 3.2*

A directory path such as /user/local/lib means:

Begin at the top level (root)
travel down one level to user
travel down one level to local
travel down one level to lib

*Caveat:* UNIX is a case-sensitive operating system and distinguishes upper- and lowercase letters. Although they may look similar

path1 = /Section3/Document

is not the same as

path2 = /section3/document

They identify different positions in the hierarchy tree.

This difference causes panic to UNIX novices when they cannot find their files. The Microsoft disk operating system also uses a hierarchy file structure. The slash is reversed, avoiding confusion with UNIX, from which it is derived.

### Advantages

Information retrieval in this model involves following a path, but each branch has more than two possible values. A binary tree is thus a special case of a general hierarchy tree. A general hierarchy tree need not have the same number of branches at each level. A linear model is one-dimensional; the hierarchy model is multidimensional. More dimensions often permit easier relationship visualization. Family genealogy charts (not surprisingly called family trees), corporate organizational charts, and chains of command are common hierarchy structures. The Dewey cataloging system relies on a hierarchy.

### Disadvantages

The hierarchy model has the same fundamental flaws as the binary tree model. The need to back-step up the hierarchy tree makes the retrieval of different data values problematic. In addition, a hierarchy model requires more internal bookkeeping than does the simpler binary tree.

### *Relational Model*

The previous models organize data in a line or in a tree. The relational model organizes data in a table with rows and columns. A table may be envisioned as an array, a matrix, or a tic-tac-toe board. Rows are called records and columns are called fields. (Memory aid: Rows and records both begin with the same letter.) Square tables have the same number of rows and columns. (See figure 3-4.)

A collection of multiple related tables, queries, forms, reports, and macros constitutes a relational database because all operations *relate* to a table. Tables may contain numeric or non-numeric data. Records and fields may be added, deleted, or manipulated, generating new tables. All power to the table!

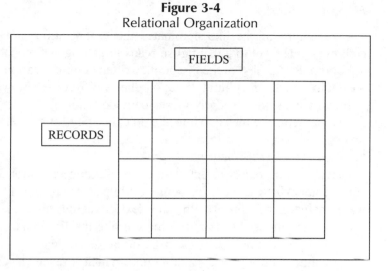

**Figure 3-4**
Relational Organization

## Advantages

The intersection of a record and field specifies a unique box within the table. *Regardless of table size, two numbers (row, column) uniquely identify the location of any particular data item.* Contrast this with previous models, which require knowledge of a path through multiple branches of a tree structure. The long paths along tree and line structures reduce retrieval performance. In the relational model, *two coordinates unambiguously locate the data.*

Manipulating relational data is a very simple process. Insert data by placing it into the appropriate box. Delete it by emptying that box. Modify it by changing its value in the box. The table easily expands with the addition of new records or fields. The table easily shrinks by removing records or fields.

In many cases, any data set that works well as a spreadsheet is amenable to a relational database structure. Relational models are thus very common in office and library environments. Records that contain multiple attributes such as author names and other fields are commonly stored in relational databases.

## Disadvantages

The position of a box in a table does not provide any ordering information. There is no intrinsic ranking, since any record may be moved. Data relationships that seem obvious in a tree are lost in a table. (We speak of family trees, not family tables.)

Tables often require extensive computer storage. A $3 \times 3$ square table uses nine elements. A table with M records and N fields contains $M \times N$ boxes. A large library relational database table may require hundreds or thousands of data storage boxes.

Table storage can be wasteful. A table with a fixed structure must allocate space even though it is not used, and empty boxes waste space. If a $3 \times 3$ table contains two blank boxes, then 22 percent of the storage capability is wasted. It is possible to split a few large tables into many small tables, but the administration of this process adds another level of complexity.

## *Hypertext Model*

The paradigm of the line dominates the organization of written human language. Hebrew reads right to left. English reads left to right. Some Asian languages read top to bottom. Regardless of the direction, written communication is linear. Question: Were these differences in cultural direction due to differences in available media, i.e., stone (tablets) versus wood (paper) versus bamboo (sticks)?

Documents are read one line at a time, one page at a time, first page to the last page (except for people who read the last pages of a whodunit mystery first). In contrast, *hypertext breaks the linear paradigm.*

Hypertext is not new. Scholars of the Talmud (a compendium of Jewish law and commentary) have used the principles of hypertext analysis for centuries. Text portions were analyzed and linked with other text, revealing inner meanings or resolving perceived ambiguities. Scholars routinely broke the linear paradigm of the page and in doing so opened a new universe of information content.

Imagine a library reading table onto which a reader has placed three books. The first book contains a poem. The second book is a dictionary opened to a page containing a word in the poem. The third book contains explanatory commentary about the poem. The reader encounters a word in the poem, looks up its meaning in the dictionary, and then refers to a discussion in the commentary. There is no physical connection between these three texts, but there is a very real though intangible connection between them within the mind of the reader. The reader creates a cognitive link from the poem word to the dictionary word to the commentary word. The links between them, embedded in the text itself, transcend the linear paradigm of the documents.

*The World Wide Web is an example of hypertext in a global multimedia networked environment.* This is in contrast with the previous example, where links reside only within the mind of the reader.

### Advantages

The power of hypertext lies in its ability to electronically connect relevant texts. The definition extends to anything that can be digitized. The physical separation of texts is irrelevant. The paradigm of distance vanishes.

The advent of the World Wide Web has already had a significant impact on library and information and retrieval. Hypertext provides extensive relevance searching as the user follows relevant links. Information need no longer be local. Indeed, the Web has become an almost indispensable retrieval and research tool.

### Disadvantages

Who makes the links? The world has many authors and many documents. There is no standard format or determination of relevance or even standards of good taste.

What links are selected? The choice of potential links is almost endless.

Who maintains the links? Directories move; computers drop off networks; people change jobs and network addresses. A reader has little assurance that the hypertext document they have just read is accurate, complete, or even up-to-date.

Where am I? The linear nature of a book or standard text page offers a clear and unambiguous sense of position. In contrast, it is easy to get lost within hypertext. If document A links to B and then to the middle of C but then branches to D and back to another portion of B, it is not always clear where you are, and perhaps more importantly, how you got there, so that you may return at another time.

Hypertext navigation is still rather crude. Forward and back motion buttons provide some measure of navigation. The "Home" button offers a fixed starting position. "Bookmarks" or "Favorites" provide shortcuts. Histories provide reference points. But these tools are limited and not always adequate in a dynamic hypertext environment.

Retrieving hypertext-organized information poses a serious challenge. The World Wide Web incarnation of hypertext involves an enormous number of links, and the number of links grows along with the number of nodes (i.e., websites). Hypertext retrieval currently involves indexing, but many studies have shown that this is not completely adequate. In contrast with more traditional retrieval methods, searching the Web by following (link) paths is not feasible because there are too many links!

Suppose for the sake of simplicity that one website contains one page. A node is a connection point. If there are only a few websites, then they can be connected forming a line, triangle, square, or other geometric shape. But as the number of websites increases, the number of possible links between them increases dramatically!

Various simplistic network meshes:

| | |
|---|---|
| The World Wide Line | 2 nodes, 1 link |
| The World Wide Triangle | 3 nodes, 3 links |
| The World Wide Square | 4 nodes, 6 links |
| The World Wide Pentagon | 5 nodes, 10 links |
| The World Wide Hexagon | 6 nodes, 15 links |

This pattern suggests the following generalization:

| | |
|---|---|
| The World Wide Web | N nodes, $N \times (N - 1) / 2$ links |

(Websites often contain multiple pages, so the number of possible connections is even greater!)

### Random Access Model (Simplified)

All of the preceding organizational models impose some sense of order on a collection of data. Ranking the data is useful, but it is not always mandated from the perspective of computer processing. The relational model conceptually puts data in a box in a table. In most cases the location of the data remains static. The organizational efficiency could be improved if the box allocation was *dynamic*.

The random access model makes optimal use of available computer storage space. The term "random" is somewhat of a misnomer. Data are not placed randomly into computer storage (that would be chaos), but into very specific storage locations directed by the operating system. It appears as random allocation, but the procedure is very well structured. The random access model is the primary model by which most computers physically store data on their hard drives.

## How It Works

Suppose Table 1 is a storage table. For the sake of simplicity, label the boxes consecutively and assume that all are the same size and each holds the same amount of data. Table 2 is an address table. It contains N rows (records) and two columns (fields). The fields of Table 2 are the data labels and their addresses in Table 1.

Suppose A is a new data value. The computer operating system places the *contents* of A into box 1. It then puts the *label* of A into the first column of Table 2 and the *address* of A into the second column of Table 2. The process repeats for other new data.

## Advantages

The address table provides immediate information on the identification and location of any data contained therein. Now suppose a data value is no longer needed. It is erased from its box and its entry within the address table is deleted. New data arrive and need a storage location. *Used space is recycled.*

Suppose data values cannot fit into their designated box. The values are broken up and distributed across multiple boxes in the storage table. Contiguous storage is preferred but not necessary. The address table maintains a dynamic record of which pieces went where, so pieces are reassembled as needed. *Data are stored wherever there is room.*

Suppose the data boxes are not of uniform size. A sophisticated algorithm assigns addresses not just by availability but also by the smallest box that is capable of storing the data. *Data organization minimizes wasted space.* Suppose a box can store a six-digit number and the new value is only a four-digit number. The operating system could dump the smaller number into the bigger box, but this wastes storage space. The operating system seeks out a four-digit box and places it there.

Suppose the address table has three columns, the third of which contains a binary (yes or no) value indicating whether the values are currently in use. If the values are no longer needed, then it is not necessary to waste computer time erasing unneeded data. *Erasure of data is replaced by changing address entries.*

## Disadvantages

The random access model is a highly dynamic and highly complex process. The address table must continually update the current state of data management. Data may be broken up, dispersed, or assigned specialized locations. Table corruption devastates this process.

In an ideal computing world, the operating system cleans up after itself. Residual data are automatically and completely recycled. In the real world, temporary files may not disappear as they should and pointers may not properly reset. Residual junk and wasted space accumulates within the storage table.

New data become more and more dispersed. The information system requires more time and resources when processing routine tasks. Computer storage becomes fragmented and affects system performance. Many computer systems require periodic defragmentation.

### Final Thoughts

This survey of data structure models is not all-inclusive. Should libraries be organized geometrically, with books organized dynamically by frequency of use (Booth 1969)? Neural networks and nearest neighbors offer additional organizing principles. How does our brain in its limited space organize the contents of our mind? How do you organize objects in your basement?

## WHO WANTS SHORT SORTS?

Sorting puts things in order, be they library books on a shelf or data in a database. Efficient retrieval relies on sorting.

### Terminology

The technical terms "sorting," "sequencing," and "ordering" are not synonymous. "Sorting" is the term of choice for data rearrangement. The word "sequencing" generally connotes a biological context; a genome sequence reveals DNA, RNA, and amino acid components. The word "order" bears various mathematical meanings (e.g., the order of a finite group has nothing to do with the order of an equation) and has various other meanings, as seen from this example:

> "I was ordered to order more tape units in short order in order to order the
> data orders of magnitude faster." (Knuth 1973, 1)

### Why Bother Sorting?

Sorting addresses several fundamental issues of information management. It can be argued that an information system expends more than half of its time arranging various sets of data into some ranked order. Sorting puts similar things together. Sorting establishes clusters, and clustering enhances retrieval.

*Sorting identifies differences.* If two files are in the same order, then the act of pairing items reveals an item present in one that is not in the other. Sorting provides a powerful information management tool for the following fiendishly elusive problems:

> Find items in group A that are not in group B
>
> Find all duplicate items in a group
>
> Order the elements of a group

*Sorting enhances retrieval.* If it is known beforehand that data have a specific ordering, then the search algorithm exploits this ordering. The process of searching ranked data is more efficient than searching random data.

*Sorting assists editing.* If edits are indexed in order, then the editing changes are sorted/merged back into the original data set effectively and efficiently, quickly and easily. Efficient editing reduces computer storage.

### Sorting Algorithms

If an entire data set can reside in a computer's high-speed memory simultaneously, then *internal sorting* is very fast. If all the data cannot be stored at one time, then the process is known as *external sorting*. External sorting overcomes a computer's memory storage limitations but requires additional access time.

Hundreds of different sorting algorithms are in common use. These methods operate via heaps, links, trees, pointers, bases, insertions, exchanges, selections, bubbles, and sinks. The processes are indeed well described by these interesting metaphors. A few fundamental methods will be discussed below.

*The insertion sort.* A single item is placed into the proper position one item at a time. Envision a poker player inserting a new card one after another into their hand.

*Example 3.3* (insertion sort)

Knuth (1973, 107) calls this a "sinking sort" because the data values "sink" to the bottom of the list. The method orders the last two elements. The next adjacent item is placed where it belongs. This step repeats.

| Original data | 60 | 45 | 10 | 7 |
|---|---|---|---|---|
| First pass | 60 | 45 | 7 | 10 |
| Second pass | 60 | 7 | 10 | 45 |
| Third pass | 7 | 10 | 45 | 60 |

*The exchange sort.* Two items are moved at a time. The items swap positions if they are out of order. The process continues until no more exchanges are needed.

*Example 3.4* (exchange sort)

This process is sometimes referred to as a "bubble" sort because data values percolate or bubble to their correct position. The method involves the selective comparison of neighboring items in a list. The first two items are compared. If the first is larger than the second, then exchange them. If the first item is smaller than the second item, then do nothing. Repeat with the next pair. The largest item bubbles to the end. Repeat the entire process until everything is sorted. The conceptual simplicity of the bubble sort has great appeal, but it uses an excessive number of operations.

Suppose there are no more exchanges after a given pass through the data. The sort is complete and the process halts automatically. *The bubble sort has the advantage that it can terminate itself.*

| Original data | 25 | 60 | 2 | 70 |
|---|---|---|---|---|
| First pass | 25 | 2 | 60 | 70 |
| Second pass | 2 | 25 | 60 | 70 |

*The selection sort.* The smallest item is located. The process repeats for the next smallest item and continues until all items are exhausted. Some variations on this method start with the largest instead of the smallest.

*Example 3.5* (selection sort)

The first element is compared to all other elements. When the smallest is found, the first element and the smallest are interchanged. The process continues with the next element.

| Original data | 25 | 60 | 2 |
|---|---|---|---|
| First pass | 2 | 60 | 25 |
| Second pass | 2 | 25 | 60 |

*The ad-hoc sort.* This is a special procedure specifically designed for a particular data set in a particular environment. The process exploits known characteristics of the data (e.g., most items are already in order, the minimum/maximum values are already known, etc.). Ad-hoc sorting methods typically excel on the data set for which they are designed but often show mediocre performance when applied to other environments.

*The quicksort.* This is sometimes called a "partition exchange sort." The last element is placed in such a position that everything to its left is smaller and everything to its right is larger. The process is repeated on one side and then the other.

*Example 3.6* (quicksort)

| Original data | 25 | 61 | 2 | 81 | 7 |
|---|---|---|---|---|---|
| First pass | 2 | 7 | 61 | 81 | 25 |
| Second pass | 2 | 7 | 25 | 61 | 81 |

*The Hat Sort* (fictional; Rowling 1997). The Hogwarts School of Witchcraft and Wizardry utilizes the Sorting Hat method to organize its student population. Novitiates don a frayed, patched hat that assigns them to one of four membership Houses. Sorting Hat assignments are irrevocable.

### Comparing Sorts

The preceding examples demonstrate the effectiveness of several common sort methods. The methods may be effective, but are they efficient? On what basis can sort operations be compared?

Raw timing tests are a crude measure of efficiency. But a production environment must also consider other factors, because the sort algorithm does not act alone; it shares its requirements with other resources within the information system. These factors can include the number of operations, running time, storage, memory, complexity, and behavior in the best-organized case, worst-organized case, and average case.

A sort method with a low number of operations but high requirements for storage necessitates external sorting, which in turn reduces overall performance. More importantly, perhaps, the efficiency of a sort method depends on the nature of the data itself. *A best-case scenario may be very very good, but a worst-case scenario may be very very bad.* This phenomenon poses a balancing problem: Is it acceptable to settle for average performance in order to hedge one's bets between two extremes?

On the other hand, a sort that can be coded simply saves people time and maintenance time. In a particular information system, these parameters may be more important than computational efficiency or level of sophistication.

Sort method comparisons remain problematic for several reasons. Different relative results occur on different data sets. Different relative results may also occur on different hardware platforms. Many vendors "tune" their methods for their specific environments and applications. The same sort that alphabetizes a non-numeric database well may be quite unsuitable for sorting checkout-counter transactions.

Counting the operations involved in a sort is not always a straightforward task. It is very much a function of computer coding, the nature of the algorithm, and assumptions about the regularity of the data. Machine operations may overlap or be skipped. The actual running time depends on storage, data swapping, and associated arithmetic. A detailed theoretical analysis of many sorting algorithms appears in Knuth (1973).

## Discussion

The bubble (exchange) sort codes easily and has a catchy name. The code detects internal ordering and automatically terminates itself. This method is useful as an instructional method but is rarely used in practice. The selection sort requires less computational effort than the bubble, but the level of computational effort remains the same irrespective of the properties of the data. The sort does not exploit preexisting ordering, and it must run to completion.

The quicksort method uses fewer operations, but why it works is less intuitive than its brethren. It performs very well in the best case but very badly in the worst case, and ironically the worst case occurs when the data are already in order! The quicksort method is often the basis for many hybrid general-purpose sort procedures.

It is not always clear which sorting algorithm performs best in a given situation. Know your data.

## EXERCISES AND RESEARCH QUESTIONS

### Exercises: Organizing

E3.1    No one knows how the brain organizes its information. The human brain may contain as many as 200 billion neurons. Suppose each neuron represents one bit of information, and a CD-ROM holds 800 megabytes. One megabyte equals 1,024 × 1,024 bytes, and one byte equals eight bits. How many CD-ROM disks are needed to perform a complete brain dump?

E3.2     Poorly organized data hinder retrieval and problem solving. Solve the puzzle entitled "Which Librarian Has the Server?" (see appendix A).

E3.3     (hierarchy model): A genealogical family tree bears hierarchical information. This information is obscured if it is organized sequentially. Record the following data on a series of linear index cards, one card per line of data. What is the relationship between Lee and Robert?

> Gladys, sister of Wilford, Martyn, Muriel
>
> Muriel, sister of Wilford, Martyn, Gladys
>
> Martyn, brother of Gladys, Wilford, Muriel
>
> Martyn, father of Richard, Robert
>
> Wilford, brother of Gladys, Martyn, Muriel
>
> Wilford, father of Lee, Mona, Michael
>
> Lee, father of Jill, Aaron
>
> Mona, mother of Jacob
>
> Michael, father of Evan

E3.4     Record the same relationships using a tree structure. What is the relationship between Aaron and Evan?

E3.5     Suppose the World Wide Web contains 200 million linked hypertext-organized documents (i.e., pages). Your boss pays you to view one page at a time, one page per second, sixteen hours a day, five days a week. Assuming no additional documents are added, approximately how much time will you need to view every page on the World Wide Web?

### *Exercises: Sorting*

E3.6     Name five common information resources that use sorted values.

E3.7     (operational count): Take three sheets of paper, each marked with a number, and sort them into increasing order by any two methods described in this chapter. Count every time a sheet moves.

E3.8     (operational count): Repeat the above process with four sheets.

E3.9     (coding simulation): Assign five students each a placard with a displayed number. Arrange the students at random. Ask another student to call out explicit instructions placing the cards in ascending order by moving the people. The students can do only what the caller *says,* not what they believe the caller *meant.* (Articulating instructions mimics writing code. Writing code is harder than it looks.)

E3.10  (order in chaos): Give seven students each a sheet of colored paper bearing a number on one side and a partial design on the other. Sort the students using any method. At the conclusion, turn the papers over, revealing a complete picture that is visible only when the papers are sorted in the correct order.

E3.11  (increased complexity): Select four volunteers. How long does it take the volunteers to sort themselves alphabetically by last name in chronological order by age? Add one more volunteer anywhere. Repeat the process and time it again.

CHAPTER 4 ▶ Retrieving Information

Create a set of rules that . . . will allow for a vendor-independent directory of every computer, user, group, printer, server, volume, and file in every department in every country in the entire world.

—Mandate of the Comité Consultatif, International Télégraphique et Téléphonique, 1989 (cited in Spalding 2000, 245)

. . . the more things we have to remember, the more help we need finding them . . . (Spalding 2000, 244)

## THE NATURE OF INFORMATION RETRIEVAL

Egyptian pharaohs used scribe-powered search engines for the retrieval of scrolls. Medieval kings used monk-powered search engines for the retrieval of sacred texts. Traditional information retrieval located *objects,* be they tablets, scrolls, or books. Contemporary information retrieval often matches terms and solves problems.

Contemporary information retrieval involves the selective identification of items by exact, partial, heuristic, or statistical techniques expedited by the processing capabilities of digital computers and networks. Keyword searching involves simple or sophisticated algorithms by which the computer locates digital strings of characters. Relevance searching often involves following paths or network links.

### Matching versus Problem Solving

Matching methods retrieve items (documents) containing specific words, terms, phrases, or other strings of characters (i.e., keywords). Matching may be exact or partial: the former is more restrictive; the latter is more general. Exact or partial matching retrieves documents with something. Relevance matching retrieves documents about something.

Retrieving a document is much easier than solving a problem. Conceptually speaking, retrieving a document involves comparing a string of words (the query) to the contents of a set of words (the document). Are the values the same or different? Yes or no. One or zero. The lowly but powerful two-valued bit has immediate information retrieval (IR) applications.

The sheer number of words, forms, stems, and synonyms make such a comparison a laborious process. Word order, format, proximity, and relationships make such comparisons complex. A partial match is even more complex, since it involves intrinsic imprecision.

Matching involves comparison. By contrast, problem solving involves identifying a solution that is revealed within a document or data collection but is not necessarily explicitly embedded within it. Problem solving contains a subtle meta-information component. There may be one solution, many solutions, or no solutions, and this information about information may not be known in advance. If there are multiple solutions, then identification of the optimal solution (if one exists) creates further meta-issues.

For example:

1. A patron wishes to read more works by a given author.
2. A physician searches for a diagnosis to a set of patient symptoms.
3. A drug company searches for experimental drugs having the best chance of success.
4. An airline seeks the fastest, cheapest, most direct route between cities.

1. Did the author indeed write more works (and possibly under another name)?
2. More than one diagnosis may match the symptoms.
3. Some, all, or none of the drugs may be therapeutic.
4. The fastest route may not be the cheapest.

Why is this important? There is no sense wasting system processing time and people time on a problem with no solution. If one knows beforehand that there is one and only one solution, then the search stops once a solution is found. Now suppose two solutions exist, but you do not know this. A solution is found and the search stops. There is no way of knowing that the second solution (which might possibly be a better solution) might have been identified if only the search had continued longer.

### When Problem Have No Solutions

There is no sense performing information retrieval if there is no solution. Not all problems have solutions. The core issue might not be well posed, or it might be inconsistently expressed. A problem might have no solution in one context but a meaningful solution in another.

Consider an aircraft beginning its landing X miles from the runway and Y feet from the ground. Knowing the plane's altitude tells us nothing about its position. Knowing the plane's position tells us nothing about its altitude. Finding the unique determination of the aircraft's location in space requires a two-information number. For that matter, knowing when this information applies is a critical third context because planes must be separated in space and in time. One single information context is insufficient to solve the problem of landing a plane.

The absence of a solution may be caused by a lack of knowledge on our part (asking the wrong question) or the inadequacy of the problem statement under its given constraints (incompatible conditions). *If a problem has no solution, then consider that the crux of the difficulty may be the inadequacy of the tools, the inadequacy of the statement, or the inadequacy of the imposed conditions.*

### Recall and Precision

Information retrieval efficiency does not imply effectiveness, and IR effectiveness does not imply efficiency. Obtaining fifty fast hits in a keyword query is quite different than obtaining fifteen highly relevant hits; the former is efficient, while the latter is effective.

Recall and precision measure the effectiveness of information retrieval (Cooper 1973; Kent et al. 1954, 1955). Recall measures the extent to which all relevant items were retrieved. Precision measures the extent to which the retrieved items were relevant. The two concepts coalesce in an ideal information retrieval system: all relevant items are retrieved and all irrelevant items are not retrieved. This would occur with perfect query design, perfect information representation, and perfect determination of relevance. This situation rarely occurs in practice, however.

Effective relevance-based information retrieval involves identifying *all* relevant items and *only* relevant items. The "all-and-only problem" hinges on the determination of relevance and the representation of information. Relevance determination is often an uncertain process, and the representation of information (whose relevance must be determined) is often inadequate or incomplete. The all-and-only problem is arguably the most fundamental problem of information retrieval. The all-and-only problem was originally called the "only-but-not-all, all-but-not-only problem" and still appears that way in some texts.

An ideal IR system should achieve both high recall and high precision. Empirical studies suggest that recall and precision act in opposition to each other. In practice, the enhancement of one tends to diminish the other. The relationship occurs so often that a deeper phenomenon may lie beneath it, but no formal proof of this has yet been found.

What is the goal of information retrieval (Swanson 1977, 1988)? Is it to enhance the number of relevant items retrieved, or to enhance the likelihood that a retrieved item is relevant? The first goal is achievable at the expense of gaining additional (undesirable) items in the output roster. This explains the common and often frustrating observation that irrelevant items often appear in a list of retrieved items. The second goal is achievable at the expense of missing (desirable) relevant items in the output list. This explains the common and often frustrating observation that fewer relevant items appear in a roster of retrieved items.

## A Numerical Example

Suppose your document collection is sufficiently small so that each item can be individually reviewed for relevance with respect to a given query. Assume that with respect to that query, the performance of the IR system is as cited below. What is the recall and precision of the IR system? (See table 4-1.)

**Table 4-1**
Information Retrieval Effectiveness Experiment

| Data set | Relevant Items | Irrelevant Items | Total |
|---|---|---|---|
| | 80 | 20 | 100 |
| **IR performance** | Relevant Items Retrieved | Irrelevant Items Retrieved | Total Items Retrieved |
| | 30 | 20 | 50 |

Recall   = number of relevant items retrieved /
           total number of relevant items = 30 / 80 = 37.5%

Precision = number of relevant items retrieved /
           number of items retrieved = 30 / 50 = 60%

The IR system identified only slightly more than one-third of all the relevant items. The recall is surprisingly low and the precision is moderate. Only slightly more than half of the retrieved items were relevant. The sum of the system's recall and precision measures is approximately 100 percent, a common empirical result.

## BOOLEAN AND BEYOND

A set is a collection of objects. Information system interactions are often diagrammed as sets. Boolean information retrieval depends on sets.

## Sets and Subsets

Library books on a shelf, socks in a drawer, and students in a classroom form sets of objects. A traditional set has an associated rule or criterion determining if something belongs to that set. Sets usually have a sharp boundary or rule delineating what is and is not contained in the set.

A set may have no elements. This special set is called the *null set*. The set of all million-dollar winning lottery tickets purchased by this author is (regrettably) a null set. The null set is not trivial because it provides the zero element for set arithmetic. The null set also engenders a critical fundamental flaw in fuzzy set theory.

A *proper subset* is a set entirely contained within a set. There may be many subsets in a set. For example, all students in a class may be divided into proper subsets based on their final grade. These subsets are mutually exclusive, since no one receives two grades. Some subsets can overlap, however.

*Example 4.1* (proper subset)

>A is the set of all children's books.
>
>B is the set of all children's books about wizards.
>
>B is a subset of A.

## Boolean and Sets

Boolean methods for using computers to search databases are based on the principles of symbolic logic developed by George Boole (1815–1864). Boolean searching relies on keywords, and the logical relationships between different keywords are expressed by terms called operators. There are three logical operators in Boolean searching: AND, OR, and NOT.

*Example 4.2*

>If A is everything inside a room, then NOT A is everything outside the room.

*Example 4.3*

>A detective examines a crime scene and compiles a set of suspects. The detective gradually eliminates the suspects until only one remains in the set, and that is the perpetrator.

Sometimes it may be logically simpler dealing with things that are not members of the set than the original set itself. Indirect reasoning is often a powerful tool in problem solving.

The union of two sets A and B is the collection of those elements that are in *at least one* of the sets. Elements can be in either or both sets but must be in at least one. A and B have a *disjunctive* (OR) relationship. The operator OR *broadens* the number of cases under consideration, since membership can be to one, the other, or both. *Caveat:* Too many unions in a query generate voluminous results.

*Example 4.4*

>A = {red, green, blue}
>
>B = {green, white, pink}
>
>The set {A OR B} = {red, green, blue, white, pink}

*Example 4.5*

>A = {articles about AIDS}
>
>B = {articles about tuberculosis}
>
>The set {A OR B} = {articles on AIDS, tuberculosis}

The intersection of two sets A and B is the set of elements that are common to both sets. Elements must be in A and simultaneously also be in B. A and B have a *conjunctive* (AND) relationship. The intersection operator *restricts* the number of cases under consideration, since membership must be in both (or all) sets. This feature is used to good advantage in the case of selective searching. *Caveat:* Too many intersections generate null results.

*Example 4.6*

> A ={red, green, blue}
>
> B = {pink, green, yellow}
>
> The set {A AND B} = {green} since this is the only color in common

> A = {lions, tigers, bears, rabbits}
>
> B = {tigers, lions, bears}
>
> The set {A AND B} = {lions, tigers, bears} Oh my!

Some information retrieval systems use *short-circuit evaluation* as an efficient means of performing multiple-intersection query operations (A and B and C and . . . ). The information system evaluates the query from left to right. It stops as soon as it encounters no more matches, since absence from one component suffices to annihilate the entire query.

Musical composition is said to have conjunctive and disjunctive components (Greenberg 2002). Conjunctive music contains notes that lie relatively close together tonally when played together, as if conceptually belonging within the same set. Disjunctive music contains notes that are tonally widely scattered apart when played together, as if in different sets. Conjunctive music sounds smooth, cohesive, lilting, or melodic. Disjunctive music sounds jagged, garish, or contains dramatic jumps.

### Rules of Combination

The order of the same Boolean operator does not matter (commutative property):

> {A OR  B}    represents the same set as {B OR A}
>
> {A AND B)   represents the same set as {B AND A}

The same Boolean operator can be regrouped (associative property):

> {A} OR {B OR C} = {A OR B} OR {C}

(The same property applies to the intersection operator, AND.)
Boolean methods are idempotent: something operating on itself returns itself.
Boolean methods support involution: for example, two NOTs reverse each other.
The NOT operator can be regrouped with mixed operators (distributive property):

> A OR {B AND C} = {A OR B} AND {A OR C}

Boolean methods have equivalent alternative forms (DeMorgan's laws):

NOT {A OR B} is the same as {NOT A} AND {NOT B}

NOT {A AND B} is the same as {NOT A} OR {NOT B}

These forms are important because sometimes an alternative form is more clear than the original.

Parenthetical grouping and rearrangement are valid for operators of the same type, *but are not necessarily valid when applied to mixed operators.* Beware! Grouping mixed operators for arbitrary convenience is a common error for both novices and experienced Boolean searchers. Doing so generates search results that are at best unexpected and at worst total nonsense. Rearrange dissimilar operators at your peril.

*Caveat 1:*     {A} AND {B OR C} is *not* the same as {A AND B} OR {C}

*Caveat 2:*     {A} OR {B AND C} is *not* the same as {A OR B} AND {C}

Why? The union (OR) and intersection (AND) operators are not opposite operations. They do not cancel or reverse each other. Be very careful if a query expression contains more than one type of operator. Clarify the meaning by appropriate use of parentheses. Mixing operations indiscriminately may yield entirely different results. The English language "or" often conflicts with the Boolean language OR. The former often connotes a sense of mutual exclusion (only one choice), while the latter means at least one (and possibly more choices).

"Lunch Special: For $4.95 you get soup or salad and sandwich"

Is this a good deal? It depends.

*Interpretation 1:* {soup OR salad} AND {sandwich}

The possibilities are: {soup, sandwich}, {salad, sandwich}, {soup, salad, sandwich}.

The Boolean OR allows either or both of the first set of selections.

The sandwich comes along with a cup of soup, a salad, or possibly both.

*Interpretation 2:* {soup} OR {salad AND sandwich}

The possibilities are: {soup}, {salad, sandwich}, {soup, salad, sandwich}.

The Boolean OR allows the left side, the right side, both sides.

The sandwich goes with the salad but not necessarily with the soup.

Depending on the interpretation (how mixed operators are grouped), you could end up with only one item (soup alone), two different items (salad and sandwich, or soup and sandwich), or three items (soup, salad, sandwich). Lunch could be an expensive cup of soup or a bargain three-course meal!

English-language homonyms coupled with variable punctuation occasionally produce the same ambiguity, often with humorous effect.

A giant panda walks into a bar and orders a beer. After consuming the beverage the panda takes out a gun, fires it several times, and exits. The furious bartender grabs the panda and demands an explanation. The panda opens a dictionary and reads: "Giant Panda, large animal indigenous to China, eats shoots and leaves . . . " (Berkowitz 2000).

The words "shoots" and "leaves" are nouns or verbs, depending on the context. This context is ambiguous. The meaning would be clarified if it were written:

> Eats shoots, and (also) leaves
>
> Eats, shoots, and (then) leaves

### Aspects of Boolean Searching

Boolean search methods have a formal analytic foundation with a simple two-valued logic and well-defined rules. The system has equivalent forms. The method has an appealing coherence.

Boolean operators are simple, powerful, and easily implemented by computer code. (The UNIX operating system implements AND/OR by the *grep* command.) Boolean methods are all or none. Sets are either relevant or irrelevant to a given query.

Similar Boolean operations are order independent. Searching for "cats AND dogs" is the same as searching for "dogs AND cats." Sometimes word order does matter, however. For example, the simple search query "Venetian AND blind" might produce information on a window dressing (a Venetian blind) or a sightless resident of Venice (a blind Venetian).

Boolean operators ignore proximity. Two words may match a Boolean query because they appear in the same document, but the match is coincidental, not relevant. They may appear in the same document but are far apart and have nothing to do with each other. Boolean operators have no intrinsic sense of weighting. Moreover, the operators do not specify relative importance. All terms are equal and have the same weight. This situation may not be realistic.

Boolean operators lend themselves to sloppy queries. A specific search expression may be ambiguous (unspecified word order). A sloppy query produces unexpected or bizarre results (search terms are too vague). A sloppy query often contains too many negations (too restrictive, producing fewer results) or improperly grouped mixed operators (unclear meaning).

Boolean methods determine relevance solely by keyword matching, not by the keywords' proximity to each other. There is no inherent sense of clustering, distance, or "closeness" between documents. Boolean methods cannot distinguish degrees of relevance except by crude measures such as term frequency. Matching keywords does not imply meaning: "VISUAL AIDS" has nothing to do with the disease "AIDS." Being "COOL" can be thermal or fashionable.

Boolean search methods presume user knowledge of the subject. A poor choice of keyword yields no results. *Keyword efficiency depends on the user.*

Boolean methods depend on language. The words in a language may be neither unique nor precise. Synonymy involves different words for the same object (e.g., beer versus brew, car versus automobile). Polysemy involves the same word having different meanings (e.g., a fan is an air circulation device and also an enthusiastic patron; a skirt is a form of dress and a form of avoidance).

Any retrieval system based on language matching encounters similar problems. Vector-based methods attempt to overcome some of the difficulties associated with simple Boolean matching.

## VECTOR METHODS (SIMPLIFIED)

Vector-based retrieval methods extend Boolean concepts. Retrieval is based not on set manipulation but on evaluation of the document itself. Every document has an associated (multidimensional) vector. Vector-based retrieval assumes that relevant documents are "close" in some well-defined sense. Vector-based methods employ a similarity principle. If a Boolean search reveals that A and B fulfill some criteria, then it is all or none. Vector methods, by contrast, quantify the extent of relevance in some sense.

A vector is a mathematical object satisfying certain properties. A collection of vectors with suitable properties is called a vector space. The analogy to library and information studies is straightforward: if document-based information is expressible as vectors, then a collection of documents may form an information space.

### Building a Document Vector

Assemble a list of keywords (important nouns, term headings, terms in the abstract, etc.) that are relevant to a set of documents. Create a table whose rows are the document names and whose columns are the keyword names. Apply the following process:

> For every document I
> For every keyword J
>> If document I contains keyword J
>> Then mark a "1" in the I-th row and J-th column of the table
> Repeat over all J
> Repeat over all I

The above pseudo-code is a way of stating a simple algorithm:

> If a particular keyword appears in a specific document
> Then put a binary value in the corresponding entry of the table

*Each document can thus be represented by a string of ones and zeros corresponding to the appropriate row in the data table. This string of ones and zeros is its document vector. The vector is a representation of the document.*

The number of components of a vector is called the dimension of that vector. The examples in table 4-2 are four-dimensional vectors because each vector has four components, corresponding to four keywords.

**Table 4-2**
Sample Document Vectors

| Document | Vector | Keyword 1 | Keyword 2 | Keyword 3 | Keyword 4 |
|----------|--------|-----------|-----------|-----------|-----------|
| 1 | {1, 0, 0, 1} | yes | no | no | yes |
| 2 | {1, 1, 1, 1} | yes | yes | yes | yes |
| 3 | {0, 0, 0, 0} | no | no | no | no |

The algorithmic rule above uses binary values. The keyword is either present or absent. Simple binary vectors process very efficiently in a digital computer. Note that every keyword has the same weight as any other keyword.

Keyword frequencies extend the idea and produce a built-in weighting scheme, hence indicating relative relevance. The more keywords, the longer the vector. A longer vector offers a more representative description of the document. If the keywords change, then so do the vector components.

Every document generates a vector, and the more documents the more vectors. Every vector is based on keywords, thus the more keywords the longer the vector. If there are N documents and M vectors, then there are $N \times M$ components. If there are 100,000 documents and 100 keywords, then the information system tracks 10,000,000 entries!

Vector-based retrieval methods do pose certain logistical and administrative questions. Typical issues include:

*How many keywords?* More keywords imply a more descriptive representation but also more components. More components cost more editorial time and processing time.

*Who sets the keywords?* Editors, administrators, authors, or automated machine scans each provide their own differing perspective. These differences may yield different retrieval results.

*Which keywords?* Different keywords produce different vectors. Different vectors produce different retrieval results.

In contrast to a static Boolean information retrieval system, *a vector-based IR system can be tuned.* Administrators may adjust the number, weight, and the keywords themselves. These actions modify the document representations, and this in turn affects the retrieval and performance properties of the information system. These actions are metaphorically akin to turning the dials of an old-fashioned radio.

### Determination of Relevance by Scoring

Vector-based methods typically establish relevance by scoring or distance measures. Scoring assumes the overall representation has a numerical value, and relevant items have similar scores. Distance assumes that clustering makes sense in an information space and that relevant items are in close proximity. Relevance by scoring means *"match my score as closely as possible."* Relevance by distance means *"match my neighborhood as closely as possible."*

Scores may be simple or complex. Suppose document A has vector = {1, 1, 0, 1}.

*Simple score* (sums)

Score = 1 + 1 + 0 + 1 = 3

*Complex score* (weighted sums)

Weights are 50%, 25%, 15%, 10%
Score = $(0.5 \times 1) + (0.25 \times 1) + (0.15 \times 0) + (0.10 \times 1) = 0.85$

*Complex score* (weighted frequencies)

The first keyword occurs four times, the second twice, the third none, and the fourth just once. Use the same weights.
Score = $(0.5 \times 4) + (0.25 \times 2) + (0.15 \times 0) + (0.10 \times 1) = 2.6$

*Complex score* (probability distribution)

Suppose empirical studies suggest that the keywords may follow a statistical distribution.
The score is the associated probabilities.

*Simple score* (global maximum)

If the document vector is {3, 5, 2, 1}, then the maximal value is 5. The second keyword dominates.
The vector {3, 2, 1, 5} has the same maximal value. The last term dominates.

Which score is correct? *All and each of them!* The professional literature abounds with discussions on the appropriateness of a given score in a given context. In the presence of so many scores, how can an information retrieval system determine which scores are close to a given query score and hence retrieve the correctly relevant documents?

The choice of scoring is a common conundrum of vector methods. Vector methods are sometimes considered ad hoc methods for this reason. *Caveat:* Different scoring techniques yield different retrieval results, making system comparisons problematic.

### Determination of Relevance by Distance

Geometric distance is well quantified. If two objects lie along the same straight line, then the distance between them is the value of the numerical difference. In practical terms, however, the shortest distance between two points is not necessarily a straight line. The shortest distance between New York and London is the line that pierces the sphere of the Earth and emerges on the other side. But the shortest practical distance between the cities is the polar arc following the curvature of the Earth. The shortest practical distance between two midtown Manhattan street corners is not through the buildings but the zigzag between blocks. The shortest distance between two offices in connected buildings might be up, across, and down if some floors connect only on certain levels.

The shortest distance between two points is not necessarily the fastest or the cheapest one. The shortest commute between my home and my job is along Route 18, but not during rush hour! Taking back roads adds three miles to the distance but subtracts fifteen minutes from the time. The New Jersey Turnpike is the fastest highway between New Brunswick and Princeton, but Route 27 has no tolls and so is cheaper.

Physical distance is defined in terms of geometry, be it curved or straight. Genealogical distance is defined in terms of offspring and generations. How do we define the distance between relevant documents?

Linear distance is not adequate for this task. The fact that two documents are physically close to each other on the same desk or shelf or that they reside on the same partition of the server does not necessarily imply relevance between them. The Dewey Decimal System classifies relevance by positional location; books of the same type cluster together. (Not all libraries do this. The mathematics library of the Courant Institute of Mathematical Sciences of New York University once arranged its books *alphabetically by author.*)

The distance between two documents can be defined as the distance between their vectors. This concept has a well-established mathematical framework based in part on the geometric model and then extended to a multidimensional setting. *Document distance measures relevance.*

Relevance by distance has the same logistical problem as relevance by score. Different measures produce different retrieval results! Critics cite this as another disadvantage of vector-based retrieval methods.

If it is possible to measure the distance between vectors, then by extension it becomes possible to measure the distance between documents. *If vectors are close in some sense, then vector-based retrieval assumes documents are too, and this closeness is a measure of relevance.*

*Example 4.7*

> The distance between documents A and B is 3
>
> The distance between documents A and C is 5
>
> The distance between documents A and D is 20

> This being the case, A and B might be considered very relevant to each other, C somewhat relevant to them, and D irrelevant to all. Boolean methods cannot easily do this sort of comparison.

Vector methods have the distinct advantage of a mathematical framework underlying the retrieval principle. These retrieval methods assume (1) documents can be represented by vectors; (2) the score or distance or similarity measure associated with such vectors determines relevance; and (3) retrieval is based on this determination of relevance.

## FUZZY INFORMATION RETRIEVAL

Fuzzy set theory (FST) overcomes some limitations of all-or-none, two-valued Boolean methods. FST has the benefit of a solid mathematical framework but lacks sensitivity.

### Infinite and Fuzzy Sets

Set-based information retrieval deals with a large but finite number of elements. This may not be of practical significance to someone who has just encountered 400,000 hits on their web search, but it does have significant theoretical value for the development of IR methods and techniques.

It is tempting to think of sets as simple, small, and confined. Infinite sets and fuzzy sets do not follow the same rules as conventional sets, though. The former pose intriguing abstract challenges, and the latter pose practical challenges.

Galileo characterized an infinite set as any set that can be placed into one-to-one correspondence with a proper subset of itself. In a crude sense this means you never run out of entries.

"Infinity" need not refer to being large. An advertisement promotes an infinite-speed electric drill. Is it very fast? Not especially, but it does have a pressure-driven trigger handle allowing a continuous range of control. Some blenders claim an infinite setting when they mean that the device remains on all the time until manually shut off.

A fuzzy set is a set without a sharp boundary. Membership inclusion in it is vague, hence the term "fuzzy." If someone asks you to meet "about twelve o'clock" near the library, then when and where is your appointment?

### Fuzzy Logic Basics

Boolean methods depend on the theory of sets. Membership (inclusion in a set) is all or none. There is no sense of partial membership. This is not always true in the real world. "More often than not the class of objects in the real physical world do not have precisely defined criteria of membership" (Zadeh 1965).

For the purposes of simplicity, a *fuzzy set* is defined as a class of objects characterized by a membership function assuming values between zero and one inclusive. The closer to zero, the lower the degree of membership. The closer to one, the higher the degree of membership. A value of zero corresponds to total exclusion, while a value of one corresponds to total inclusion. A conventional Boolean set has a fixed membership boundary. FST boundaries are unclear, no longer sharp or precise. They are "fuzzy," hence the name.

*Example 4.8* (fuzzy set membership function)

Let F be a membership function whose value ranges from zero to one. Suppose F operates on a domain set of elements {red, green, blue}. Let its values be:

| | | | |
|---|---|---|---|
| F acting on | yellow | 0 | yellow does not belong to the set |
| F acting on | red | 0.5 | red is half inside and half outside |
| F acting on | green | 0.75 | green is 75% inside and 25% outside |
| F acting on | blue | 1.0 | blue is completely inside |

## Basic Operations of Fuzzy Sets

If fuzzy set methods are an extension of Boolean methods, then they must revert to the Boolean model for the two special cases of inclusion and exclusion. The appropriate membership function involves a minimum and maximum relation (Zadeh 1965; Bellman and Giertz 1973; Sage 1990).

If A and B are two fuzzy sets with membership function F, then the union of two fuzzy sets is the smallest set containing both A and B, and the value is the maximum of F(A) and F(B).

The intersection of two fuzzy sets is the largest set contained in both A and B, and the value is the minimum of F(A) and F(B).

The complement of a fuzzy set A is everything outside of set A, and the value is $1 - F(A)$.

*Caveat:* Strictly speaking, a membership function does not operate on the set but on each individual member of the set, but this is a general discussion, so the author takes the liberty of dispensing with mathematical rigor. A formal expression of fuzzy logic principles appears in Zadeh (1965) and Bellman and Giertz (1973).

*Example 4.9*

Based on Zadeh and others, suppose X is 30% in set A and 50% in set B.

The value of the membership function of the union equals:

maximum $(0.3, 0.5) = 0.5$

The value of the membership function of the intersection equals:

minimum $(0.3, 0.5) = 0.3$

The value of the membership function of the complement of A equals:

$1 - (0.3) = 0.7$

Unions and intersections act as switches. A union acts like a parallel switch; an intersection acts like a series switch. (A parallel circuit with two switches will be live if at least one switch is closed. A series circuit will be live only if both switches are closed.) In contrast, fuzzy set unions and intersections act as sieves, and their associated membership functions correspond to mesh sizes. The metaphor is relevant because a switch is absolute (all or none), while a sieve is relative (varies).

## Issues

Bookstein (1980) constructed a disturbing example demonstrating a fundamental flaw in fuzzy logic. Suppose two documents contain indexed terms and each term has a weight. The relevant query is: mesons AND scattering. (See table 4-3.)

If the query is ranked on the basis of membership weights, then which document is retrieved? The answer may surprise you.

There is only a small variation in meson values, but a large variation in scattering values. This suggests that Document 2 has the higher weight (0.99) and should be selected. Not so. The larger membership value (0.40) occurs in Document 1, so it is selected over Document 2! Fuzzy retrieval lacks sensitivity! The lack of sensitivity stems from the choice of membership functions. The maximum and minimum functions act *globally,* not locally.

Why choose the maximum and minimum functions as membership functions? Bellman and Giertz (1973) examined the problem of self-consistency and derive properties of membership function from basic principles. They prove that minimum and maximum functions are not the only viable candidates, but they are the simplest. An extensive analytic discussion on alternative membership functions appears in Sage (1990, 175–81), but the discussion is not for the algebraically faint of heart.

**Table 4-3**
Fuzzy Query Example

| Document | Term, Weight; Term, Weight | Membership Function |
|---|---|---|
| 1 | (mesons, 0.40; scattering, 0.40) | 0.40 (minimum) |
| 2 | (mesons, 0.39; scattering, 0.99) | 0.39 (minimum) |

### Other Disturbing News

The complement of a set is everything outside the set. The union of a set and its complement should logically contain everything. The intersection of a set and its complement should contain nothing. Both statements are true in a Boolean context, and both are false in a fuzzy set context.

*Example 4.10*

Suppose a fuzzy set has a membership function F for a set A.

The membership function of the union of fuzzy sets A and ~A has the value:

maximum [1, 1 – F] but this is not necessarily 1

The membership function of the intersection of A and ~A has the value:

minimum [1, 1 – F] but this is not necessarily 0

The essence of the problem lies in the *inherent ambiguity of the NOT operator within a fuzzy context.* Bellman and Giertz refer to this difficulty as "fuzzy negation." The authors suggest a possible solution that is more reasonable than rigorous. Disallowing the NOT operator (removing the offender) removes the problem but also reduces the power, flavor, and appeal of Boolean methods.

Consider these differences between traditional Boolean and FST methods:

The union of a traditional set and its complement is everything.

The intersection of a traditional set and its complement is the null set.

The union of a fuzzy set and its complement should be everything, but it is not.

The intersection of a fuzzy set A and its complement should be null, but it is not.

The results are counterintuitive. These results should not be surprising, because a sense of *"belonging" is not really meaningful in fuzzy set theory.* The boundary between a fuzzy set and its complement is neither distinct nor sharp, and that is what makes all the difference (Robertson 1978).

## INVERTED FILES

Many information systems use indexing as an efficient means of file, data, or document retrieval. An index entry provides a pointer that says, "Here I am!" These pointers enhance information retrieval.

### Pointers to Retrieval

Information retrieval by inverted files involves a multistep indexing process wherein the data set rows (documents) and columns (words) exchange roles. Since the row data becomes column data and the column data becomes row data, the result is called an inverted file. Information pointers are effectively reversed.

One characteristic of inverted file retrieval is that most computational overhead occurs during initial preprocessing, but the final result permits very rapid retrieval. Static data sets such as journal archives in which few changes occur are especially amenable to this kind of reversed indexing.

For example, a library database consists of 100 book records. The records are arranged by author name, and the fields are subject keywords. In a corresponding inverted file, each record is a subject keyword, and each field is the author name.

### How It Works

The data are initially organized by documents. The initial step removes "stop" words that bear low information value but occur frequently within the text (e.g., "a," "an," "the"). Stop-word removal expedites indexing with a minimal loss of information.

Index every remaining word in every document. An index is a pointer that reveals where information resides. A high-resolution index might store the location of each document, page, paragraph, sentence, and word number. A low-resolution index might store only the document and page.

Invert the information contained within the documents by filling in the values:

Word (I) = {Document (J), Page (K), Sentence (L), Word (M)}

*Example 4.11*

If "cat"  = {Document (1), Page (2), Sentence (3), Word (5)}
= {1, 2, 3, 5}

Then the word "cat" appears in Document 1, Page 2, Sentence 3, Word 5

*Example 4.12*

Suppose a very simple (low-budget!) data set consists of two documents.

The first document contains two sentences, and the second contains one sentence.

Assume stop words have already been eliminated.

Document 1:  HIV causes AIDS. Avoid unsafe sex.

Document 2:  AZT slows AIDS.

Form the index set. (See table 4-4.)

Alphabetize the word roster. Since the word order is rearranged and every word has an associated vector, the vectors are automatically rearranged. (See table 4-5.)

**Table 4-4**
Word Indexing

| Word | Document Number | Sentence Number | Word Number | Vector |
|------|-----------------|-----------------|-------------|--------|
| HIV | 1 | 1 | 1 | {1, 1, 1} |
| Causes | 1 | 1 | 2 | {1, 1, 2} |
| AIDS | 1 | 1 | 3 | {1, 1, 3} |
| Avoid | 1 | 2 | 1 | {1, 2, 1} |
| Unsafe | 1 | 2 | 2 | {1, 2, 2} |
| Sex | 1 | 2 | 3 | {1, 2, 3} |
| AZT | 2 | 1 | 1 | {2, 1, 1} |
| Slows | 2 | 1 | 2 | {2, 1, 2} |
| AIDS | 2 | 1 | 3 | {2, 1, 3} |

**Table 4-5**
Inverted File Indexing

| Word | Document Number | Sentence Number | Word Number | Vector |
|------|-----------------|-----------------|-------------|--------|
| AIDS | 1 | 1 | 3 | {1, 1, 3} |
| AIDS | 2 | 1 | 3 | {2, 1, 3} |
| Avoid | 1 | 2 | 1 | {1, 2, 1} |
| AZT | 2 | 1 | 1 | {2, 1, 1} |
| Causes | 1 | 1 | 2 | {1, 1, 2} |
| HIV | 1 | 1 | 1 | {1, 1, 1} |
| Sex | 1 | 2 | 3 | {1, 2, 3} |
| Slows | 2 | 1 | 2 | {2, 1, 2} |
| Unsafe | 1 | 2 | 2 | {1, 2, 2} |

Here comes the magic. Retrieval is very efficient because the words are now in sorted (alphabetical) order. The words are in order. Each word has an associated vector. The vector is a pointer. The retrieval system jumps directly to the position pointed to by the vector. There is no need to traverse a possibly long path (as might happen in a tree hierarchy) or follow a line (as might occur in sequential storage).

This method has the advantage that the precise address of each component appears in an index and the index has a rapid lookup capability. The method's disadvantage is that new data disrupt the alphabetical ordering and require re-creating the index file. Inverted file structures are often used for data that are frequently retrieved but not frequently updated.

## EXERCISES AND RESEARCH QUESTIONS

### Exercises: Retrieval

Information cannot always be retrieved by simple pattern matching. Always understand the nature of the problem you are trying to solve.

E4.1    According to the Bible, how many animals of each species did Moses bring aboard the Ark?

E4.2    Who was the first president of the United States to declare war?

E4.3    Would you rather be attacked by hungry cannibals, hungry carnivorous fishes, or by lions that have not eaten in three months?

E4.4    The U.S. Constitution mandates that the president must be born in the United States but need not be buried within the United States. Name any president who is not buried in the United States.

### Exercises: Boolean

E4.5    A classroom consists of five men and four women. Their eye colorings are blue and brown. Their hair colorings are black, brown, and blonde. Are the gender subsets mutually exclusive? Why are the hair and eye color subsets not mutually exclusive?

E4.6    Examine the advertising of various appliances in a department store. How many use the words "infinite" or "infinity" as a descriptive term?

E4.7    The imprecise nature of language is often conducive to fuzziness. Listen for fuzzy descriptors in a nearby conversation (e.g., words like "big, pretty, fine").

E4.8    A library consists of three groups:

    A = {circulation, administration, youth services}

    B = {technical services, media services, music}

    C = {youth services, music}

Verify that {A} OR {B AND C} is *not* the same as {A OR B} AND {C}.

CHAPTER 5 ▶ Networking Information

The essence of networks is connectivity. There are job networks, social networks, power networks, phone networks, computer networks, and, of course, paper cups and string.

## NETWORK TOPOLOGIES

A network topology is the "shape" of the network. The question "Is your network in good shape?" assumes more than one level of meaning. Every topology brings with it a variety of properties that assist in the connection of information.

### Bus Topology

The word "bus" derives from the Latin word *omnibus* ("for all"). It is the simplest topology for uniform connectivity. All computers connect along a single line. The connection cable is called a segment. The segment is closed at each end by terminators defining the segment. Linear communication is conceptually simple and easily maintained, but if the cable breaks or the terminators fail, then all communication ceases along the bus. (See figure 5-1.)

**Figure 5-1**
Bus Network Topology

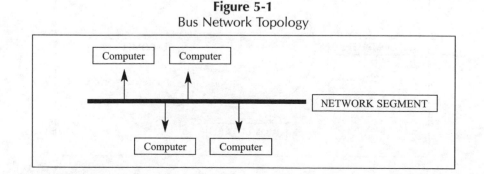

Joining a computer to a bus topology involves attaching it to the segment. Removing a computer from the same network merely involves detaching it. Bus topologies are simple, inexpensive, and straightforward. They are used in simple local area library or office networks and in small individual segments of wide area networks.

Communication traffic increases as more and more computers attach to the bus. Increased traffic generates noise as multiple signals travel the same line at the same time. Signals wait; signals fade with distance; and signals collide. A break in the line stops any further communication. Increased traffic reduces performance. (Imagine several million computers vying for Internet access along the same line.)

## Ring Topology

We can sing at the same time, but we cannot talk at the same time. A bus topology permits multiple simultaneous communication sessions, but it can easily get out of control. But suppose that computers are connected in a circle instead of a line. Data communication travels in one direction and every computer repeats the signal around the ring.

Every computer connects directly or indirectly to every other computer. In contrast to a bus topology, the signal is unidirectional, so collision and interference do not occur. Each computer repeats the full signal onward, so signal strength is not diminished regardless of the number of computers that exist on the ring. (See figure 5-2.)

A special file or signal called a *token* moderates communication on the network. Only the computer with the token sends the message. The token passes to the next computer when the message is sent. Each computer waits its turn. The basic principle is akin to a Talking Stick device used for teaching children social communication skills. The child with the Talking Stick speaks and all others listen. The Talking Stick token prevents everyone from talking at once. One wonders if a network engineer got the idea from a kindergarten teacher?

**Figure 5-2**
Ring Network Topology

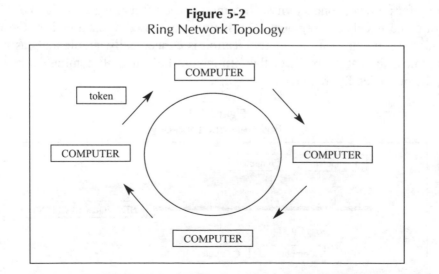

The token ring topology maintains high-speed communication and reduces network noise, but only one computer communicates at a time. (Imagine multiple computers vying for the Internet but only one at a time.) A ring costs more than a bus, but it is a useful alternative if the local area network administrator does not want reduced performance as more computers are added to the network. If the ring breaks, then all network communication stops. Some vendors offer "self-healing" rings. A token ring should not be confused with a Tolkien Ring.

### Mesh Topology

Bus and ring topologies for small local area networks share a common drawback in that a single failure of the connecting medium annihilates signal transmission, and networking stops. Creating redundant paths eliminates this problem. A mesh topology provides fault tolerance because every computer is connected to every other computer. (Imagine every computer on the Internet being physically connected to every other computer.) Backup paths sustain network operation. This topology requires more cabling and hence has a higher cost. (See figure 5-3.) It is used in small networks where connection reliability is of prime concern.

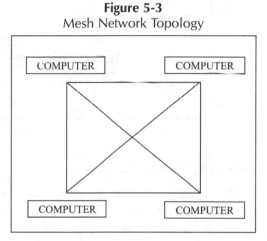

**Figure 5-3**
Mesh Network Topology

### Star Topology

A *hub* serves as a common connection component between the cables and segments in a star shape. If a network cable or a segment fails, then only that specific computer or portion of the network fails. The remainder of the network functions normally. This topology is used if a network requires a higher level of performance and reliability. Hubs are expensive and must be reliable, for if the hub fails, then everything fails. (See figure 5-4.)

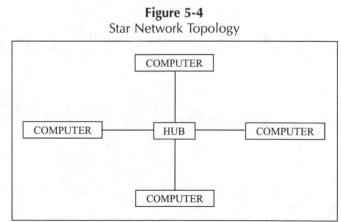

**Figure 5-4**
Star Network Topology

### Star-Bus Hybrid Topology

A star-bus hybrid topology consists of two or more independent star topologies connected by a cable segment. Additional stars are added as needed. This mixed shape has all the advantages and disadvantages of each individual topology. If any computer fails, then the overall network is not affected. (See figure 5-5.)

**Figure 5-5**
Star-Bus Hybrid Network Topology

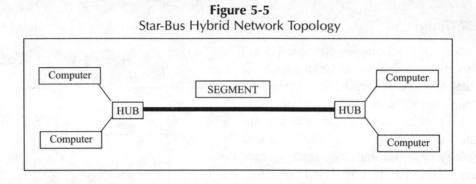

### Star-Ring Hybrid Topology

In this topology, the hub components of several star networks are themselves connected in a ring. A token is passed along them. A single computer failure does not bring down the network, and network noise is reduced. (See figure 5-6.)

The Internet as a network of networks uses all of these topologies plus variations on their themes. Every local network administrator strikes a balance between cost, reliability, and performance.

**Figure 5-6**
Star-Ring Hybrid Network Topology

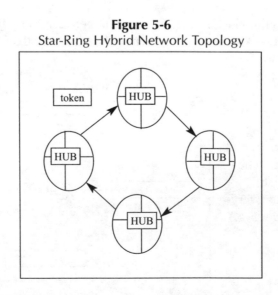

## BRIDGES, SWITCHES, ROUTERS, AND GATEWAYS

A land bridge connects one landmass with another. A network bridge connects one network segment with another network segment. A smart bridge recognizes if the sender and receiver of a signal are on the same segment, localizing the transmission and expediting internal communication. Bridges often split segments, allowing load balancing and more efficient network operation. A bridge reduces network bottlenecks and performance degradation resulting from too many computers attached to the same segment.

A network switch is similar to a network bridge except that a switch connects the source and destination directly by an internal connection. This connection is retained for the duration of the communication. Every connection takes full advantage of the bandwidth (carrying capacity) of the medium. The concept of a network switch derives from a telephone switchboard. When two people make a phone call, there is a direct and dedicated connection within the telephone network for the duration of the call. The connection is released and becomes available to others at the completion of the call.

A router operates as an intelligent switch or bridge. It tracks all addresses within its network by a routing table, and it is aware of the *best path* between any two points. If a path becomes disabled for any reason, the router supplies an alternate path. Routers can screen data signals or block signals containing corrupted or unknown addresses.

A gateway passes signals across different architectures. It repackages disparate signals across networks. A gateway is an interpreter.

CHAPTER **6**    ▶ Securing Information

Who has access to what resources where, when, and why? Information security involves the computer, the network, the server, and their data.

## PHYSICAL, DATA, SERVER, BACKUP, AND NETWORK SECURITY

### *Physical Security*

Barriers block access. Physical barriers include locked cabinets, doors, rooms, and buildings. Any accessible workstation or server is potentially vulnerable.

A deadbolt lock is better than a spring lock. A hardened lock is better than a regular lock. A welded lock is better than a screw-in lock. If the lock is solid but the plate is weak, then physical security is weak. A strong lock on a weak door serves little purpose. *Security is no stronger than the weakest component.* This general principle applies equally well to software (permissions), hardware (barriers), and high-tech filters (retinal scans, fingerprints, voiceprints, DNA scans, etc.).

Physical security involves protection from the elements. Pipes can break; ceilings leak; lightning strikes and power stops; air conditioning fails; fires can start. Nature has a way of humbling us.

Many data centers are designed for machines, not for people. Servers do not move, but people do, and people need alternative escape routes. If electronic locks do not disengage properly, resulting in people being trapped and injured, then legal action will cost the negligent organization dearly. (This author has seen staff hide a brick near a sealed window . . . just in case.)

Water-based fire extinguishers are commonplace but are ineffective for electrical fires. Provide the appropriate extinguisher for the appropriate environment. Test alarms. Much like a parachute, an alarm system must work properly the first time it is needed! Practice evacuation drills. No one should be exempt from fire drills—not even staff with big egos.

## Data Security

Employ a judicious use of user rights and permissions. *Staff should be granted the minimal access privileges necessary to do their jobs.* Keep permissions current. Managing permissions by group is easier than managing permissions by user.

Every user receives baseline permissions and access rights. If a user enters a group, then they should inherit the permissions associated with that group. If a user leaves a group, then they lose the permissions of the group. Users move to and from groups as mandated by their jobs. If the administrator grants enhanced access privileges to a group, then every member of that group now receives those rights immediately and simultaneously. Equally important, nonmembers do *not* receive the benefit. Assigning users to multiple groups as appropriate makes complex levels of security much more manageable.

## Server Security

Servers should be physically isolated in secure areas and be accessible only by authorized personnel. *Servers should run the minimum number of background utilities necessary to perform their tasks.* Remove inappropriate default values, accounts, and settings and modify them to more secure values.

Maintain an up-to-date system complete with all relevant vendor upgrades, service packs, and security patches. Back up the system prior to an upgrade. Be aware that some upgrades or enhancements may introduce new vulnerabilities. *Not every upgrade is necessary for every computer.*

Follow the configuration principle "Deny first, then allow" (Allen 2001, 43). No one likes dealing with an irate user, but it is easier to hear a user squawk and fix the problem than it is to provide open access and plug holes later. Disable what you do not need.

An information system may be better served by many individual machines performing specific tasks than by fewer machines having multiple tasks and multiple vulnerabilities. Dedicated devices such as web, print, log-in, application, file, mail, and backup servers may have incompatible security needs when combined on the same machine.

Limit server access to only those staff supporting a specific application on that server. Minimize direct access. Document all system changes. Perform regular diagnostic maintenance checks. Log system, application, and security events. Study the log and tune your system appropriately.

## Backup Security

If losing data costs time or money or critically impacts normal operations, then a backup policy is a necessity, not a luxury. Accidental and intentional disasters happen. Protect your information.

Backup security involves the ability to restore lost or deleted files. Retain backup copies in a secure location in which they are physically isolated from the originals. Two copies of the same file on the same disk do not make a safe backup. Protect your data and guard your backup. Develop a disaster recovery plan. What would happen if your office had a fire tomorrow? How long would it take to recover? What must be recovered? *Could you recover?*

## Principles of Backup Security

Secure the access and removal of all data storage media such as backup tapes and backup disks. An unlocked room of backup media is a treasure trove to the wrong person or a person with the wrong motivation. Distribute the media. Secure the area. An unsecured console allows the mischievous and malevolent both quick and easy access. If it is easy to get something into a backup room, then it is probably easy to get something out.

Backups are either localized (manual) or centralized (automatic). The right form depends on the needs of the organization and the peace of mind of the administrators. Backups should be performed on a regularly scheduled basis.

Local backup involves changing storage media on each individual computer. This mode is reasonably effective for small computer clusters in close proximity to each other such as in a local area network or computer lab or library setting. Do not rely on users making their own backups.

An automatic centralized backup involves deploying multiple storage media on a single backup computer rather than single media on multiple computers. Centralization provides greater control. A centralized service schedules backups, thus guaranteeing the files are indeed backed up. Backups should never interfere with production services.

A centralized service enforces policies, tracks media, and logs actions. Data restoration occurs from a single controlled console. If backup media are encrypted on a centralized backup server, then the motivation for theft decreases because the media cannot be read anywhere else.

## Basic Backup Strategies

An effective backup strategy involves planning. Be selective. Which files must be backed up? How often should they be backed up? How long should copies be retained? A haphazard backup policy is only slightly better than no policy at all.

Encourage users to back up their work on networked drives, not on their own local drives. Networked drives are easily incorporated into a centralized backup strategy and provide central distribution points.

A *full backup* copies everything whether or not it has changed. The information system thus always has a full and complete replica of itself. File restoration is straightforward and relatively simple. Nevertheless, scheduled full backups are often discouraged in many enterprise environments because they are time-intensive and contain redundant information.

A *differential backup* includes only those files backed up since the last full backup. Differential backups require less processing time than full backups. Restoring the system requires only the latest full copy and the latest differential copy. Each differential copy contains all the changes from the one before.

An *incremental backup* includes those files backed up since the last full backup or the last differential backup. This process requires even less time, because only files changed since the last backup activity are copied. Each incremental backup includes only the most recent changes from the one before. This type of backup typically spreads files across multiple storage media, hence finding a specific item becomes a complicated procedure. If the entire system is restored, then incremental copies must be processed in a specific order.

A backup is based on capturing either all files (changed files and unchanged files) or only changed files. A full backup captures all data all the time, but it is also wasteful. Why continually back up hundreds of files that have never changed? Incremental and differential backups capture only changed files, hence they operate quickly. Every file has an associated archive bit set to 1 if the file needs to be backed up and 0 if not. If a file has changed, the incremental backup copies the file and then resets the archive bit to 0 (i.e., once the change has been recorded, the file is backed up only once). The differential backup does not clear the archive bit (i.e., it keeps a running copy of the changes). An incremental backup is faster to back up but slower to restore. A differential backup is slower to back up but faster to restore.

## Storage Media Replacement

Disks can fail, often with little warning. Storage media can rip and tear or lose magnetic coherence. Record when a backup disk or tape enters service and replace it periodically. Avoid the temptation of squeezing in another few weeks of use. Replace it *before* it fails.

## Backup Media Storage

Storing backup media near their computers conveniently saves processing time, but one accident to them becomes a dual disaster. Information systems have been devastated by minor pipe bursts. If backup tapes are stored in the computer room and a ceiling water pipe breaks, then the backup is damaged as well as the computers.

Most organizations achieve adequate protection by storing backup media away from normal activity and securing them from fire and theft. Off-site storage provides an additional level of security. (*Note:* Maximum security is available by storing backup data in a guarded underground vault deep within the mountains. This level of security is rarely needed.)

## Rotation, Rotation, Rotation

A daily full backup provides maximum protection, but it also requires high overhead. This is neither practical in space nor efficient in time. Rotating media enhances the efficiency of backup measures.

The son (or daughter) method involves making a single full backup every day. Each backup generates a child offspring, hence the name. Recycle the tape. This method is simple and coverage is comprehensive, but it is not recommended as a general-purpose method. The storage medium eventually wears out, and data recovery is only available one day back.

The father/son method involves multiple media and a suitable mix of full, differential, or incremental backups. Data recovery is available more than one day back. The grand-father/father/son method is similar but provides even more comprehensive recovery.

### Network Security

Network security involves controlled access to networked resources. Networks are extremely complex entities with an intrinsic duality of purpose. A good network pro-motes the communication of information; a secure network restricts the communication of information. Network security involves resource access, perimeter monitoring, intru-sion detection, and firewalls.

A breach of network security is by no means obvious. If someone steals another person's wallet, then the loss is easily detected. Suppose a person copies a file, renames the copy, and then transfers it to another location deep within a network directory. The theft is not so obvious. The rapidity and near-invisibility of network transactions makes network crimes almost perfect crimes. Neither the victim nor the authorities may ever know that a crime has been committed (Ratzan 1993).

## FIRST LINE OF DEFENSE: THE LOWLY PASSWORD

In 1980 a computer cracked a three-letter user password within fifty-eight seconds by brute force checking. Contemporary computer hardware is hundreds of times faster, and contemporary software is considerably more intelligent than devices of yore. A strong password policy provides a solid first line of defense against unauthorized access.

Network access should require authentication. Authentication is typically based on something you know (password), something you have (swipe card), or something you are (retinal scan, DNA, etc.). Authentication imposes control. The process of authenti-cation lets authorized people in and keeps unauthorized people out.

An effective information security policy includes password management. Deploy passwords, control them, and assure acceptable criteria. Users often balk at password restrictions. They perceive passwords as interruptions of normal work flow—until their work is compromised. No, your password cannot be "your_name1" even though it is easily remembered. Information managers must continually emphasize to the user: *Anyone with your password . . . can do what you can do . . . can see what you can see . . . can change what you can change . . . can go where you can go.*

Users think in terms of their own needs and not that of the enterprise as a whole. Impose too much of a password burden and users will typically bypass security by the "principle of least effort." Passwords will be written down in obvious locations, for example.

## Password Management

Users want simple, short, easily remembered, rarely changed passwords . . . or better, none at all. Good password management policy involves a multilayered approach. The following criteria serve as useful guidelines:

*Password length.* Long passwords are more secure than short passwords.

*Password complexity.* Complex passwords are more secure than simple passwords. Complex passwords contain mixed-case letters, numbers, and symbols.

*Password aging.* Change passwords within a time window. Block access if the password has not been changed. Disable accounts if they are not active.

*Password recycling.* Do not reuse passwords. Users subvert this by choosing password X, then password Y, and later reverting to X. Stop this ploy by implementing password history checking.

*Password authority.* The user must authenticate themselves before any password change. Telephone contact is not acceptable. (How do you know I am who I claim to be?) Some organizations do password resets only during certain times of the day, or they may issue temporary passwords valid for only one log-in.

*Password blocks.* Disable log-ins after a specified number of unsuccessful password attempts. The user must reestablish access by contacting administrators or wait a specified period of time. Password blocking discourages brute force checking. Unfortunately, blocking can also create a simple "denial of service" attack. If I know your log-in name and intentionally use the wrong password several times, then you will be locked out!

## How Secure Is Your Password?

The Roman alphabet contains 26 letters. If a password consists of only lowercase letters, then each position can be one of 26 possibilities. If the information system allows 26 single-case letters and 10 digits, then each position can be any of 36 values. If the policy supports an uppercase/lowercase/digit mix, then the number of possible values for each position increases to 62. The idea can be extended further by the use of punctuation. (*Caveat:* Some information systems use certain punctuation as reserved symbols.)

If a password is three characters long, then the number of possible passwords is:

| | |
|---|---|
| Single-case letters: | $26 \times 26 \times 26$ |
| Single-case letters and digits: | $36 \times 36 \times 36$ |
| Mixed-case letters and digits: | $62 \times 62 \times 62$ |

These values are even more striking with passwords up to five characters long. (See table 6-1.)

The simple expedient of using uppercase/lowercase/digit symbols over single-case letters dramatically increases the number of possibilities.

Choosing complex four-character passwords containing mixed-case letters and digits over simple four-letter, single-case passwords makes brute force password checking thirty-two times more difficult. A complex eight-character mixed password is more

**Table 6-1**
Password Possibilities

| Characters | Single-Case Letters | Mixed-Case Letters and Digits |
|:---:|:---:|:---:|
| 3 | 17,576 | 238,328 |
| 4 | 456,976 | 14,776,336 |
| 5 | 11,881,376 | 916,132,832 |

than a thousand times more difficult!

This being said, *one sloppy password can wreck a secure information system*. It does not matter if there are billions and billions of possible cases if a password is easily guessed. Do not use common words or phrases. Do not use your name or that of a family member or significant other. No pet names, office numbers, phone numbers, or birth dates.

This author once worked for a firm where passwords were based on the user's last name. Once the pattern was realized, *anyone* could make an educated guess about the password of another. The fact that there were billions of possible password combinations was irrelevant. *Pattern recognition eliminated virtually all of them.* (The password policy was later changed.)

### Choosing a Good Password

Many ultrasecure information systems do not give users the option of choosing their own password. The user is presented with a string ten or more characters long containing a random mixture of symbols. The system prescreens the string for embedded words, log-in names, and ID numbers.

Passwords should be easily remembered but not easily guessed. A useful password-generation technique involves the suitable manipulation of a literary text. Select a line from a favorite song, poem, or quote. Form a password based on letters from each word. (This method presumes the text is not in plain sight on the user's wall!) Substitute the letter "o" with the symbol zero, number words with number symbols, and use capitalization.

*Example 6.1*

> Ipa2tf              I pledge allegiance to the flag
> Is0aatm           I sing of arms and the man

(The latter is a phrase in Virgil's *Aeneid,* or use the original Latin!)

> 0wabAM          Oh, what a beautiful morning

(Note that "morning" is replaced by AM.)

## VIRUSES, WORMS, TROJAN HORSES, LOGIC BOMBS, AND OTHER NASTIES

A computer is a complex machine. A network is a complex medium. There are those among us who exploit these imperfections as vulnerabilities.

Computer mischief has increased over time and, regrettably, so has its level of sophistication. More access is now available from the proliferation of personal computers and the advent of global networking. Data access was more easily controlled in the era of mainframe computers, which were housed inside locked rooms with limited facilities and only a few users. Network access can now be almost instantaneous. (It can be argued that a baseball webcast is heard sooner by those sitting at a computer than by spectators at the ballpark because the former receive their information at the speed of light and the latter at the speed of sound.)

A computer program is a set of instructions. A computer *virus* is a program that modifies the actions of a computer without the knowledge or consent of the computer's operator. A virus satisfies two special criteria: the program must execute itself and the program must reproduce itself.

The concept of a computer virus was originally dismissed as an abstract concept with little practical application. The expression "computer virus" is itself a metaphor. Metaphors express the unfamiliar in terms of the familiar. A computer virus infects and must be cleaned, disinfected, sterilized, deactivated.

Computer viruses execute and replicate by many different modes of procedure. Their unwelcome modifications may include file corruption, file deletion, special text or video displays, erratic behavior, or system crashes. Even benign viruses can be dangerous.

*Omnes viri in multes partes divisa est.* ("All viruses are divided into specific categories.") More categories will probably be developed over time. The nature and activity of a computer virus depends on the nature of the computer platform on which it acts.

*File infector viruses* infect executable files. These nasties remain in the computer's memory, so files processing through that memory also become infected. *Boot sector viruses* infect the system area and are always memory resident. *Master boot sector viruses* are similar to boot sector viruses, but the latter tend to retain a legitimate copy of system files elsewhere on the computer. *Multipartite (polypartite) viruses* infect both boot-up records and program files. *Macro viruses* infect data files. A macro virus exploits the programming language of another application for its delivery and impact.

A *Trojan horse* is an impostor program. It poses as one function but in fact does something else. The name derives from an ancient historical event. After a ten-year siege of Troy, the Greek army suddenly abandoned its encampment, leaving behind a giant wooden horse. The Trojans opened the city gates and brought the horse into the city, unaware that the horse contained hidden Greek soldiers. Later that night the soldiers emerged, opened the city gates, and signaled the Greek fleet. The city of Troy fell within hours.

A Trojan horse differs from a virus in that it does not replicate. It must be "invited" in by the host. This commonly occurs in conjunction with a file download or the opening of an e-mail attachment. Trojan horse programs may provide unauthorized and unwelcome access to the information system by outsiders.

A computer *worm* is a program that replicates itself without need of a host. Worms do not infect files. Worms use networks as conduits. Their replication consumes bandwidth and file space, wreaking havoc in their path.

A *logic bomb* is a code snippet that is triggered by an event or condition. The event may be a date, time, or an internal variable reaching a threshold value. The trigger may have a known time of deployment (trigger time) or occur at a random time. A logic bomb typically aborts a process or displays a screen message, much to the dismay of the user. Good software engineering practices implemented by reputable vendors filter out most logic bombs in commercial applications.

An *e-mail bomb* is a variation on the same theme. This type of attack delivers excessively large messages or attachments, overwhelming the target host. Blocking an e-mail bomb involves restricting the size and extent of e-mail traffic between the source and the target.

*Shoulder surfing* is the simple low-tech act of standing behind a user and looking over their shoulder as they enter their password. This ploy is especially effective if the user password is a geometric pattern on the keyboard. Do not use keyboard patterns as the basis for a password!

*Password grabbers* capture passwords. The information system displays what appears to be a normal log-in screen, and the user enters log-in information. A warning message appears. The user believes they made a typographical error and enters the information a second time. The second attempt is successful. In fact, the initial screen is an impostor, a log-in screen look-alike. The impostor program captures the user's log-in and password, writes the information to an obscure file for future harvesting, disables itself, and then activates the real log-in screen.

This ploy was common in public computer labs, where no one would detect the perpetrator planting the code on the target machine(s). The ploy can be defeated by periodically rebooting the computers, thus terminating the offensive program; by requiring a specific keystroke sequence that activates a trusted screen (such as "Ctrl-Alt-Del"); or by automatically resetting the machine after each log-off.

### Mass-Mailing Methods

"Malware" exploits social engineering. The user receives an e-mail from a trusted friend (or the user's mother!). A friend would never send anything bad, so the message is opened. The message was *not* from your friend and it *did* contain something bad. You have become the next victim. A hidden program captures your e-mail address book and then sends a message to all or some of the people contained therein. They open the message, believing it originated from you. The cycle continues.

This modus operandi has several variations. For example, the message you receive ostensibly contains a warning against these attacks. Being the responsible person you are and believing the message came from a presumably trusted source, you open the message, hoping to stop the spread only to become an unsuspecting victim. These social engineering ploys spread rapidly, a credit perhaps to our social courtesies but dangerous to the network. Their rate of growth is extraordinary. An infection can go global within hours.

### Intruder Knowledge and Attack Sophistication

Attacks on network information security no longer require a high level of intruder expertise. Almost anyone with the right tools, all too easily obtained, can launch an attack against an unsuspecting target (Stoll 1989). The effectiveness of such an attack depends on the cleverness of the approach and the laxity of the victim. Recent innovative attack styles include denial of service, cross-site scripting, packet spoofing, zombies, staged attacks, website defacement, and the exploitation of obscure vulnerabilities in lesser-known applications. It is likely that more attacks will come. Networked information security relies on constant vigilance.

## A DANGEROUS SCRIPT

> "It takes a carpenter to build a house, but any jackass can tear it down."
> —variously attributed to Mark Twain, Sam Rayburn,
> Harry Truman, or Tom Foley

Computer software systems are extremely complex constructs of code, pointers, and data composed of millions of harmoniously interlaced instructions. Security may not be the prime consideration in their design. As a result, a simple script can wreck a computer system. The script discussed below is short, simple, elegant, and devastating. *It does not take a lot of code to do a lot of damage.* Some important implementation features of the script have intentionally been withheld as a precaution. Nevertheless, do not try to run this script on your own computer (or on others'!).

### Analysis of the Script

The following snippet of programming code was described by Steven Bellovin at a 1988 computer security seminar held at Princeton University. It demonstrates the simplicity of a former classic vulnerability.

```
Line 1   While [ .TRUE. ]
Line 2   Do
Line 3   mkdir .dummy
Line 4   cd .dummy
Line 5   Done
```

Line 1 initiates a block of code that repeats itself (loop). The code begins at the "Do" statement and continues until it encounters the "Done" statement.

Most computer languages support loops. Well-written code controls its loops, however. If there were no control, then loops would execute at the wrong time. If a special condition is true, then the loop is executed (the process repeats) or else the loop stops. The condition is typically linked to a counter incrementing up to a given value, decrementing down from a given value, or comparing a variable to a special value. For example, a condition of the form

> While [ number_of_students .LT. 25 ]

repeats as long as the number of students remains less than twenty-five, then it stops.

The script in the first example is syntactically correct, but the threshold condition is permanently TRUE by (bad) design. The loop always repeats. It never ends. This structure is known as an infinite loop.

Line 3 creates a new directory. Dotted file names are generally system configuration files. The operating system hides such files from prying eyes lest users accidentally alter critical information. This line intentionally creates a hidden directory.

Line 4 changes the active working directory to the newly created hidden invisible directory. All further action now takes place inside a directory the user does not see and probably does not know exists.

Line 5 marks the end of the loop. The loop continues because of the TRUE condition. The process creates another (hidden) directory inside the first hidden directory and moves there. The process repeats.

The never-ending loop produces a nested box effect akin to a set of Russian nested dolls. A hidden directory contains a hidden directory which contains a hidden directory which contains a hidden directory . . . ad infinitum. The unsuspecting victim sees none of it.

### What Is the Danger?

Suppose each directory uses one byte of computer storage. If the computer repeats the loop hundreds of thousands of times every second, then these same number of bytes are allocated to a never-ending set of embedded directories hidden one within the other. *The accumulated nested directories rapidly exceed the computer's available storage capacity, halting the computer for lack of space.*

The damage is done quickly, automatically, and silently. The computer "hangs." The user sees nothing because the culprit directories are hidden.

### Prevention

The script as written applies to a specific computing platform. It will fail if applied as is to other environments. A quota system provides a simple and effective defense against it.

There was a time not so long ago when any user had access to any resource on an information system. This was a bad idea. A quota system allocates a specific area or extent of resources to a given user, restricting the number of files or the space used by those files or both. A quota manager program continually monitors resource usage, canceling a job if the user exceeds a threshold.

Suppose a malicious user plants the danger script. It silently consumes storage space. A quota manager program detects the aberrant processes or activity. The process immediately shuts down, damage is localized to the individual user, and administrators take appropriate action (Ratzan, "Network Jumping," 2001; Ratzan, "While True Do," 2001).

## MISDIRECTION

Misdirection is a standard ploy in magic, politics, and computer security. By changing the focus of our attention, it allows an improper or suspect act to go undetected and unchallenged. It can be easy to misdirect the unsuspecting. If a file seems to come from a known source, then it becomes less suspect. *The social value associated with the sender exceeds a cautionary threshold.* Politicians make speeches that misdirect the thinking of their listeners through the arts of persuasion and metaphorical manipulation. Misdirection controls perspective and thus action (Wilson 1962).

### Misdirecting Information by the French Drop

The stage magicians Penn and Teller have demonstrated and explained a principle of misdirection with a simple illusion known as the French drop.

A professor asks a student for a number between one and ten. The student states the number aloud. Suppose the number is five. The professor counts out five cards, hands back the deck, and asks the student to do the same. The student counts out five cards, showing the fifth card to all other students but not the professor. That card is hidden in the deck.

The professor shuffles the cards, mumbles a few magic words, and claims the secret card will percolate to the top. The top card is displayed . . . and it is not the correct card. The embarrassed professor tells another student to open a sealed envelope given to them at the onset of class. The student opens the envelope. Lo and behold! It contains a large copy of the secret card! The professor bows graciously and accepts the applause.

The key is misdirection. The initial student believes they have free will, since they randomly chose a number between one and ten. How could the professor possibly know their choice in advance and place the card in the proper position?

The trick works because the choice of number is irrelevant. The professor prepares the deck in advance with the secret card placed on top. The professor emphatically repeats the chosen number (five) aloud and with great flourish counts that number of cards into a pile in front of the student. When the pile is placed on the deck, the secret card goes to the fifth position of the full deck. The student focuses on the counting process. The professor tells the student to count the cards the same way.

The professor deftly places the pile back onto the top of the deck and hands the deck back to the student. Unbeknownst to the student, the secret card is now in the fifth position of the counted-out pile. The student counts the cards and shows everyone the fifth one, never realizing that the secret card was forced to its current position without their knowledge.

The identity of the secret card was known in advance. The trick was to place it into a location where the student would "discover" it. *In fact, the student was never in control.* This principle is often exploited in the distribution of infected software.

## Misdirection and Information Transfer

The next example (Kleber 2002) demonstrates information transfer by misdirection.

A professor hands a deck of cards to his teaching assistant, who asks any student to select any five cards at random. The assistant places four of the five cards on the table in plain sight. After a moment of appropriate drama, the professor mysteriously identifies the hidden fifth card to the amazement of all.

The student focuses his attention on selecting the five cards. The student knows there are an enormous number of possible choices. There are

$$52 \times 51 \times 50 \times 49 \times 48 = 311{,}875{,}200 \text{ possible hands}$$

The student is not aware that the assistant will relay information to the professor revealing the identity of the cards. The audience's attention is focused on the cards, not on the actions of the assistant.

A standard deck of cards contains thirteen cards of four suits (club, heart, diamond, and spade). According to the Dirichlet pigeonhole principle, *in any choice of five cards at least two have the same suit.* The assistant who sees all five cards selects the first card to be shown as one of the matching-suit pair. The other member of the pair will be the secret card. The professor now immediately knows the suit of the hidden card because it is the same as the first card on the table.

What is the relation between one card of the matched-suit pair and the other? Imagine a clock face with thirteen entries labeled sequentially from ace (1) to king (13). *One of the matched-suit cards will always be within six units of the other as one moves around the thirteen-faced clock.*

The first card the assistant displays is numerically within six of the other. The professor now knows the suit of the hidden card and the numerical value of the displayed card (= base number). If the assistant can somehow relay a number between one and six, then the professor adds it to the base number and obtains the face value of the hidden card. Voila!

Simonson and Holm (2002) offer this example:

> The matched suit cards are the 4 of diamonds and 7 of diamonds
>
> The 4D is three units away from the 7D
>
> The assistant shows the 4D
>
> If the assistant can somehow relay the number 3
>
> Then the professor knows the hidden card is the 7 of diamonds

One card is already exposed. Three others are yet to be displayed. There are six possible ways to arrange the three remaining cards. The professor and assistant must decide in advance on the correspondence between the order of three cards and the numbers one to six. The professor now knows the suit, the base number, and the value to be added to the base number. With appropriate drama the professor predicts the hidden card, and amazes the students with his professorial powers of prognostication.

The process of coded information transfer can be accomplished in many different ways. The choice of scheme makes no difference, but the assistant and professor must agree to the same method. For example, the value is coded based on the size ordering of the cards or the relative positioning of the cards.

## EXERCISES AND RESEARCH QUESTIONS

### *Exercises: Securing*

E6.1    What is the backup schedule of your organization? Why is it so?

E6.2    Suppose a password is seven characters long, all lowercase letters. You know the first five (they form a user name). How many cases does a brute force attack need to check all the possibilities?

E6.3    Why are "zxcvbnm" and "qazwsxedc" bad passwords? Hint: Look at the keyboard.

*Research Question 6.4*

Some information systems mandate password changes every thirty days, while others require changes every six months. Discuss the balance between user convenience and tighter security involved in these different policies.

### *Exercises: Misdirection*

*Research Question 6.5*

Examine the metaphorical language used by a political candidate. At what point in their logical argument(s) is the audience redirected from an objective stance to a subjective perspective?

*Research Question 6.6*

Study the way people behave when they receive an object from a friend or colleague or a stranger. How can this social engineering be exploited in passing a foreign object to someone without eliciting their suspicion?

*Research Question 6.7*

What social safeguards do people commonly use in order to avoid being fooled? What factors motivate people to disregard these safeguards?

## CHAPTER 7

▸ Concealing Information

Public information should be shared. Private information should be secret. How can Alice send private information to Bob securely across an insecure public network? She can do so by using cryptography.

*Cryptography* is the art and science of concealing information by enciphering it using a secret key, and of later revealing that information by deciphering it using the secret key. *Cryptanalysis* is the art and science of revealing or recovering enciphered information without possessing knowledge of the key, i.e., "code-breaking." *Cryptology* is the scientific study of these secret communication methods and embraces both cryptography and cryptanalysis.

## CODES AND CIPHERS

### Not So Long Ago on a Cold Drizzly Night . . .

Two men step out of the shadows. They approach each other cautiously, their hands clenching not-so-hidden weapons.

"The cuckoo eats sassafras," says one man.

"My brother loves matzoh balls," replies the other.

"The pickled herring is too sweet," says the first.

Each man removes a torn dollar bill from his pocket. The ragged edges align. The pair exchange a sealed envelope and vanish into the night . . .

### Today in a Well-Lit Office . . .

Alice types a secret message into her computer. She encrypts the information using Bob's public key. The message travels across a global network at the speed of light to where Bob decrypts it with his private key. A secure message passes across an insecure network, but only Alice and Bob know its contents.

### Vocabulary

A *code* replaces words or symbols with other words or symbols. A codebook contains the correspondence terms between them. The sender uses the codebook for encryption. The receiver uses the codebook for decryption. For example, the World War II British code words 03680C, 36276C, and 50302C corresponded to the phrases "shipped at," "shipped by," and "shipped from," respectively (Trappe and Washington 2002).

Postal ZIP codes and telephone area codes are common public codes. Military operations often bear code names. Operation Overlord and Operation Neptune were the code names for the land and sea operations of the Allied invasion of Normandy in 1944.

Tales of secret codes and secret messages abound in world literature. The reader is referred to classic tales such as "The Adventure of the Dancing Men" (Doyle), "The Gold Bug" (Poe), and *A Journey to the Center of the Earth* (Verne). The first two tales involve monoalphabetic ciphers. The last tale involves encryption by writing backwards.

Secret decoder rings may be fun, but codes have several logistical problems. A code cannot deal with unanticipated or unexpected words outside its codebook. Every sender/receiver pair must have the same version at the same time, and the codebook must always be secured. If the codebook is captured, then all messages encoded using it become vulnerable.

A *cipher* (Middle English *cifre,* from Medieval Latin *cifra,* "to be empty") differs from a code. A cipher substitutes each letter or symbol of the message with a different letter or symbol according to a rule or algorithm defined by a secret key. The operation of the rule cannot be easily reversed by anyone trying to decipher the message without knowledge of the key. Codes generally work on a word level, while ciphers work on a letter level.

Ciphers and codes both use keys for encryption and decryption. A code key has only one form (a codebook). A cipher key has many possible forms. Ciphers are often more versatile than codes. Codes and ciphers are used to deduce the true message (plaintext) from the encrypted hidden message (ciphertext).

The terms "cryptology" and "cryptography" first appeared in a 1641 book by John Wilkins as their Latin forms, *cryptologia* and *cryptographica. Cryptologia* was Anglicized to "cryptology" by 1645 and *cryptographia* to "cryptography" by 1658.

*Symmetric cryptography uses a single shared key.* The same key is used for both encryption by the sender and decryption by the receiver. Successful symmetric cryptography requires that both parties have the same key at the same time and no one else has that key at that time. This situation may be feasible for clandestine communications between two people, but it presents massive logistical issues when used on a larger scale.

*Asymmetric cryptography* uses *different* keys. The encryption key used by the sender differs from the decryption key used by the receiver. Public key encryption, for example, uses a public key (known to anyone) and a private key (known only to its owner). The keys are not selected arbitrarily. They form a bonded, matched pair with a strong one-way mathematical relationship.

Keys can consist of numbers, words, or phrases. Computers use bit-string keys. Keys can even be tones. The fictional character Gwildor unlocks a dimensional gateway using a musical key (motion picture: *Masters of the Universe* 1987). The actress Whoopi Goldberg realizes that the secret code key is "B-flat," the musical key of the spy's code name (motion picture: *Jumpin' Jack Flash,* 1986).

## Classifying Ciphers

A *substitution cipher* replaces one letter by another in the same position (A becomes G, B becomes Q, etc.). A *monoalphabetic substitution cipher* replaces one letter by the same letter every time. A *polyalphabetic substitution cipher* replaces a letter with any of several different letters according to different cipher alphabets.

Simple newspaper cryptogram puzzles are usually monoalphabetic substitution ciphers. The letters retain the original positioning, so their inherent grammatical and linguistic structures remain intact, revealing clues about the secret message. For example, if an encrypted sentence begins with ZFJ, a cryptanalyst might guess that it represents THE and hence decrypt three important letters.

A *Caesar substitution cipher* transposes each letter of the alphabet three letters down the alphabet (A becomes D, B becomes E, etc.). This trick is very old; a military treatise on the subject appears in *Lives of the Caesars* by the Roman historian Suetonius. The *general Caesar cipher* shifts a letter N units down the alphabet where the number N ranges from 1 to 25. (If the offset factor equaled 26, then a letter would cycle back to itself.)

A Caesar cipher decrypts easily if it is detected. Find the offset and shift all the letters appropriately. In fact, it always deciphers easily, because there are at most twenty-five possible offsets. A sliding paper strip imprinted with the alphabet is an effective low-tech cryptographic computer for this type of cipher.

*Rot-13 cipher* encryption is a special case of the generalized Caesar cipher. It is commonly used within Internet newsgroups to hide offensive messages or spoiler messages from the curious eye. Rot-13 encryption shifts (*rot*ates) a letter thirteen letters down the alphabet. Rot-13 has a unique advantage over other Rot- methods because applying Rot-13 both encrypts and decrypts.

A *transposition cipher* retains the original letter but moves its position further down the word. A substitution cipher replaces; a transposition cipher shifts.

## Frequency Analysis and Other Decryption Methods

Substitution ciphers are amenable to attack by frequency analysis of the occurrence of particular letters or symbols. For example, the most common letters in English are E, T, A, I, O, and N. Grammatical conventions "force" certain letter combinations. For example, "the" is a frequently used word in the English language. A frequency analysis of the most commonly occurring character string in a ciphertext can sometimes identify that string as representing the word "the." Familiar quotes are often recognized despite encryption:

*Example:*   AC  DB  OE  NCA  AC DB        (*Hamlet* 3.1)

The letter T is very common, so the first word is TO. The remainder of the expression is easily decoded.

It is interesting to observe that Edgar Allan Poe ("The Gold Bug," 1965 edition) uses the distribution:

{E, A, O, I, D, H, N, R, S, T, U, Y}

This difference demonstrates an intriguing linguistic shift over several generations.

Transposition methods are not effective for enciphering short messages because there are few possible rearrangements. For example, transposing the letters in "cow" generates only six possible arrangements {cow, cwo, owc, ocw, wco, woc}. Short transposed cipher messages are amenable to brute force attack by checking every possible rearrangement of the letters (or symbols) of each word or character string.

Long, complex messages make brute force attacks impractical but not impossible. Smart brute force attacks exploit linguistic rules, grammatical forms, and pattern recognition. Dictionary attacks test common word stems. Grammar excludes many nonsense combinations. Many seemingly random patterns (e.g., qwertyuiop and 1234567) are recognizable patterns.

## KEY ISSUES

Effective encryption depends on the quality of the key. If a key is insecure, then so is the encryption and hence the information it secures. *Key management must be a critical aspect of any information security policy.*

"Key lifetime" involves the duration of the key's viability. *The longer a key remains viable, the longer it remains vulnerable.* A short key lifetime assures a small window of vulnerability.

"Key length" involves the size of the key. *The longer the key, the more possible encryptions.* If a key is only one bit long, then there are only two possible cases. If a key is N bits long, then there are $2^N$ possible cases. Ten additional bits increases the number of cases by a factor of 1,024, more than one thousand-fold! (See table 7-1.)

**Table 7-1**
Key Length and Cases

| Key Length (bits) | Number of Possible Cases |
| --- | --- |
| 1 | 2 |
| 2 | 4 |
| 10 | 1,024 |
| 30 | 1,073,741,824 |
| 56 | ten thousand trillion (approximately) |
| 128 | one hundred trillion trillion trillion (approximately) |

Size alone does not a secure key make. Some algorithms are fundamentally weaker than others, regardless of the key length. "Not all 128-bit algorithms are created equal" (Trappe and Washington 2002, 7). Keys should be generated as randomly as possible.

If a key is predictable, then it contains patterns. Code-breakers using brute force attacks can exploit patterns.

"Key distribution" involves the act of passing keys to all authorized persons and to no unauthorized persons. (This is a variation on the all-and-only problem of information retrieval.) Symmetric cryptography has major problems involving authentication and control when large numbers of keys must be distributed.

Keys must be secured. Public key/private key encryption only works effectively if the private key remains private. If the key is stored in an accessible location (perish the thought, taped to the computer), then security crumbles. All the technological and algorithmic sophistication in the world cannot compensate for lax key security.

"Key recovery" addresses the simple but crucial question of key loss. The recovery of privately held keys impinges on many jurisdictional and civil rights issues. Who should know your key? When and how should they use it? Suppose you lose your private key. What happens?

> *Scenario 1.* Nothing happens. Your loss. Too bad.
>
> *Scenario 2.* Authorized agents hold complete copies of all keys in "escrow" and replace them if they are lost. But *quis custodiet ipsos custodes?* ("Who watches the watchers?")
>
> *Scenario 3.* Several authorized "trustees" hold partial copies of all keys. No single person can reconstruct the entire key and hence decrypt a message. The potential for abuse decreases, but the complexity of the authentication infrastructure increases.

## THE UNBREAKABLE ONE-TIME PAD

At least one encryption/decryption scheme satisfies the triple criteria of being simple, secret, and secure. The method is commonly known as the *one-time pad.* It has the distinction of being *completely unbreakable* if properly implemented.

The one-time pad has several variations, but the basic principle works as follows. The sender and receiver both have an identical copy of a pad inscribed with one random number per page. The message is encrypted using the first random number as the key. Once the message is received and deciphered, both parties destroy that page of the key pad. The key is never used again, hence the name "one-time pad." The next message uses the random number key on the next page, etc.

The one-time pad method is unbreakable because the key changes on a message-to-message basis, so that the decoders, even if they manage to decipher one message, are soon confronted with the next message, which has a completely different key, and hence they never have enough consecutive examples in the same key to decipher the messages.

Producing pseudo-random numbers is easy. Producing truly random numbers for a cryptographic key is surprisingly difficult. People do not generate random numbers well. People make patterns.

Singh (1999, 123) offers the example of the typist pressing keys on alternating sides of the keyboard. Would this process produce a random string of letters? No. This process is structured in the sense that half of all letters will originate from one side of the keyboard and half from the other.

The best random numbers come from natural events such as radioactive decay. Carrying a Geiger counter on the battlefield is not practical, however. Random numbers must be distributed to a large number of authorized people immediately and simultaneously. The destruction of used keys must be synchronized. *If the enemy captures one copy of the one-time pad, then secret communication becomes vulnerable.* One-time pads are used for extremely secret and extremely secure communication between a small number of people. One can envision the White House, 10 Downing Street, or Kremlin hot lines using such a process.

## SYMMETRIC (ONE-KEY) CRYPTOGRAPHY

Symmetric cryptography utilizes a single secret key that is shared by the sender and receiver. The Data Encryption Standard (DES) was the United States government's standard for symmetric cryptography in the late 1970s. It consisted of a symmetric 56-bit key that had initially been developed by Horst Feistel and International Business Machines.

DES became independent in 1976 and later received a U.S. patent. The patent expired in 1993, but DES had already become available for public use prior to that date. DES was considered by many as being unbreakable due to the sheer enormity of possible cases. It became a commercial standard. Many believed that no civilian agency could amass the computing power necessary to crack the key. They were wrong.

In 1997–98 the RSA Data Security Company issued a $10,000 challenge to crack DES. The key was found five months later. A new challenge was issued the following year. DES was cracked within forty days. The next challenge was achieved within five days. This achievement was especially significant because the dedicated computer used to crack the key was built from common off-the-shelf components. In January 1999 the combined effort of globally networked machines across the Internet cracked DES within twenty-two hours. A secret message could be deciphered within a single day. DES is now no longer considered secure.

Triple DES is a variation on DES using a 112-bit key. Triple DES encrypts the message three times using sophisticated mathematical operations. *Multiple encryption does not necessarily imply the new key is three times more secure.* Triple DES has replaced DES for many applications. DES was later replaced by Rijndael (pronounced "Rhine Doll" or "Rain Doll") as a government standard. It operates with a 128, 192, or 256-bit key. The algorithm encrypts with a multilayered approach, each of which provides security for different levels of protection.

Regardless of the specific implementation, a single-key system is intrinsically simpler than a dual-key system. Symmetric key systems typically operate 100 to 1,000 times faster than their asymmetric counterparts (Microsoft, *Cryptography,* 2000, 791). Asymmetric cryptography is thus not generally used for large messages.

## ASYMMETRIC (TWO-KEY) CRYPTOGRAPHY

### *Alice and Bob Send Secrets*

Alice sends secret information to Bob. He needs the key. How does she relay a secure key across an insecure medium? How does he know the information comes from her? (Alice and Bob, along with an eavesdropper named Eve, traditionally appear as characters in cryptographic literature.)

Alice and Bob could meet at a prearranged place and time to pass the secret key. This action involves the simultaneous coordination of two different people in space and time. They must either know each other or must authenticate one another.

A key might be sent through a third party. This obviates the need for a mutual meeting but introduces a loss of control. The third party could lose, copy, sell, nullify, or alter the key. A fourth party could intercept the key from the unsuspecting third party. The key cannot be sent via a public medium such as postal mail, fax, or phone because these methods are generally insecure.

Alice could encrypt the key and relay it to Bob. But how would Bob decrypt the encrypted key? He would need a key for that key. The problem folds onto itself.

The preceding scenario relates to the simple case of two people and one key. The problem becomes much more complicated if multiple people require the same key at different places and different times. How can keys be distributed simultaneously, securely, and reliably over insecure telecommunications media?

The solution is asymmetric cryptography, which uses two keys. Alice and Bob each have their own public and private key. The public key can be shared by anyone and passed to anyone. The private key must remain secret, known only to its owner.

The public and private keys form a matched pair. Crume (2000, 236) describes this as "Whatever you do with one key can only be undone with the other." *In theory,* if the link between the two keys is known, then one can be derived from the other. *In practice,* there is a strong and special functional relationship between them that is easily performed in one direction but made as difficult as possible in the other. Deriving the private key (reversing the function) is difficult *by design.*

The following example demonstrates the basic process of public/private cryptography:

> Bob publishes his public key.
>
> Alice obtains Bob's public key.
>
> Alice encrypts her message using Bob's public key.
>
> She sends the encrypted message to Bob.
>
> Bob decrypts the secret message using his private key.

Here are the salient points:

> Bob's public key encrypts.
>
> Bob's private key decrypts.
>
> Alice (and the world!) knows Bob's public key.
>
> Bob's private key cannot be determined even though the public key is known.

Passing the public key does not compromise security, nor does passing the encrypted message. Only Bob knows his private key and only he can decrypt the secret message.

## Authentication

Authentication provides a means of assuring the identity of the sender. *Knowledge of a secret shared key does not guarantee the sender is who they claim to be.* Suppose Alice wants to send a message to Bob using a shared key. She sends the key and it is intercepted by Eve. Eve sends a message to Bob. (Eve's relayed message may or may not be the original message.) How does Bob know if it came from Alice or from Eve?

Eve could receive Alice's message, read it, and pass it on to Bob, or she could change it and then pass it on to Bob. Bob has no way of determining the validity of the sender or, for that matter, knowing if the message was altered.

A digital signature can authenticate the message. A digital signature is analogous to a signed document. The security of a digital signature lies in the fact that the message and the identity of the sender are intertwined by means of a special hashing function. A hashing function produces a number called a "message digest value." It accepts any size input but produces a fixed-length output. It processes quickly, and the original message cannot easily be recovered from the digest value. *If any portion of the message is altered (even by one bit), then the hash value changes.* The digest value marks message integrity.

*Integrity test:* If the message value from the digital signature matches the message value computed from the message itself, then the message was not altered. If the values do not match, then the recipient immediately knows that the message was altered.

*Scenario:*

> Alice encrypts her message with her private key.
>
> She runs a hashing function against the message, deriving a message digest value.
>
> She encrypts the message digest value with her private key.
>
> She sends the encrypted message and message digest to Bob.
>
> Bob decrypts the encrypted message and message digest using Alice's public key.
>
> He runs the hash function against the message and gets a message digest value.
>
> If the values match, then all is well.

## How and Why It Works

*Public/private key cryptography only works properly if the private key remains private.* If someone steals Alice's private key, then that person in effect becomes Alice. That being said, what prevents anyone who knows Alice's public key from deriving her private key? The two keys are related by a functional relationship. The security of the matched pair of keys is dependent on the nature of that relationship.

The functional relationship between a public key and its corresponding private key lies in the ease of operating in one direction and the difficulty of operating in the other. Two-way functions are not suitable in cryptographic methods. Consider the following example where addition is a two-way function:

> Suppose private key = 5, the public key = 3, and 8 is the known relationship
>
> Given the public key (3), the private is easily found (8 − 3 = 5 = private key)

## One-Way Functions and Prime Factorization

Cryptographers, computer scientists, and mathematicians work to determine suitable candidates for one-way operations. Prime numbers offer one example. Multiplying two large prime numbers together is easy. Reversing the process (finding the prime factors of a large number) is hard.

> EASY →
>
> $863 \times 997 = 860,411$
>
> HARD ←

If a number is very large (200 digits long?), then prime factorization becomes fiendishly difficult. A brute force approach checking all the possible divisors requires a high computational overhead. Consider the effort involved in factoring a 100-digit number. The prime number theorem shows that the number of primes less than or equal to that number is:

> $10^{97}$ primes (approximately)

By comparison, the number of electrons in the universe is:

> $10^{90}$ electrons (approximately)

## One-Way Functions and Discrete Logarithms

A modulo function has cyclical arithmetic properties. A twelve-hour clock face operates modulo12 because the same time repeats every twelve hours. It makes sense to say:

> $9 + 6 = 3$     (six hours after nine o'clock is three o'clock)
>
> $2 + 12 = 2$     (twelve hours after two o'clock is also two o'clock)

The discrete logarithm problem is a generalization of this cyclical process. Singh (1999, 263) cites the easy/hard pair:

> *Easy:*   Pick X. Compute $453^X$. Divide by 21,997. What is the remainder?
>
> *Hard:*   Find X so that $453^X$ divided by 21,997 equals 5,787

The specific math formula used is not important. The core idea is that the process involves simple operations in one direction and difficult operations in the other.

If a one-way function forms the basis for a secret key, then encryption must be easy but decryption must be difficult. On the other hand, the overall process must be simple, otherwise it will not be of practical value. It serves no purpose if the sender transmits secret information quickly but the recipient requires days to decipher it. A trapdoor makes the evaluation easier. Asymmetric cryptography has two fundamental guidelines: (1) public and private keys are bonded, and (2) the private key is a trapdoor.

A trapdoor has immediate practical considerations in a computer network because hundreds of messages may be decrypted at any given moment. If a trapdoor scheme were not available, then the action of multiple encryption/decryption would reduce overall system performance.

### Two Implementations

The key-agreement process developed by Whitfield Diffie, Martin Hellman, and Ralph Merkle uses the principles of modulo and cyclic arithmetic as the basis for a secure key. The basic process appears below. It appears complex, but the computer does all the work anyway.

> Alice and Bob both agree on an index number and a prime number.
>
> Alice selects her own secret number.
>
> Bob selects his own secret number.
>
> Alice's computer calculates her public key from her numbers by a special formula that involves the index number, the prime number, and her secret number.
>
> Bob's computer calculates his public key similarly.
>
> Alice sends her public key to Bob.
>
> Bob sends his public key to Alice.
>
> Alice's computer calculates the secret shared key using the formula:
>
> Alice's secret key = (Alice public key) × (Bob public key)
>
> Bob's computer calculates his secret shared key using the formula:
>
> Bob's secret key = (Bob public key) × (Alice public key)

But mathematically the keys match. So Alice and Bob now have a secret shared key. The communication of information is secure.

Does it matter if their public key is intercepted? No. Deriving the missing values is difficult. Is the key itself insecure? No. The key is never transmitted. Each party calculates the needed value independently.

### The RSA Method

The RSA method of encryption is named after the last initials of its developers: Ron Rivest, Adi Shamir, and Leonard Adelman. This algorithmic method received a U.S. patent and later entered the public domain. RSA information security uses prime number factorization as the source of public and private keys instead of the discrete logarithm problem. The basic idea follows the discussion of Singh (1999, 379).

Alice chooses two secret and very large prime numbers.

She computes a value based on those numbers.

She chooses an encryption value.

She calculates a decryption value.

She forms a public and private key based on pairs of these values.

Alice publishes her public key.

Suppose Bob wants to send a message M to Alice. He knows her public key.

Bob encrypts a coded message and sends it to Alice.

Alice decrypts the message.

The salient points of this process are:

The large primes are known only to Alice.

Their product is sufficiently large that it is not easily factored.

Bob knows the public key.

Only Alice knows the private key.

The private key cannot be easily determined from the public key.

The public key and private key are linked.

The relationship is easily undone by Alice's knowledge of her private key.

## THE SECRET HISTORY OF PUBLIC KEY CRYPTOGRAPHY

Diffie, Hellman, and Merkle usually receive credit for the development of public key encryption. Rivest, Shamir, and Adelman usually receive credit for development of the RSA method. Secret codes being what they are, the public history of public key cryptography may not be totally correct.

According to Singh (1999, 280), the British government claims that the theory of public key encryption was initially developed at the top-secret General Communications Headquarters (GCHQ) in Cheltenham, England. Its development occurred several years before the work of Diffie, Hellman, and Merkle. GCHQ was associated with Bletchley Park and the cracking of the secret German Enigma code.

The original idea of public key encryption is credited to James Ellis (1969), who developed the notion after reading a paper discussing the transmission of secure voice signals over insecure telephone lines. The paper suggested *adding controlled random noise at the sending end and removing the same noise at the receiving end*. If such noise was indeed random, then any signal interception could not be deciphered except by the sender who introduced it at one end and an authorized receiver who removed it at the other. The concept was then called nonsecret encryption. An appropriate one-way function for accomplishing this was not easily identified, however. The concept remained theoretical because contemporary technology could not support sufficient resolution.

In 1973 Clifford Cocks (a number theorist) joined GCHQ. He recognized that prime numbers supplied a possible manipulative function. But the level of available computer power was inadequate for the proposed algorithm, and the method was deemed impractical. During 1974 Cocks explained his ideas to Malcolm Williamson (a cryptographer), and the team together developed the basic concepts of public key encryption. Their results could not be made public due to the secrecy imposed by GCHQ. Many of the same ideas were later rediscovered by Diffie, Hellman, Merkle, Rivest, Shamir, and Adelman.

*Historical note:* It is possible that the U.S. National Security Agency (NSA) was aware of the work of Ellis, Cocks, and Willamson. Did Diffie and company hear of their research when dealing with the NSA? Ellis, Cocks, and Williamson received public acknowledgment in December 1977. Ellis had died one month earlier.

## OTHER CRYPTOGRAPHIC SYSTEMS

### Navajo Code Talkers

The grammar of the Navajo language is significantly different from most other languages. Verbs are not conjugated solely on the basis of tense or gender, but may incorporate subject and relative adverbs. In some cases a single word expresses what would be an entire sentence in English (Singh 1999, 99).

The U.S. Army used the Native American Choctaw language for secure military communications during World War I. (Very few German eavesdroppers could understand Choctaw.) The U.S. Marines later refined this concept, selecting Navajo as the language of choice. Why choose Navajo? Apart from its linguistic complexity and speed of communication, it was estimated that there were only thirty known non-native speakers of Navajo and none of them were Japanese.

Military communication is critical, but military telephone and radio communications are not secure. The enemy spoke English and knew its idioms. The Navajo language served as an effective and secure form of military communication. "A Navajo message could never be faked and could always be trusted . . . " (Singh 1999, 198).

The language was modified for military use. This not only made it more secure, but also prevented the enemy from forcing any captured non-Code Talker Navajo soldier to serve as an unwilling translator. Authorized code words formed a special vocabulary. Words that were neither in the Navajo language nor appeared in the authorized list were spelled out using the first letters. Substitute words minimized repetition and the possibility of word pattern detection. (See table 7-2.)

The contribution of approximately 400 Navajo Code Talkers to the U.S. war effort was not declassified until 1968. Public recognition did not fully appear until much later. *The Navajo language as an encryption technique holds the distinction of one of the few codes in history that has never been broken.*

*Sociological footnote:* Many Navajo tribal members believe in *chindi,* spirits of the dead that revenge themselves on the living unless there are appropriate ceremonial rites. It is very difficult to perform ceremonial rites in the middle of a battlefield situation amidst human carnage. The Navajo Code Talkers not only braved the living enemy but the vengeful dead amongst them.

**Table 7-2**
Navajo Code Talkers Dictionary (sample)

| Military Units | Navajo Form | Literal Translation |
|---|---|---|
| corps | din-neh-ih | clan |
| platoon | has-clish-nih | mud |
| *Officers* | | |
| major general | so-na-kih | war chief |
| colonel | atsah-besh-le-gai | silver eagle |
| *Countries* | | |
| America | ne-he-mah | our mother |
| Germany | besh-be-cha-he | iron hat |
| Russia | sila-gol-chi-ih | red army |
| *Planes and Ships* | | |
| dive bomber | gini | chicken hawk |
| aircraft carrier | tsidi-moffa-ye-hi | bird carrier |
| submarine | besh-lo | iron fish |
| *Actions* | | |
| abandon | ye-tsan | run away from |
| accomplish | ul-so | all done |

(Navajo Code Talkers Exhibit, National Cryptologic Museum, Fort George Meade, Maryland)

## Quantum Cryptography

A binary digit (bit) has only two possible states and hence only two possible values (0, 1). A quantum bit (qubit) would exist as a linear superposition of these two states. In a sense, a qubit-based computer would exist in multiple states at the same time. Parallel operations would enhance computational speed.

It is theoretically possible to create a quantum prime-factoring algorithm and a quantum discrete logarithm algorithm. This accomplishment would resolve several hard problems and would counter the basis for RSA and other encryption methods. Quantum cryptography could use the properties of photon transmission. It would provide an intrinsic protection against eavesdropping because any interception would result in modifications of the photon polarization. Alice and Bob would know with certainty if their message were being overheard or modified.

Implementing quantum computing and quantum cryptography has technical difficulties, however. Quantum de-coherence loses information as the system interacts with its environment. The components must thus act in isolation, involving special electromagnetic shielding for excruciatingly short intervals of time. Quantum-based events are not completely understood. But *audentes foruna iuvat* ("fortune favors the brave").

## STEGANOGRAPHY: HIDING INFORMATION IN PLAIN SIGHT

Cryptography hides meanings. Steganography (Greek *steganos,* "covered"; *graphein,* "to write") hides messages. In the former case, the enemy captures a secret message and works toward its decipherment. In the latter case, the enemy is unaware that a secret message exists. Information is secured by its not being noticed.

Steganography secures information by stealth; if a message is intercepted, then its secret information may still remain obscured. But if a hidden message is recognized for what it is, then all security is compromised. Steganography is sometimes coupled with cryptography for an additional layer of security.

Classic steganography includes invisible ink and microdots. The ancient Greek historian Herodotus (Singh 1999, 3–7) relates the story of Histaiaeus, who wrote a secret message on the shaved head of a messenger and waited for the messenger's hair to grow back. The messenger later traveled inconspicuously throughout the land, then shaved his head at the destination and revealed the message. Chinese military history refers to wax balls revealing their contents upon careful melting.

During the fifteenth century secret messages were written on hard-boiled egg shells using an ink composed of vinegar and alum. The writing was absorbed through the porous shell and became readable on the inner egg only after the shell was removed. There are hundreds of recipes for invisible ink. (Author favorite: Ordinary milk. Heat gently and charred carbon brings forth the message.)

Imprinted microdots have been used for a very long time. Carrier pigeons carried photographically reduced diagrams and documents in the nineteenth century. Magic lanterns (early slide projectors) projected the image onto walls for easy reading. A current variation on the microdot concept involves encoding changes in the bit values of digitized photographs posted on the World Wide Web. The human eye cannot distinguish these subtle shade gradations and so they are not noticed, but they are easily detected by a computer.

Hiding messages in plain sight transcends cultures. Tobin (1999) has proposed that quilt designs secretly coded information on safe lodging, food, waterways, and escape routes for runaway slaves following the Underground Railroad during the American Civil War. Secret messages imprinted as ancient Chinese symbols drove the plot in one episode of the television series *Kung Fu: The Legend Continues* (episode 59; "Deadly Fashion").

Secret messages have been concealed within text and later decoded by marking off equidistant letter sequences (ELS) starting from a given initial letter. The code works if the recipient knows the text, the starting point, and the offset sequence. To anyone else the secret message is never revealed. Some believe that secret messages are already embedded in the Bible and other classic works (Drosnin 1997). Their rationale is based on the unexpected appearance of special words derived in this manner. This rationale has serious statistical flaws, given the enormous number of possible letter combinations in most texts.

## EXERCISES AND RESEARCH QUESTIONS

E7.1    Why is the name "Morse code" actually a misnomer?

E7.2    Why does a thirteen-character shift (Rot-13) both encrypt and decrypt?

E7.3    Frequency analysis fails for nonstandard words because grammatical rules are broken (or at least bent). Decrypt the following first few lines of a poem by Lewis Carroll ("Jabberwocky"):

> *Wnoorejbpxl*
> 'Gjnf oevyyvt, naq gur fyvgul gbirf
> Qvq tler naq tvzoyr va gur jnor:
> Nyy zvzfl jrer gur obebtbirf.
> Naq gur zbzr enguf bhgtenor.

E7.4    Why is the following paragraph unusual?

This is a most unusual paragraph. How quickly can you find out what is so unusual about it? It looks so ordinary you'd think nothing was wrong with it, and in fact, nothing is wrong with it. It is unusual though. Why? Study it, think about it, and you may find out. Try to do it without coaching. If you work at it for a bit it will dawn on you. So jump to it and try your skill at figuring it out. Good luck! —Unknown

E7.5    Cite several English grammatical rules or conventions that are useful in decryption.

E7.6    Find the prime factorization of 100 and 30,030.

## Research Question 7.7

Show that "stega" (as in steganography) and "stego" (as in stegosaurus) do not have the same root.

## Research Question 7.8

What is the currently largest known prime number? How many digits does it have?

## Research Question 7.9

What English word contains three consecutive sets of double letters? It relates to someone who keeps books. (Read backwards: repeekkoob)

*Research Question 7.10*

How effective is frequency analysis when applied to cultures that have a strong oral tradition but no letters/words in a written tradition?

*Research Question 7.11*

Are there any known cases of hiding information in or by music?

CHAPTER **8**    ▶ Measuring Information

## BIBLIOMETRICS: MEASURING THE PRINTED WORD

Bibliometrics quantifies the qualities of the printed word. It assumes that information exchange by means of printed media contains patterns, and these patterns are measurable.

### In the Beginning Was the Word

Bibliometrics uses statistics to recognize and measure patterns of publication within a particular field or area of study. For example, it uses quantitative analysis to measure the nature of professional journals in a given field, the nature of the articles within those journals, and the nature of the words within those articles. In other words, it examines the diffusion of information by the written word.

Bibliometrics was a field of study before it had a name. Early studies began with hyperbolic relationships (Auerbach, 1913), followed by major contributions on frequency distributions (Lotka, 1926), citation analysis (Gross and Gross, 1928), least effort principles (Zipf, 1932), scattering (Bradford, 1934), bibliographic coupling (Kessler, 1961), and journal impact factors (Garfield and Sher, 1963).

The word itself first appeared in French as *bibliometrie* (Otlet, 1934), then "librametrics" (Ranganathan, 1948), and later assumed the Anglicized form "bibliometrics" (Pritchard, 1969). An early form called *naukometrika* or *naukometria* was developed in the Soviet Union between 1930 and 1966.

Bibliometrics is sometimes associated with the related disciplines of scientometrics, infometrics, and scientography. The first specializes in biological and physical sciences, the second deals with general information flow, and the third is concerned with the visualization of information.

### Validity and Citations

Bibliometrics is not without its controversy. Statistics and measurements abound, but the interpretation and generalization of them are often problematic. Results may not scale to larger data sets, or they may not generalize from one environment to another. *Metrics must have meaning transcending the special case.*

Critics claim that bibliometric results are easily manipulated. For example, journal publications are presumed to be the basic unit of scientific information transfer. Suppose that three bibliographic citations per published page is deemed par, but five citations per published page is deemed scholarly. A prospective author desirous of distinction adds more references to their text. This simple act alone does not necessarily make the paper more scholarly. The problem lies with the perceived linked relationship between citation distribution (a quantitative concept) and academic worth (a qualitative concept).

Citation analysis can yield skewed results. What does it mean if my paper contains twice as many citations as yours? Does it suggest that my paper is better than yours? No. Boosting a citation count is an easy trick quickly learned by opportunistic authors.

Printed text citations are static and inert, while hypertext citations are dynamic in character. Citation analysis assumes new dimensions on the World Wide Web. Citations link authors and ideas, a relevance chain put in place by the author for the benefit of the reader. Common forms of citation can include the following:

| | |
|---|---|
| background | oneself |
| corrections | unpublished works |
| homage | criticisms |
| inaccessible sources | sources of physical constants |

Table 8-1 offers some classic bibliometric measures. Citation counts suffer from several potential flaws. Traditional citation analysis treats every citation equally, thus skewing results. Self-citations introduce bias. Dropping names in a multiple-authored list removes credit.

## Laws of Bibliometrics

Bibliometrics claims several laws that are useful for the purposes of insight, but which should not be considered as inviolable laws in the same sense as laws of physics or nature. They are merely organizing principles.

**Table 8-1**
Classic Bibliometric Measures

| Measure | Meaning |
|---|---|
| Mass citation count | number of citations |
| Immediacy influence index | author/article influence over a given time period |
| Citation ratio | average citations per page |
| Bibliographic coupling | similarity between source documents |
| Co-citation analysis | relationships between two cited documents |

### Lotka's Law

Lotka's law describes the scientific productivity of authors in a particular field as measured by their frequency of journal article publication. In a set of N authors:

> *The number of authors producing K publications is approximately equal to $N / (K^2)$*

This law of scientific productivity has appeal because it includes the formalism of an inverse square law akin to many natural science phenomena. (See table 8-2.)

**Table 8-2**
Theoretical Application of
Lotka's Law (N=100)

| Number of Published Papers (K) | Number of Authors Writing K Papers |
|---|---|
| 1 | 100 |
| 2 | 25 |
| 3 | 11 |
| 4 | 6 |

In this example, 25 percent of the authors published two papers and 6 percent produced four papers. The number of highly productive authors is very small. This qualitative assessment is not unexpected, but it is now quantifiable.

The number of publications is not necessarily a good or adequate measure of scientific productivity. *Lotka's law measures production, not content or impact.* The professional literature of every field contains many cases where a single article by a single author with a single new idea revolutionizes the field. There are (regrettably) many cases where authors generate multiple papers essentially having the same content and thus little productivity.

Inverse square laws appear often within the physical sciences. Perhaps it is satisfying that such a theoretical property also appears within the communication of information. This being said, the exponent value (2.0) in Lotka's law may be a function of the academic discipline and not a law of human information transfer. Voos (1974) claims the value can be 3.5, and so Lotka's law may not be an inverse square relationship at all.

## Zipf's Law

Zipf's law is used as a predictive measure for the frequency of occurrence of particular words within texts. It is derived from the following empirical observation:

> Rank the words in a document in order from most to least common
>
> Multiply the rank of each word by its frequency of appearance
>
> Zipf's law states that:

$$(Word\ rank) \times (word\ frequency) = constant$$

A Zipf analysis involves information-laden words, not stop-words (e.g., a, an, the), since the latter have low information content. It applies to sufficiently long texts. (See table 8-3.) Note that short, terse manuscripts skew word distribution. Also, the constant is a function of the specific text, not a universal value to all texts at all times.

The constant associated with this text is $C = 26,500$. The product of rank and frequency is not truly a constant, but the relationship

**Table 8-3**
Zipf's Law Applied to *Ulysses*
(James Joyce)
(The tenth, hundredth, and two-hundredth
most common words)

| Rank | Frequency | Rank × Frequency |
|---|---|---|
| 10 | 2,653 | 26,530 |
| 100 | 265 | 26,500 |
| 200 | 133 | 26,600 |

(Palmquist 2002, citing Potter 1988)

between rank and frequency is intriguing and remarkable. *Something* is affecting the composition of the text.

*Zipf conjectures the existence of a least-effort principle.* People use familiar words more often than unfamiliar words. This process minimizes cognitive, linguistic, or communicative effort. *Zipf's law may be not so much a law as a manifestation of human behavior.*

The measures of recall and precision are often discussed in the context of information retrieval effectiveness and the laws of bibliometrics. Full discussion of this topic and examples appear in chapter 4 ("Retrieving Information").

## Bradford's Law

Bradford's law involves journal productivity as measured by the number of journals containing relevant articles in a given field. Suppose a large number of professional journals are ranked according to the number of articles each carries on a given topic during a given time. Starting from the top of the ranking, let Zone 1 consist of those journals containing one-third of all published articles on the topic. There are relatively few journals in Zone 1.

Zone 2 consists of journals in the ranking with the middle third of all the articles published. It requires more journals to achieve that same number of articles. Zone 3 consists of those journals in the lower third. This set requires even more journals. In a sense Zone 1 represents highly productive journals, Zone 2 consists of moderately productive journals, and Zone 3 has less-productive journals. Bradford's law states that:

> There is a geometric relationship between the number of journals (N) in each zone and the ratio is $1: N : N^2$.

Bradford's zone grouping demonstrates the existence of a core nucleus of highly productive journals. This core produces a significant portion of articles on the given subject. It takes more less-productive journals to obtain the same number of articles. (See table 8-4.) This is a scattering effect.

Bradford's law has several useful applications. A library must have 100 percent of all journals to have 100 percent of all the articles published on a given subject. This is highly impractical and is not cost-effective. Bradford's law allows libraries to "hedge their bets." Suppose a collection of 40 journals contains 66 percent of all the articles on the

**Table 8-4**
Sample Bradford Distribution (N = 5)

| Zone | Number of Articles | Number of Journals | Theoretical Value |
|------|--------------------|--------------------|-------------------|
| 1 | 429 | 9 | 9 |
| 2 | 499 | 59 | 9 × 5 = 45 |
| 3 | 444 | 258 | 9 × 5 × 5 = 225 |

(Palmquist 2002)

given subject. If a library subscribes to these 40 journals, then on average two out of every three articles requested by users are readily available.

*Bradford's law suggests two possible collection development strategies.* The first strategy involves allocating funds for as many of the productive journals as possible in order of their ranked productivity. A few highly productive journals cover a significant portion of the topic area. The second involves setting a coverage goal (say 75 percent?) of all articles on a topic and purchasing journals toward that goal according to Bradford distribution guidelines.

## SABERMETRICS: MEASURING BASEBALL INFORMATION

Sabermetrics (from the Society for American Baseball Research, or SABR) measures baseball information. Sabermetrics is "the search for objective knowledge about baseball" (James 1988).

### *In the Big Inning . . .*

Sabermetrics compares the performance statistics of different players at the same time, the same player at different times, and different teams at the same or different times. A sabermetric analysis might compare old records with new records even if the teams no longer exist. It is possible to compare the Brooklyn Dodgers with the New York Mets, for example.

Sabermetrics predicts likelihood, measures performance, and evaluates events. Its measures, or metrics, include win/loss, batting average, runs, losing streaks, hot hands, home field advantage, and optimal batting lineups. Baseball records contain an astounding amount of data. Every major league run, hit, pitch, and error that has *ever* occurred appears in the record books. Fans claim this body of data adds to the aura of the game.

Not all agree on the validity or application of the methods used. Sabermetrics may only be trying to quantify measures in a qualitative world. The decision is left to the reader.

### *Who Wants to Know What?*

Team owners, coaches, players, sportswriters, and fans perceive the game from varied perspectives. Some follow the game with fervor and passion. A select few with vested interests pursue every possible advantage, and this is what they ask:

> Is player A better than player B, or is team C better than team D?
>
> What is the optimal batting lineup?
>
> How much does a player contribute to the team's overall success or failure?
>
> Who is the best hitter, pitcher, catcher, fielder?
>
> How much is a player worth in terms of a trade?
>
> Is a lucky streak or a losing streak real?
>
> Should a left-handed player bat against a right-handed pitcher and vice versa?

### Validity of the Measures

Performance in baseball may not be predictable. Any stockbroker will affirm that past performance never guarantees future performance. Weather, peer pressure, and injuries affect player performance, as do motivation, fear, and fatigue. A quantitative measure with qualitative components is subject to variability.

A simple team model assumes that all players are equivalent, while a complex model involves individual characteristics. Some models dismiss the impact of qualitative factors, assuming they average out over time.

### Baseball Simplified

Baseball is a game with two teams of nine players. The teams take turns batting and fielding. The batting team tries to produce runs. The field team tries to produce outs. An inning consists of one team's turn at bat and one turn in the field. Most games run nine innings. The team with the highest score of runs wins the game.

Playing baseball involves extraordinary physics. The collision of a ball and bat occurs in less than one-thousandth of a second. The ball typically hits the bat in excess of 90 miles per hour in one direction and leaves the bat in excess of 100 miles per hour in the other. The ball reverses direction and gains velocity in approximately 0.001 second, about one-tenth of a blink of an eye. The batter applies 6,000–8,000 pounds of force on the ball at the moment of impact. The decision to swing or not swing the bat must be made within one twenty-fifth of a second. A discrepancy of more than one-hundredth of a second can send the ball foul. A pitch loses speed at about one mile per hour for every seven feet thrown (Adair 1994).

Baseball is a leisurely pastime and a simple game with complex strategies. Consider the following commentaries:

> "You will learn about relativity faster than I learn baseball." —Albert Einstein
>
> "Baseball is like church. Many attend, few understand." —Leo Durocher
>
> "Baseball is 90 percent mental, the other half is physical." —Yogi Berra
>
> "Baseball is the only field of endeavor where a man can succeed three times out of ten and be considered a good performer." —Ted Williams

According to *The Guide (*August 2002), Yogi Berra is the only member of the Baseball Hall of Fame with seven entries in *Bartlett's Familiar Quotations*.

### Batter Measures

Most sabermetric measures are observable: swing the bat, hit the ball, run the base, catch the ball. Other measures are statistical abstractions. (See table 8-5.)

The batting average measures all hits regardless of type. Batting 400 means a batting average of 0.400. The difference between a superlative batter (0.400), a good batter (0.300), and a mediocre batter (0.200) is only one-tenth.

**Table 8-5**
Some Standard Batter Metrics

| Metric | Definition |
|---|---|
| Single, double, triple | type of hit |
| Batting average | hits/official at-bats |
| Slugging average | bases achieved/ official at-bats |
| Home runs | home runs |
| RBI | runs batted in |

(official at-bats = plate appearances – walks, sacrifices, hit by pitch)

The slugging average measures the ability of a batter to achieve a single, double, triple, or home run. It measures hit quality. The total bases is calculated by:

$$\text{total bases} = (1 \times \text{singles}) + (2 \times \text{doubles}) + (3 \times \text{triples}) + (4 \times \text{home runs})$$

Slugging average differs from batting average because a batting average treats every hit equally. The batting average measures the probability of getting to *some* base. The slugging average measures the probability of getting to a *higher* base.

## Pitcher Measures

The pitcher throws the ball to the batter. The pitcher is the first line of defense of the team in the field. Standard pitcher metrics include games won, games lost, runs allowed, walks, and strikeouts.

## Advanced Metrics

If player A has a higher batting average but fewer triples than player B, and player B has a lower batting average but more triples than player A, then who is the better player? James (1982) suggests that:

$$\text{runs created} = [(\text{hits} + \text{walks}) (\text{total bases})] / [(\text{at-bats}) + (\text{walks})]$$

The first numerator term measures the ability of getting on base. The second term measures the ability of moving around the bases. Lindsey (1963) suggests basing the slugger average on linear weights where each base hit has a value. It is unknown if the weights change from season to season.

$$\text{runs} = (0.41 \times \text{singles}) + (0.82 \times \text{doubles}) + (1.06 \times \text{triples}) + (1.42 \times \text{home runs})$$

*Scoring runs is important, but scoring more runs than your opponent is even more important.* James (1982) claims that player contributions to team performance are measured by:

$$\text{runs-to-wins} = (\text{wins}) / (\text{wins} + \text{losses})$$

(This statistic sometimes appears as a sum of squares formula.)

Winning games may not necessarily measure pitcher performance. Thorn and Palmer (1993) assert that this measure is fundamentally flawed because winning games may be more a function of team batting success than of pitcher throwing ability.

Bennett and Flueck (1984, 378–80) suggest a "player game percentage" that measures individual players' contributions to winning games. The player contribution is a function of every event in which the player participates.

### Event-Driven Measures

Does sabermetrics support the existence of a slump (losing streak) or a "hot hand" (winning streak)? Does performance depend on the playing field surface? Is the home field advantage real? Are night games more or less successful than day games? Are hits more likely in one inning over another?

The analysis of these multiple simultaneous variables creates a greater challenge for sabermetrics. This does not stop sportscaster speculations, however. Some may speculate that a left-handed batter might do better against a right-handed pitcher during a night game on the home field, but only if the game is played on grass and not later than the seventh inning.

Lindsey (1963) analyzed 1,800 major league games and concluded that the average number of runs correlates with the inning number. The data suggest that more hits occur in the first inning than in any other inning. Fewer runs occur in the second inning than any other inning in the game.

Albert (1994) asks what the probability is that event A will occur given that event B has already occurred. This approach suggests that most of the time there is no statistical significance on performance *with two important exceptions*.

> Batters tend to perform better within their own ballpark (the home field advantage)
>
> Batters tend to perform better when facing pitchers of the opposite arm

### Prediction

Is the outcome of a baseball game predictable? If the answer is yes, then there would be no point in playing. If the answer is no, then enjoy the game. Can sabermetrics predict outcome? Its advocates say yes, but its detractors claim no.

Some sabermetric predictors are reasonably successful. The minor league statistics of players often predict their major league performance. This should not be surprising, since major league players usually originate from minor league pools.

Does players' age predict their sabermetric performance? Baseball folklore suggests that player performance declines rapidly after age twenty-seven. The rule of twenty-seven has not been substantiated, however.

### Optimal Batting Lineups

A baseball team consists of nine players. Each player takes a turn at bat in a predetermined order set by the coach. Does a specific player arrangement increase the probability of the team winning?

The number of possible batting lineups is:

$$9! = 9 \times 8 \times 7 \times 6 \times 5 \times 4 \times 3 \times 2 \times 1 = 362,880 \text{ lineups}$$

This number is so large that it is likely many possibilities have not yet been used.

It is unclear if an optimal lineup exists. Baseball coaches and sportswriters set their preferred batting orders depending on a variety of factors. (See table 8-6.) These factors include raw power, on-base average, internal politics, knowledge of the opposing team, and just plain intuition.

**Table 8-6**
Proposed Optimal Batting Lineup (Dearing, Kolodzie)

| Batter Position | Dearing: Factor | Kolodzie: Factor |
|---|---|---|
| Leadoff | high on-base percentage, high speed | high on-base, low total bases |
| Position 2 | second-best base percentage | high on-base, high total bases |
| Position 3 | best hitting average | low on-base, high total bases |
| Position 4 | best power player | low on-base, low total bases |
| Position 5 | best clutch player | not important |
| Position 6 | best on-base, slugging percentage | |
| Position 7 | next best on-base, slugging percentage | |
| Position 8 | worst on-base, slugging percentage | |
| Position 9 | high on-base percentage, less speed | |

(Dearing 2002; Kolodzie 2002)

An optimal lineup may not exist because the game intrinsically has too many subtleties and human variations. Freeze (1974) contends that differential batting order affects less than three wins per team per season.

Bukiet, Harold, and Palacios (1997, 14–23) consider the idea of dynamic transition matrices. A comprehensive simulation for all 362,880 possible batting orders requires excessive computer time. A real game would have long since finished, so the researchers searched for a near-optimal batting lineup, assuming that only the best and worst players make a difference. (This calculation only required a few minutes.) The model suggests that:

> The best batting position for the pitcher is lineup position number 7
>
> The best hitter should be in lineup position number 2
>
> The pitcher should always be as far away as possible from the best batter

Their general optimal batting order appears in table 8-7.

**Table 8-7**
Optimal Batting Lineup
(Bukiet, Harold, and Palacios)

| Batter Skill Ranking | Optimal Batting Order Positions |
|---|---|
| Best      1 | positions 2, 3, 4 |
| 2 | positions 1–5 |
| 3 | positions 5–6 |
| 4 | positions 5–6 |
| 5 | positions 1–2 or 5–7 |
| 6 | any position except 8, 9 |
| 7 | positions 1 or 6–9 |
| 8 | positions 7–9 |
| 9 | positions 7–9 |

provided . . .

> The second or third best batter must be placed immediately before or after the best batter

> The worst batter must be placed four to six positions after the best batter

> The second-worst batter must be placed four to seven positions after the best batter

(Bukiet, Harold, and Palacios 1997)

## WEB METRICS

Web metrics uses bibliometric methods to analyze data about websites on the Internet. Web engineering metrics consider packets and pings. Web user metrics consider content and commerce. The World Wide Web can be measured from many perspectives.

### So Many Metrics

Web-based communication lends itself to an abundance of potential metrics. Web metrics obtains and analyzes raw data from logs. Server-based logs track activity from the web source to users, such as pages requested from it. Client-based logs track activity from client applications. Network-based logs track traffic-related data. The analysis of server log files can answer such questions as how many visitors a website has, where the visitors come from, which pages they request the most, how long they stay on the website, and so on.

Quantitative analysis does not always apply well to qualitative user behavior, however. *Virtually every digital bit transfer measures something,* but *having data is not the same as understanding it.* Being measurable does not imply being meaningful!

The metrics of a website can be examined and analyzed from several general perspectives, including those of commerce, content, activity, management, and the network. The last-named category includes IP hosts, browser referrals, browser types, files transferred, and other sanitized summaries devoid of human meaning. It provides environmental information, but reveals nothing about the actions or intents of users.

Content metrics offers some degree of insight into the user mind-set, and assumes that a site's content and design impact upon user actions. These factors drive users to come and explore the site, then hook them after they arrive. In contrast, commerce metrics describes the process between the click-here and the pay-now. Time-based metrics provides more insight into website use than simple scalars such as tallies (bean counts) and ratios.

Collecting the IP addresses of a site's users may not be a reliable web metric. Some networks use dynamic host name addressing. The user IP address changes from session to session, confounding interpretation for the web metric analyst.

### CENDI

CENDI is an umbrella committee composed of members from the U.S. Department of Commerce, the *E*nvironmental Protection Agency (and the Department of Energy), the *N*ational Aeronautics and Space Administration (and national libraries), and the departments of *D*efense and the *I*nterior. CENDI produces a list of web metrics and their practical uses and has issued multiple publications, reports, and presentations. (See table 8-8.)

**Table 8-8**
Common Web Metrics

| Common Label | Relates to: |
| --- | --- |
| Sales | web advertising or product selling |
| Site traffic | visitor number |
| Hits | access |
| Failed hits | hits with bad status codes |
| Page view | popularity |
| Referrers | sources |
| Requested pages | page popularity |
| Time spent | user interest |
| Browser | web access |
| Operating system | platform |
| Length of visit | design effectiveness |
| Kind of query | search effectiveness |
| Time of visit | traffic |
| Hot keywords | active terms |
| Unique hosts | distinct sources |
| Page downloads | information requests |
| Subscribers | registered users |
| Customers | purchasers |
| Repeat customers | loyal customers |
| Log-in name | authenticated users |

## EXERCISES AND RESEARCH QUESTIONS

### Exercises: Bibliometrics

E8.1    Evaluate Lotka's law based on N = 1,000 authors. How many authors can be expected to produce five articles?

*Research Question 8.2*

Perform a frequency count and word ranking of a recently submitted paper or manuscript. Does Zipf's law apply?

*Research Question 8.3*

How might the frequency distribution of letters impact on the frequency distribution of words?

*Research Question 8.4*

How might Zipf's law reveal when new words enter the vernacular?

*Research Question 8.5*

Suppose every text had the same Zipf constant. How might this impact writing styles, cataloging, and the organization of text?

### Exercises: Sabermetrics

E8.6    Each baseball sportscaster has his own sabermetric style. Tabulate the types of batting and pitching measures cited by your local sportscaster. Which occur most often in his commentary?

E8.7    Do sportscasters adequately explain the basis for their baseball metrics?

E8.8    Create a new type of baseball statistic. Refine it using data from one team. Based upon a single trial, does it predict performance when applied to another team?

*Research Question 8.9*

Batting .400 demonstrates superlative performance, yet the batter may fail to get on base most of the time. Suggest the reasons for this discrepancy.

*Research Question 8.10*

Ascertain the age distribution of players from several teams. Does player performance drop after age twenty-seven?

*Research Question 8.11*

Estimate the total number of professional baseball games ever played, using any convenient means. If every game had a unique batting order, have all possible lineups occurred?

### Exercises: Web Metrics

E8.12    Why would deriving conclusions based on website users' IP addresses be problematic?

E8.13    Suggest a means by which a hit-count web metric might be artificially inflated.

E8.14    Which web metrics does your local web manager actively collect?

## CHAPTER 9

▶ Counting Information

The counting method we learn is neither special, natural, nor necessarily better. You can count by beads, bowls, fingers, and sliding sticks. You can count forces, chess moves, words, family names, rabbits, Friday the 13ths, disks, lotteries, and poker hands. It's what you count that counts.

## COUNTING TOOLS

### The Abacus

The abacus is an ancient calculating tool related to the counting board. The term "abacus" originally meant a "flat board" composed of wood or slate and holding a layer of sand upon which words and figures could be traced and then retraced. The name derives from either *abak* (Phoenician, "sand"), *abax* (Greek, "legless table" or "sand tray"), or *avak* (Hebrew, "dust"). The abacus is a manually operated digital computer that remains in common use in East Asia and the Middle East.

A counting board used sand-filled grooves or painted lines as column markers and pebbles as tangible numerical representations. The Salamis Tablet (Babylonia, ca. 300 B.C.E.) was a counting board of marble. Remigius of Auxerre (C.E. 900) described counting boards that used colored sand. If ordinary sand was used, then the sand was called "learned dust." Cicero scolded arithmetically challenged Romans as *numquam eruditum illum pulverem attigistis* (having "never touched learned dust," Kaplan 1999, 52).

But counting styles change. In post-medieval Europe the gradual adoption of Arabic numerical notation, with its decimal placeholders and use of the zero, eventually rendered the abacus superfluous as a counting tool.

The classical Chinese abacus (*suan-pan*) consists of a modest-sized rectangular frame enclosing an upper and lower partition separated by a horizontal bar. Rods or wires strung with sliding beads extend across both partitions. The number and shape of beads determine the type of abacus.

Each rod in a typical Chinese abacus is strung with two beads in the upper portion and five beads in the lower portion (the 2/5 form). Each rod in a typical Japanese abacus (*soroban*) contains one bead in the upper portion and four beads in the lower portion (the 1/4 form). There are also less common 3/4 and 1/5 forms.

The Chinese abacus uses round beads, while the Japanese abacus uses diamond-shaped beads. Each upper bead represents a unit of five, and each lower bead represents a unit of one. Upper beads are Heaven beads, while lower beads are Earth beads.

Each rod represents a positional power of ten. Reading right to left, the rods represent ones, tens, hundreds, etc. The number ten can be expressed as two upper beads (5 + 5), one upper bead and five lower beads (5 + five ones), or one single bead in the next column. Many post-World War II abaci contain a mark every three positions, acknowledging the comma used in expressing Western currency.

The Roman abacus had a Roman numeral positioning system. The Aztec or Meso-American abacus (*nepohualtzitzin,* C.E. 900–1000) utilized maize kernels threaded through strings and may have belonged to the 3/4 form family.  The Russian abacus (*schoty*) was not beaded to powers of ten but to the national currency and hence used primarily for fiscal transactions.

The abacus is not an arithmetic artifact. Professional abacus repairmen still ply their trade (*Shanghai Star,* March 1, 2001). This author has seen an abacus serving alongside an electronic cash register at a Chinese restaurant in Manhattan. Some skilled abacus operators acquire the remarkable ability of mentally visualizing bead positions, resulting in extraordinary powers of mental arithmetic. McLeish (1991, 70) suggests that ancient abacus operators exploited patterns in their calculations. These patterns evolved to sophisticated algorithms discovered only much later in western Europe.

European counting board operators in the Middle Ages were known as abacists. Mathematicians (such as they were) were called algorists. The former used numbers as tools for commerce (practical applications), while the latter used numbers for philosophy (metaphysics, abstract mathematics). A schism developed between abacists and algorists. This dichotomy may have hindered the development of Western science and mathematics.

An abacus is usually but not always a handheld counting tool. As of this writing, the largest model  contains 91 beads and weighs 380 kilograms. The smallest model has beads consisting of individual molecules (*Guinness* 2002, 124).

### Why It Works

*An abacus is a counting machine.* Adding and subtracting involves a tally with appropriate power given to each representative column. Each bead represents a uniform value. Each column represents a uniform multiple. The abacus is a *digital* computer in contrast to the slide rule as an analog computer.

For example, consider the problem 8 + 4 = 12. The eight can be expressed as one upper bead (= 5) plus three lower beads (= 3). The value of four can be expressed as two sets of two lower beads. Adding two lower beads to the three lower beads makes the bottom equal to five beads, or equivalently one more upper bead, thus making two upper beads, or equivalently one bead in the next rod. The abacus then has one bead in the left rod and two beads in the right rod, making ten and two, equaling twelve.

The abacus has the unusual computational property that column operations can be performed in any order because only the final bead position matters. An experienced abacus operator pairs selective numbers (nine with one, eight with two, etc.) requiring only a single motion to the next column. This process vastly reduces the number of movements and enhances speed.

## The Slide Rule

The slide rule is a mechanical calculating tool in which two ruled components with specially marked scales slide past each other doing arithmetic. It was the computational tool of choice for a very long time.

Some slide rules are practically works of art. Many manufacturers constructed specialized rules for chemical, electrical, mechanical, commercial, or military applications. These rules provided rapid evaluation of pressure, frequency, wavelength, and other quantities. Their scales were based on the specific problems they were designed to solve. Some slide rules now command high prices from collectors as objets d'art.

The English mathematician William Oughtred (1574–1660) developed the current model of the "sliding rule" based on a caliper design of Gunter (1620). Slide rules were commonly made of metal, wood, or plastic. They could be straight, round, large, small, simple, or elaborate.

A standard ruler uses a *uniform* scale. The distance from one marked unit to another is the same everywhere along the rule (e.g., a meter stick contains increments of one millimeter). A slide rule uses a *graduated* (proportional) scale. The distance between units is not the same everywhere. Its markings appear bizarre to the novice operator, and there are no decimal points!

Multiplication and division use the scales labeled C and D on the slide rule. The number two is positioned at 0.3010 the length of the rule, the number three is positioned at 0.4771 its length, and the number nine is positioned at 0.9542 its length. The astute reader might recognize that these positions correspond to the base-ten logarithms of the values. Slide rule multiplication and division is based on common logarithms (from Greek *logos,* "proportion," and *arithmetik,* "number").

Many people cringe upon hearing the word "logarithm." A slide rule manipulates logarithms transparently. If A and B are any two positive numbers, then the logarithm of a *product* is the *sum* of their logarithms, and the logarithm of a *division* is the *difference* of their logarithms.

Since the slide rule uses a logarithmic scale, addition replaces multiplication and subtraction replaces division. *Calculating a product (or quotient) merely involves sliding one slot forward (or backward) along the appropriate scale and reading off the result.* A skilled operator could calculate (285 × 312) / (54 × 14) within a few seconds.

Only the final position of the slide marker matters. The operator pairs terms with the same order of magnitude, reducing relative error. Slide rules operate with significant digits, not decimal points. The numbers 1, 10, and 100 are all represented in the 1 position, as are one-tenth, one-hundredth, etc. The numbers 21 and 210 are represented in the same position. *The slide rule operates on all orders of magnitude.*

The slide rule could do complex operations, but it could not do simple addition or subtraction. A slide rule is not a counting machine. The device was rugged, inexpensive, low maintenance, reasonably accurate, and eminently portable. *Sic transit gloria.*

The atomic physicist Enrico Fermi was asked to estimate the force of the first atomic bomb even though he was miles away from the point of detonation. He threw some paper scraps on the ground and observed the angle and distance of their dispersal after being struck by the blast's shock wave. He worked at his slide rule and announced the result in a few moments. His value was confirmed hours later by scientists who had calculated the values by hand.

## COUNTING METHODS

An arithmetic problem is solved. How do you know that the answer is correct?

The eyeball method validates data by looking at the result. Is the result reasonable? If you know your data and the result looks wrong, it probably is.

The comparison method validates data by repeating the calculation. This method is effective *provided the same mistake is not made twice.* Avoid this pitfall by repeating the operations in a different order (e.g., adding up instead of adding down) or by a different grouping. Or have someone else compute the value and compare results. (The word "computer" originally referred to a person, not a machine. During World War II, teams of "computers" were assigned tasks of calculating artillery shell trajectories from tables and formulas. Common results between different teams validated their results.)

### Casting Out Nines

Casting out nines provides a quick and easy way to check addition. The original arithmetic problem is cast in terms of the number nine and is then compared to the final result. If the cast sum equals the original sum, then the answer is correct.

Casting out nines deletes any appearance of the digit nine or any sets of digits that add to nine, and then adds the remaining digits. Here is the process for numbers A and B:

> Cast out nines in A and write them in a new column
>
> Cast out nines in B and write them in a new column
>
> Add the first column (original numbers)
>
> Add the second column (cast-out numbers)

If the results match, then the addition is correct. If not, there is an error.

*Example 9.1*

Verify $314,159 + 146,283 = 460,442$

| Original | Cast Out | |
|---|---|---|
| 314,159 | 5 | (cast out 4 + 5 and digit 9; add 3 + 1 + 1 = 5) |
| + 146,283 | 6 | (cast out 6 + 3 and 8 + 1; add 4 + 2 = 6) |
| 460,442 | 11 | (original sum on left; cast sum on right) |
| 20 | 2 | (add the digits) |
| 2 | 2 | (add those digits; they match!) |

**Why It Works**

Decimal numbers are represented by the digits zero to nine. It is easy to show that adding the digits of a number has the same remainder as the original number when divided by nine.

*Example 9.2*

> 314,159 divided by 9 equals 34,906 with remainder 5
>
> The digit sum of 314,159 is  3 + 1 + 4 + 1 + 5 + 9 = 23
>
> 23 divided by 9 equals 2 with remainder 5

This remainder property works because $9 = 10 - 1$, and arithmetic is done in base ten.

We should not be too biocentric as regards this remarkable result. If we had eight fingers and did arithmetic in base eight, then the same trick would be known as "casting out sevens."

**The Russian Peasant Algorithm**

Russian folklore claims that peasants unskilled in the art of multiplication but experienced in the ways of commerce performed transactions using bowls with pebbles. The Russian peasant algorithm splits a multiplication problem into an addition problem with two columns (sets of bowls) and rows of operations. The contents of one column are successively doubled, while the contents of the other are successively halved. Any remainder is discarded.

The process continues until the second column resolves to the value of one. Rows with even entries are ignored (here crossed-out), and the entries of the first column are summed. The result (pebble count) is the product of the two numbers.

The algorithm operates as follows:

> Double the value in the left column, halve the value in the right column
>
> Repeat with the new set of values; when halving, ignore remainders
>
> Stop when the right column value equals 1
>
> Ignore even-number entries
>
> Add the first column. The value is the product of the two original numbers

*Example 9.3*

The Russian peasant algorithm applied to 54 × 37 = 1,998:

| | Double | Halve | |
|---|---|---|---|
| Row 1 | 54 | 37 | |
| Row 2 | ~~108~~ | ~~18~~ | (discard the remainder; even values so ignore) |
| Row 3 | 216 | 9 | |
| Row 4 | ~~432~~ | 4 | (discard the remainder; even values so ignore) |
| Row 5 | ~~864~~ | ~~2~~ | |
| Row 6 | 1,728 | 1 | (STOP) |
| Add | 1,998 | | (tally non-crossed off rows) |

## Why It Works

The Russian peasant algorithm relies on a regrouping principle based on binary numbers. Consider the multiplication problem 6 × 8 = 48. This problem is the same as finding the area of a checkerboard 6 squares on one side and 8 squares on the other, or a checkerboard 12 squares on one side and 4 on the other, or a board 24 squares on one side and 2 on the other.

Doubling on one side compensates for halving on the other. *Each row represents a different regrouping of the same problem.* What happens to the remainder?

Halving divides by two. The remainder is either 0 (even number) or 1 (odd number). If the number is odd, then the remainder is discarded and the contribution of the remainder is lost. Or is it? Adding the rows not crossed-off incrementally picks up the missing values.

The process relates to binary numbers because doubling and halving involve powers of two. *The Russian peasant algorithm is a conversion process.* Numerical values are converted from one base to another and back again.

## From Pebbles to Pictures and Boats

Eves (1976, 237–38) cites the ancient art of *gelosia* (lattice grating) for long multiplication and *galley* (scratch) for long division. Both methods employ a *graphical approach to arithmetic.* Multiplication involves movement across the diagram. Crossed-out components produce a lattice design for multiplication or a boat design for division. Both methods are attributed to the early Hindu tradition.

## *Chisenbop (Finger-Based Math)*

At some time in the distant antediluvian past, a humble hominid formed a remarkable association between the fingers on its hand and the objects before its eyes. This fundamental observation became the basis for counting.

Chisenbop is an ancient Korean method for doing simple math using the ten fingers as a "digital" computer. One common form of chisenbop uses the right hand for single-digit values (1–9) and the left hand for the tens digits values (10–90). A closed fist represents zero. Fingers mark position and value. Fingers move up/down, on/off a surface, and are displayed/hidden depending on the style of the operator.

The finger positions are read according to the guidelines in table 9-1:

**Table 9-1**
Chisenbop Finger Positions and Their Values

| Value | Position (right hand) | Value | Position (left hand) |
|-------|----------------------|-------|---------------------|
| 0 | closed fist | 0 | closed fist |
| 1 | pointer finger | 10 | pointer finger |
| 2 | index finger | 20 | index finger |
| 3 | ring finger | 30 | ring finger |
| 4 | pinky finger | 40 | pinky finger |
| 5 | thumb | 50 | thumb |
| 6 | thumb/pointer finger | 60 | thumb/pointer finger |
| 7 | thumb/index finger | 70 | thumb/index finger |
| 8 | thumb/ring finger | 80 | thumb/ring finger |
| 9 | thumb/pinky finger | 90 | thumb/pinky finger |

For example, the {right thumb up, left thumb up} combination represents 5 + 50 = 55.

Fingers may also represent powers of two for binary arithmetic (one, two, four, eight, etc.). There is a common misconception that finger math has limited value because it deals only with small numbers. Not so. Lieberthal (1983) suggests fingers as multiples of 100.

Surprisingly, finger-based subtraction can be performed *without "borrowing"* (Lieberthal 1983). *Finger-based math provides an alternative and innovative means for teaching arithmetic to those individuals for whom traditional methods are inappropriate or unsuccessful.*

Lieberthal also provides many examples of multiplication using a "carrying" technique. Appropriate values are (digitally) transferred without knowledge of multiplication tables. It is claimed that persons with learning disabilities can multiply using this simple technique.

## COUNTING THINGS

### Astrology and the Delivery Room

Followers of astrology believe that the configurations of celestial objects influence human behavior. How well does this belief hold up to scientific analysis?

Do celestial objects exert a greater gravitational attraction on newborns than the medical staff in the delivery room? Do celestial objects generate tidal forces across the cosmos against the newborn, subtly affecting its psychc and development? Planets and stars have enormous masses but are also enormously distant. Obstetricians have small mass but are nearby. Whose force dominates (Ratzan 1975)?

## The Method

Newton's law of gravity describes the gravitational force between objects. The force is the product of their masses multiplied by the gravitational constant divided by the square of the distance between them. Based on calculated values (and excluding the Earth itself), the Moon exerts the greatest force on the newborn of all nearby celestial objects, followed by Jupiter, the obstetrician (at very close range), Saturn, Venus, the obstetrician (at medium range), and finally Mars. This supports Carl Sagan's contention (1975, 123) that Mars exerts less force than the doctor, but it also shows that his contention is not true for all planets.

Does this analysis provide scientific credibility for astrology? Not necessarily. The fact that forces are measurable does not mean they are effective. The displacement caused by the gravitational force of the Moon is approximately 0.000017 meters, or approximately the distance of two red blood cells placed end to end. The displacement caused by the force of the physician at close range is about one-tenth of one percent of the diameter of a single red blood cell. The tidal forces from planets are so small that they do not disturb the hydrostatic equilibrium of blood flow.

How much closer must the obstetrician stand to the newborn so that he or she generates a force exceeding that of all the planets? Substitute the Jupiter value into the force equation and solve for the associated distance. This yields the surprising result: *The physician need only hover over the child at a distance of 0.16 meters (6.3 inches) to dominate the influence of any celestial object except the Moon.* If the obstetrician remains at a distance of 0.5 meters, she must then increase her mass to 900 kilograms (1,980 pounds). Moving closer is preferred.

The accurate astrologer should pay more attention to the configuration of personnel in the delivery room (and perhaps the magnetic field generated by the overhead light) than to the configuration of the planets. One last and important question remains. Under what sign would the child be born? Clearly, the *"Oxygen in Use–No Smoking"* sign.

## Counting Games of Chess

Chess is a game easily learned but not easily mastered. No one really knows the number of possible games of chess.

## The Game

The game of chess is played by two players with a board eight squares on a side and containing alternating black and white squares. Each player has sixteen pieces. Every piece has a rule specifying the manner in which it can navigate the board.

The pawn has little power. It moves forward only one square at a time, except for its initial move (one or two spaces) and diagonal capture. Pawns block more powerful pieces and are often sacrificed for strategic advantage. A rook travels straight. The bishop slides diagonally. The knight leaps over pieces.

The queen is the most powerful piece. It can move straight or on the diagonal, forward or backward, thus bearing the power of the pawn, the bishop, and the rook. In contrast, the king is the most vulnerable piece and must be protected at all times, since the purpose of the game is to attack the king in such a way that it has no escape (checkmate).

Chess involves much more than successively capturing pieces until the king can be checkmated. Strategic positioning is often crucial. There are hundreds of classical strategies (Queen's Gambit, Poisoned Pawn, etc.) with myriad variations. The game is an exquisite mental exercise of logic and tactics, patience and courage.

Chess folklore suggests the game was first introduced in India with the name *chaturanga* ("four corps," indicative of four army divisions) and later called chess from the Persian word *shah* ("ruler"). Legend says the game derived from a courtier explaining to a king how an army could be defeated without destroying all of its soldiers. Kasner and Newman (cited in Newman 1956, 4:24–27) assert the inventor was Sissa Ben Dahir, grand vizier to King Shirham.

The supposed origin of the game has a dark side. The king was so delighted by the game that he granted the courtier anything he desired. The man asked for one grain of wheat to be placed on the first square of the chessboard, two grains on the second square, four grains on the third square, and that it be so doubled for each successive square. The king thought this a trivial request and ordered it done, but the powers of two accumulated so quickly that the royal warehouses were soon emptied of grain that was needed to place on the squares. The first chess master was jailed, exiled, or executed according to different versions of the story.

Number of grains on a square N    1, 2, 4, 8, 16, 32, . . . $2^{(N-1)}$

Number of grains on last square    $2^{63}$ (approximately more than one billion billion)

Total number of grains on all squares    $(2^{64}) - 1$

Table 9-2 shows the increase in the number of grains for just the first two rows of the board.

**Table 9-2**
Grains per Chessboard Square

| | Number of the Square | | | | | | | |
|---|---|---|---|---|---|---|---|---|
| *Row 1* | 1 | 2 | 3 | 4 | 5 | 6 | 7 | 8 |
| *Grains* | 1 | 2 | 4 | 8 | 16 | 32 | 64 | 128 |
| *Row 2* | 9 | 10 | 11 | 12 | 13 | 14 | 15 | 16 |
| *Grains* | 256 | 512 | 1,024 | 2,048 | 4,096 | 8,192 | 16,384 | 32,768 |

The total number of grains on all squares is:

18,446,744,073,709,551,615 grains (approximately 18 billion billion)

This is more grain than existed on the entire planet. No wonder the king was upset!

## The Long and Short of It

Counting squares and grains is straightforward, but how does one count games of chess? What is the shortest possible game, for example? The following actions constitute possibly the shortest game with two moves per player:

*Example 9.4*

A very short game of chess:

| *White* | *Black* |
|---|---|
| King bishop pawn to king bishop pawn 3 | King pawn to king pawn 3 |
| King knight pawn to king knight pawn 4 | Queen to king rook 5; MATE! |

## Estimates

Estimating the number of moves in a chess game seems a reasonable task. Each side has the same initial placement of pieces. Neither side has any strategic advantage. White moves any one of eight pawns (one space or two) or any one of two knights (left or right). The number of White's first possible moves is:

(8 pawns × 2 choices) + (2 knights × 2 choices) = 20 possible choices

Black has the same set of twenty choices in reply to each of White's twenty choices. The number of possible board combinations after the first pair of moves is:

(20 White choices) × (20 Black choices) = 400 possible combinations

Schwarzkopf (1994) claims the following counts (table 9-3).

**Table 9-3**
Moves and Chess Positions

| Move | Possible Chess Positions |
|---|---|
| Move 1 | 20      (after White 1) |
| Move 2 | 400      (after Black 1) |
| Move 3 | 5,362   (after White 2) |
| Move 4 | 71,852 (after Black 2) |

Comment: Not all chess scholars agree on the precise count.

The number grows so rapidly that it is unclear how to count the count. The following discussion provides estimates based on different perspectives and assumptions.

## The Shannon Count

Assume there are two players each with sixteen pieces, and each piece can move a maximum of thirty-two possible ways. There are

32 × 32 =1,024 board positions

Assuming that most games end in forty or fewer plays, then the maximum number of chess games is:

$(1,024)^{40} = 10^{120}$ moves (approximately)

(one followed by 120 zeros)

By some topological estimates this number exceeds the number of atoms in the universe.

How valid are these assumptions? Some pieces are blocked and *cannot move* to their full potential. Most tournament games range from thirty to forty moves per player. Very long games can and do occur. One tournament game lasted 269 moves and more than twenty hours (Nikolic vs. Arsovic, Belgrade, played February 17, 1989). It was a draw (*Guinness* 2002, 597).

Some pieces have strategic positional value leading to attack or checkmate, in which case *they should not move*. Some pieces have *more movement than others*. A king usually moves only one space at a time. A queen slides forward, backward, or diagonally to a maximum of twenty-eight possible positions.

The board contains *a variable number of pieces* at different times of play because captured pieces are removed from the board. If a pawn survives its perilous journey across the board, then it can be promoted to a queen, adding more potential moves to its repertoire. Counting moves is also made more difficult because at the onset of a game there are more board pieces but less available space. In the endgame there are fewer pieces but more available space.

## A Combinatorial Approach

An alternative approach counts the number of arrangements thirty-two objects have over sixty-four squares. This approach counts the game independent of the properties of the pieces themselves. Shannon (1950) derives the smaller estimate:

$10^{43}$ moves (approximately)

(one followed by 43 zeros)

A binary approach considers that there are thirty-two chess pieces on the board, and at any given moment either a piece moves or it does not. In this scenario the estimated number of possible chess moves is:

$10^{63}$ moves (approximately)

(one followed by 63 zeros)

How valid is this argument? It counts all positions, *many of which are impossible* according to chess rules. For example: a bishop always remains on its initial color; a king cannot be placed in jeopardy; a blocked piece has restricted movement or none at all.

## The Stewart Count

Stewart (1971) suggested that most chess counts do not exploit a little-known rule: if no piece is captured and no pawn is moved within fifty moves, then the game is a draw.

*(Note:* Contemporary computer analysis has shown that this rule may not always apply.)

The Stewart analysis is as follows. There are 8 pawns on a side. Each can move up to 6 positions, so there are $8 \times 6 = 48$ available pawn moves per person and a total of $48 \times 2 = 96$ moves. There are 32 pieces, but kings cannot be captured, hence $32 - 2 = 30$ removable pieces. The total number of available moves for one player is less than or equal to:

$$50 \times (96 + 30) = 6{,}300$$

and the number of player moves is twice that:

$$2 \times 6{,}300 = 12{,}600$$

Table 9-4 lists player options.

Possible moves are given in table 9-5.

The number of distinct games of chess is less than or equal to:

$$334^{12,600} = 10^{31,799} \text{ (approximately)}$$

(one followed by 31,799 zeros)

**Table 9-4**
Maximum Possible Moves
by Chess Piece

| Piece | Maximum Possible Moves |
|---|---|
| Pawn | 6 |
| King | 8 |
| Rook | 14 |
| Bishop | 14 |
| Queen | 28 |
| Knight | 8 |
| Castling | 1 |

How valid is this argument? *It counts moves that might never be played.* For example, successively capturing pieces or surrendering powerful pieces for the sake of capturing lesser pieces are counted but not recommended. This counting approach yields an enormous number of junk moves that would and should never be played.

*Note:* A chess master may indeed sacrifice a powerful piece for strategic advantage, but this is not done lightly. In contrast, there are special board configurations with the unusual property that every possible move invariably leads to checkmate!

How many possible games of chess are there? It depends on how and what you

**Table 9-5**
Net Chess Moves

| Pieces | Type | Moves |
|---|---|---|
| 8 | pawns | 224  (if every pawn is promoted) |
| 1 | king | 8 |
| 2 | rooks | 28 |
| 2 | bishops | 28 |
| 1 | queen | 28 |
| 2 | knights | 16 |
| 2 | castling | 2 |
| | Total = | 334 |

count. The number is so enormous that it is likely that any given game has never been played before or may ever be played again. In that sense every game of chess is a unique experience.

### And as to Checkers

Chess and checkers ("draughts") are played on the same board, but the rules of checkers are simpler than those of chess. Checkers originated in the twelfth century in the border areas between France and Spain. Schneider (2002) estimates the number of possible games of checkers, assuming there are approximately sixty moves in a match and only three serious strategic moves at any time. The number of possible combinations is:

$$3^{60} = 10^{28} \text{ (approximately forty billion billion)}$$

How valid is this analysis? It assumes game length and possible moves. Some checker scholars disagree. Alemanni (2002) claims $10^{20}$ is a better estimate.

Why does the chess estimate exceed the checkers estimate? Checker movement is unidirectional. Only kings can move backward, and jumping is limited. In contrast, chess movements are multidirectional, since many pieces can and do retrace their steps. Some pieces leap over others with impunity. The checkers estimate considers only *serious* and *realistic* moves per play, while the chess estimate counts *all possible* moves per play.

## Counting Words

Information is borne on words. How many possible letter combinations does the Roman alphabet contain, and how many of these are meaningful words in English?

### How Many Words?

There are 26 letters in the Roman alphabet. Counting English words can be recast as counting the number of possible arrangements of 26 letters taken one at a time, two at a time, three at a time, etc. (See table 9-6.)

The first column count incorporates all possible arrangements, most of which are nonsense. Two-letter words such as AT are counted, but so is UQ. The second column count avoids double letter arrangements because no letters are repeated, but misses possible words because many use double letters (Boo!). *Neither count above incorporates or considers normal usage.*

**Table 9-6**
Counting English Words

| Numbers of Letters in the Word | Number of Words | Number of Words |
|:---:|:---:|:---:|
| (N) | (allow repeated letters) | (no repeated letters) |
| 1 | 26 | 26 |
| 2 | 676 | 650 |
| 3 | 17,576 | 15,600 |

An N-letter word allowing repeated letters has:

$26^N$ arrangements

An N-letter word with no repeated letters has:

$26 \times 25 \times \ldots (26 - N + 1)$ arrangements

For example, if a letter is Q, then the next letter must be U and all other possibilities vanish. Counting words involves more than counting 26 letters taken some at a time, since order matters. (See table 9-7.) The word NO is not the same as ON, even though they use the same letters.

**Table 9-7**
Two- and Three-Letter Words
Using the Same Letters (sample)

| Number of Letters | Sample Words |
|---|---|
| 2 | (no, on), (ha, ah), (am, ma) |
| 3 | (are, era), (rat, tar), (rat, art) |

## How Many Are Meaningful?

There are 26 possible one-letter words, but only three (A, I, O) are viable in common usage. This makes a signal-to-noise ratio of $3/26 = 0.115$. Does this same signal-to-noise ratio persist through multi-letter words? If so, then about 11 percent of all Roman-alphabet combinations would be meaningful in English, and about 89 percent would be nonsense!

Consider the case of two-letter English words. There are $26 \times 26 = 676$ possible two-letter words. How many legitimate two-letter words are there? One estimate follows.

Two-letter English words must be either a vowel-consonant or a consonant-vowel. There are 6 vowels (a, e, i, o, u, y) and 21 consonants. Observe that the letter Y can be either a vowel (as in BY) or a consonant (as in YE), making:

$$(6 \times 21) + (21 \times 6) = 252 \text{ possible words.}$$

A roster of two-letter words reveals there are approximately 22 consonant-vowel words and 23 vowel-consonant words, making:

$$\text{signal-to-noise ratio} = (22 + 23) / 252 = 0.17$$

The signal-to-noise ratio of two-letter words here is remarkably close to the signal-to-noise ratio of one-letter words. Is this an interesting coincidence or is it representative of a deeper pattern? The topic of linguistic signal-to-noise ratios warrants further study. For example, for words up to and including a given length, do most spoken languages display a similar ratio, and if so, what might be the reason?

## *Counting Votes: The United States Electoral College*

The U.S. Electoral College system was developed as a means of reducing the power of big states over small states. With few exceptions it followed the overall will of the people until the 2000 presidential election, when an extremely close vote threw the entire system into temporary confusion. The article cited below foreshadowed later political controversy.

What follows below is the original text (Ratzan 1977) introduced into 1977 congressional testimony by Senator Birch Bayh (D-Indiana). The article's results were correct for political data available at that time. These empirical results have changed with time, but many of the article's speculations still warrant consideration. The reader is encouraged to extend them.

## Some Mathematics of the Electoral College
Hearings before the Subcommittee on the Constitution
of the Senate Committee on the Judiciary

Elementary statistics coupled with computer analysis reveal that some long-standing political campaign maxims are in fact false. An example of this is the (incorrect) notion that "As Maine goes, so goes the nation."

Have our political pundits in fact successfully analyzed the American body politic? The analysis is taken from post-1824 presidential elections, since prior to that date political party distinctions are unclear. Here is a model of the Electoral College procedure.

Each individual belongs to a particular geographic region (a state). Each state has a preassigned electoral weight associated with its federal representation. The individual casts a single ballot for party A or party B (henceforth we use R or D, mindful of political parties). The weight factor of that state goes to the winner of the popular majority in that state on an all-or-none basis. The electoral weights are then summed over all states. (Split electoral votes and obscure political parties are ignored in this model.)

The rationale from a strict popular vote is that electoral weights reflect geographic distribution, with more populated areas having greater national impact then less populated ones. Unfortunately, this system allows for several types of perversities. It is possible that the electoral vote will not strictly reflect the will of the people [2000 election!]. It is possible to be elected with neither party receiving a popular majority (i.e., a minority election). It is possible to win an election but have fewer popular votes than one's opponent, or win a popular majority and still lose the election!

Based on past values, the probability of having a majority election is nearly twice as great as that of having a minority election. From this it can be shown that if there is a high turnout on election day, then the R party has a better chance of success, but if there is a low turnout, then the D party has the best chance of success. Therefore it is not in D's best interest to bring out the vote!

What information can be gleaned from the past performances of a given state? Do states tend to vote along party lines, and what states have the best voting records? These probabilities can be calculated, producing some rather surprising results.

By 1977 there was only one region which has consistently voted along a single party line (District of Columbia)! Every other state has fluctuated more or less, but Vermont and Iowa were most likely to vote for party R, while the District of Columbia and Arkansas were most likely to vote for party D.

Each state can be considered as an independent voting entity. Multiplying the associated probabilities ascertains the odds of winning a specific demographic area. This analysis suggests that a strategy of "hit the heavy" is not effective. The probability of capturing the electoral votes of the three major states (California, New York, and Pennsylvania) is quite small. The odds of winning enough heavyweights to secure the election are almost negligible. An alternate strategy is to "go with the winners."

A party can attempt to win over those states that have shown the highest incidence of success in matching the overall national choice. Do not put faith in the political maxim "As Maine goes, so goes the nation." As of 1977, New Mexico had an accuracy rate of 94 percent in selecting the ultimate electoral victor (followed by Illinois, New York, and Pennsylvania). Alas, poor Maine does not even make the top ten list—another burst political balloon.

Ah, but there is a subtlety afoot. There is little benefit in knowing that a state has a high probability of matching the national choice if it has a low probability of voting along a certain party line. One may well ask that *if* a state were swayed in a specific direction, how would it affect these odds? Based on prior probabilities when Arkansas, Hawaii, Missouri, and North Carolina went R, so did the nation; but when Alaska, Arizona, California, and New Mexico have gone D, there has never been an overall R victory.

---

The preceding article has not been presented here for serious prediction purposes, but there are some who feel that political elections are too important to be left to the people. If this analysis is too obscure, there are always the auspicious augurs of tea leaves and zodiac signs.

## Counting Surnames

Family surnames mark hereditary descent. Different cultures use different surname systems. What is the likelihood your family name will survive through the generations?

### A Surname Tells Who We Are

The patrilineal system passes the family name along the male line. The patronymic system gives the second name of the child a variation on the first name of the father (e.g., Williamson). Some Russian surnames use the *-ich* or *-ova* suffixes, indicating a child is the son or daughter associated with their father (e.g., Ivanovich, son of Ivan; Ivanova, daughter of Ivan).

Many male Semitic surnames designate lineage by the form "X ben Y" where *ben* or *bin* means "son of" (e.g., Judah ben Levi = Judah, son of Levi; Osama bin Laden). A fully qualified Hebrew name might be Velvel ben Levi ben Velvel ben Melech. A parental relationship is sometimes generalized to a region (e.g., David Ben Gurion = David, native son of the Gurion region).

There are approximately 100,000 Japanese surnames, 500 Chinese surnames, and a few hundred Korean surnames. In the case of Korean surnames, 43 percent are either Kim, Lee, or Park (Roberts and Roberts 1983). Some Native American cultures use their names as trait labels, not hereditary labels, so there is less information regarding lineage based on name alone.

### Surname Derivations

English surnames often derive from lineage, location, or tasks. (See table 9-8.) Surnames can also derive from language modification or ruler fiat. My maternal grandfather bore the name Udell, from the Russian form of the French form U' de Lev (= "from the Levites"). My paternal great-grandfather bore the name Ratzan, from the Hebraic priestly blessing *K'hayn y'he rah tzon* ("So it may be God's will"), or possibly from an edict of the czar, who ordered that men identify themselves by the town in

**Table 9-8**
Surnames

| Type | Examples |
|------|----------|
| Lineage | Davidson, Anderson |
| Locations | Dell, Lake |
| Occupations | Miller, Smith |
| Things | Clay, White |

which they were born (Ratzenia). The surname Katz may have originated from *Kohan Tzadek* ("Supremely Holy Priest"), the title bestowed upon Aaron, brother of Moses.

## An Ominous Problem?

The study of eugenics began with the control and enhancement of animal breeding stock and, by extension, the advancement of human society. Early European demographers observed that many British peerage surnames had died out. Did the fact that these men left no living descendants imply a genetic deterioration? If surnames traced lineal heritage, then in time would only a few family lines survive?

Francis Galton posed the following problem to the *Educational Times* in 1873:

A large nation of whom we will only concern ourselves with the adult males, N in number, and who bear separate surnames, colonise a district. Their law of population is such that, in each generation, a0 per cent of the adult males have no male children who reach adult life; a1 have one such child; a2 have two; and so on up to a5 who have five. Find what proportion of the surnames will have become extinct after r generations . . . (Smith and Keyfitz 1977, 399–406)

## The Solution

The solution to this problem has since been named the Galton-Watson branching process. (The proper name is the Galton-Watson-Bienayme' process, including the name of a French mathematician who investigated the same problem in 1845 but whose work was not discovered for another century.) The general process has applications to the study of explosive nuclear chain reactions, something clearly never envisioned by the authors.

The probability of producing K male heirs can be obtained from either empirical data or theoretical distributions. The probability of family name extinction is the solution to a special characteristic equation (Bailey 1964, 58–61; Keyfitz 1968, 406–10; Keyfitz 1977). Feller (1968, 298) shows that after a sufficient number of generations there are either no descendants or a great number of descendants.

The classical theoretical model contains many simplifying assumptions, including the following ones. Names are passed by the patriarchal system. The likelihood of a male heir is always constant for all generations. The same probabilities apply to every parent every time. Generations do not overlap. New surnames are not added to the pool of names.

## Some Examples

*Example 9.5*

Assume that a family produces at most two male heirs, and that the probabilities of producing zero, one, or two male heirs are equally likely. What is the probability of family name extinction?

The probabilities of male heirs are each one-third, since there are three equally likely cases. Table 9-9 shows the probability of extinction after four

**Table 9-9**
Extinction of Family Names:
Theoretical Distribution

| Number of Generations | Probability of Extinction |
|:---:|:---:|
| 1 | 0.333 |
| 2 | 0.481 |
| 3 | 0.571 |
| 4 | 0.671 |

**Table 9-10**
Extinction of Family Names:
Empirical Data

| Number of Generations | Probability of Extinction |
|:---:|:---:|
| 1 | 0.237 |
| 2 | 0.346 |
| 3 | 0.410 |
| 4 | 0.450 |

(Galton and Watson 1874; cited in Keyfitz 1977, 405)

generations, based on solutions to the characteristic equation (Keyfitz 1977, 403, citing Galton and Watson 1874).

The likelihood of surname extinction increases with each generation, and the name eventually dies out. The largest drop occurs during the first two generations (33 percent during the first generation, 48 percent in the second). Approximately half of the occurrences of the family surname vanish by the end of the second generation!

*Example 9.6*

Assume that a family produces up to five male children. The probability of producing K male heirs can be derived empirically from government records. What is the probability of surname extinction? (See table 9-10.)

The likelihood of producing K male heirs differs since the data is empirical, not theoretical. The probability of surname extinction increases at a much slower rate. There is almost a 50-percent extinction rate by the fifth generation. Feller (1968, 294), citing the results of Lotka, claims that the American family has a 48-percent chance of producing no male heirs, a 21-percent chance of producing one male heir, and a 12-percent chance of producing two male heirs.

It is important to remember that the surname pool is always in flux. New names constantly enter the system through foreign immigration. The fashion of grafting (hyphenating) the name of the wife to the name of her husband generates an enormous number of new candidate surnames. It might be interesting to ponder the impact of a matronymic naming system.

## Counting Fibonacci Rabbits

A boy bunny and girl bunny play in the field. Rabbits can mate at the age of one month. At the end of the second month, the female rabbit produces a pair of bunnies. If the rabbits never die and females always produce one male and one female offspring every month, then how many pairs of rabbits will there be after one year?

## The Rabbit-Counting Problem

Leonardo Pisano (Leonardo of Pisa; Filius Bonaccii, son of Bonaccii; Fibonacci) posed the counting problem above in a thirteenth-century text (*Liber Abaci,* "Book of the Abacus"). Here are the values:

| | |
|---|---|
| Month 1 | (1 pair) |
| Month 2 | original female has her first offspring (2 pair) |
| Month 3 | original female has more offspring<br>original offspring has her offspring (3 pair) |
| Month 4 | original female has more offspring<br>original offspring has more offspring (5 pair) |

A diagram quickly reveals a pattern known as the Fibonacci sequence:

1, 1, 2, 3, 5, 8, 13, 21, 34, 55, 89, 144, 233, 377 . . .

*Agricultural note:* The bunny-counting problem is not realistic because brother and sister bunnies mate, rabbits never die, and each pair produces exactly two offspring (always male and female). A more realistic scenario is the Dudeney cow problem (cited by Knott 2001). Suppose a cow produces a female calf when it is two years old and another female calf every year thereafter. How many female calves will there be in twelve years if no cows die?

## The Fibonacci Sequence Itself

The Fibonacci sequence contains an abundance of intriguing and almost mystical relationships. The *Fibonacci Quarterly* continually publishes newly discovered relationships. The following are a few samples:

*Terms.* With the exception of two starting terms, *every number in the Fibonacci sequence equals the sum of the two numbers that precede it.*

*Triads.* Select any three consecutive numbers in the Fibonacci sequence. Multiply the two end numbers together and subtract the square of the middle number. The result always alternates between plus or minus one *no matter which consecutive triad is chosen.*

$$2, 3, 5 \rightarrow (5 \times 2 - 3 \times 3) = 1 \qquad 3, 5, 8 \rightarrow (8 \times 3 - 5 \times 5) = -1$$

*Ratios.* Compute the ratio between any two consecutive terms in the Fibonacci sequence. *The sequence of ratios steadily converges to a special value known as the "golden ratio"* whose value is termed $\phi$ (phi), possibly after the Greek artist Phidias, who purportedly used the ratio in his sculptures (Knuth 1973, 79).

The entire Fibonacci sequence can be defined abstractly irrespective of rabbits and cows. It is a sequence whose initial two values are both one, and every next term is the sum of the previous two. What does this mean? The current value is a function of previous values. *The sequence models a process with a latent memory.*

## Counting Fibonacci Leaves, Bees, Fingers, and Plants

The biological process of morphogenesis (forming shape) occasionally demonstrates a two-level structural memory. A flower, petal, or branch receives developmental information from its last two prior states. The process is a two-step deterministic one.

The coneflower bears 34 internal spirals and 55 external spirals. Some species of daisies contain 21 or 34 spirals. Some pine cones have 5 spirals in one direction and 8 in another, while pineapples have 8 or 13. (See table 9-11.)

**Table 9-11**
Floral Fibonacci Values

| Plant | Ratio of Turns to Leaves |
|---|---|
| Elm, linden, lime | ½ |
| Beach, hazel, blackberry | ⅓ |
| Oak, cherry, apple, holly, plum | ⅖ |
| Poplar, rose, pear, willow | ⅜ |
| Pussy willow, almond | ⁵⁄₁₃ |

(Knott 2001)

The ubiquity of Fibonacci values suggests more than coincidence. Is there a subtle biochemical two-step process at work? Could the Fibonacci distribution relate to the physics of optimal seed-packing design? Is the Fibonacci sequence representative of a significant interaction between biology and physics?

A honeybee colony includes a special female called the queen bee. If the queen's eggs are not fertilized, they develop into males. If the queen mates with a male, then the eggs develop into females. The ratio of females to males in a honeybee hive is approximately the ratio of Fibonacci terms (Yanega, 1966; cited in Knott 2001).

Is it a biological coincidence, accident, or design that humans have two knuckles per finger, three parts per finger, and five fingers per hand? Is it surprising that the ratio of the longest finger bone to the middle finger bone or the ratio of the middle finger bone to the shortest finger bone is approximately the ratio of Fibonacci terms?

Lucas numbers are similar to Fibonacci numbers but have different starting values. Many plants that do not exhibit Fibonacci patterns do exhibit Lucas patterns. The ratio of consecutive Lucas numbers approaches the same special ubiquitous Fibonacci ratio.

## The Golden Ratio

The ratios of successive numbers in the Fibonacci sequence approach a number called the "golden ratio." This ratio's *exact* value is the solution of a linear difference equation whose positive solution is:

$$\text{golden ratio} = \phi = [1 + \text{square root of } 5] / 2 \quad \text{(exactly)}$$
$$= 1.618033989 \ldots \quad \text{(approximately)}$$

## The Golden Ratio and Art

Why does a sequence of numbers derived from the propagation of rabbits appear in the world of petals and flowers and fingers? If the golden ratio is so ubiquitous in the world of biology, then it should not be surprising that it also appears in the world of art. Is there something intrinsically resonant in the information-processing capacity of our brain that makes this ratio so appealing?

The ancients observed that if the ratio of A to B was the golden ratio, then so was the ratio of (A plus B) divided by A. Does this reveal something about the manner in which our eyes see the world?

The "golden rectangle" is a box whose length-to-width ratio equals the value of the golden ratio. The golden rectangle appears in the Parthenon of Athens and a Parisian home designed by Le Corbusier. Leonardo da Vinci used the rectangle for the dimensions of his painting *St. Jerome;* Seurat used it in *La Parade;* and Piet Mondrian employed it for *Place de la Concorde* (Bergamini 1963, 95–97).

*Example 9.7*

Here are some strange properties of this mysterious number:

Phi times itself equals $\phi$ plus one

One divided by $\phi$ equals $\phi$ minus one

Phi equals one plus (one divided by (one plus (one divided by (one plus (one divided by . . . etc.)

The American Mathematical Society claims that this makes $\phi$ the most irrational number (Livio 2002).

## Counting Friday the 13th

Friday the 13th conjures up images of mishaps, bad luck, and generally a day worth avoiding. The reason behind this ominous day lies deep in folklore, yet the 13th day of a month is more likely to fall on a Friday than on any other day of the week!

### An Uncommon Fact of the Calendar

The current solar calendar incorporates 365 days divided into seven-day weeks. The number 365 is not evenly divisible by seven, so there are not exactly 52 weeks in a year. The value 365 also does not exactly describe the Earth's rotation around the Sun. These aberrations make some calendar dates more likely than others.

Baxter (1969) examined the frequency of days of the week. Consider a 28-year period ending in a leap year and remaining in the same century. It can be shown that January 1 is equally likely to fall on any day of the week. Based on this result, it is possible to calculate the number of times January 1 falls on a given day over a 400-year period. Since January 1, 1968, fell on a Monday, the likelihood that the 13th of the month falls on a given day of the week is shown in table 9-12.

**Table 9-12**

Day of the Week Frequency for the 13th Day of the Month

| Day of the Week | Frequency |
|---|---|
| Monday | 13 |
| Tuesday | 13 |
| Wednesday | 15 |
| Thursday | 12 |
| Friday | 16 |
| Saturday | 12 |
| Sunday | 15 |

*The thirteenth day of the month is more likely to fall on a Friday, then Wednesday or Sunday (equally), then Monday or Tuesday (equally), and lastly Thursday or Saturday (equally).* Being a common occurrence, Friday the 13th should be embraced, not avoided!

### Counting the Tower of Hanoi

Legend says that at the beginning of time, temple priests received instructions that sixty-four golden disks, each slightly larger than the other, were to be moved across three poles. No larger disk could be placed upon a smaller one. At the completion of this task, the temple would disappear and Time would end. This legend is the basis for a puzzle known as the "tower of Hanoi." (See figure 9-1.)

### A Ring Puzzle

The tower of Hanoi puzzle was developed in 1883. Place the disks on pole 1 from largest to smallest, with the smallest on top. Move disks successively from pole 1 to pole 2 and then to pole 3, following the rule that no larger disk may rest upon a smaller one. Movement is straightforward until a large disk is forced upon a smaller one, negating the move. Can the task be completed? If so, how many moves are needed?

The solution involves an enormous number of moves, so the world should exist for at least some time. One strategy is easily demonstrated (with disk A being smaller than disk B, which is smaller than C, etc.).

> Two disks (transfer in three moves):
>> Move A to pole 2
>> Move B to pole 3
>> Move A to pole 3 . . . done!

**Figure 9-1**
Tower of Hanoi Puzzle

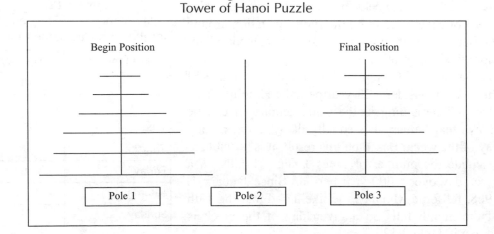

Three disks (transfer in seven moves):

| | |
|---|---|
| A to pole 3 | A to pole 1 |
| B to pole 2 | B to pole 3 |
| A to pole 2 | A to pole 3 . . . done! |
| C to pole 3 | |

A pattern quickly emerges. (See table 9-13; see also Newman 1956, 4:24–25.)

At the rate of one disk per second without stopping, the task requires hundreds of billions of years. More time is needed if the priests take a lunch break.

This same huge number appears prominently in the legend about the origin of chess. Is there a *cultural association* between doubling grains on an Indian chessboard and the movement of rings across three poles in Hanoi? This association has never been investigated. Newman (1956, 4:24–28) has noted that assuming everyone has two parents, four grandparents, eight great-grandparents, etc., then a person can have about $2^{64}$ ancestors over the past 2,000 years!

**Table 9-13**
Tower of Hanoi Moves

| Number of Disks | Number of Moves for Completion |
|---|---|
| 2 | 3 |
| 3 | 7 |
| 4 | 15 |
| N | $(2^N) - 1$ |

The complete sixty-four disk tower of Hanoi puzzle requires:

$$2^{64} - 1 = 18,446,744,073,709,551,615 \text{ moves}$$

Arthur C. Clarke (1987) wrote a science fiction story called "The Nine Billion Names of God" that is loosely based on the tower of Hanoi puzzle. An enlightened order of monks commissions a massive information system that, instead of moving disks around on poles, will enumerate all the names of God in the belief that the stars will vanish and Time will cease. The chief engineer of the project is skeptical, but then . . .

## Winning the Lottery

> "Gamble with your head, not over it." —Gamblers Anonymous

People select or are assigned lottery numbers in return for a potentially large prize. The cost is low and the lure is high. How can one win the lottery?

### Lucky Numbers

Part of the lottery's lure is the misconception that some numbers are luckier than others. There are *no* lucky numbers in a fair lottery because by design every number is equally likely to be chosen in the drawing. The number 999 is just as likely to be selected as the number 314. If you selected number 124 and the winner was 125, then were you oh so close? No. The number 742 is just as close. Numerical distance is irrelevant.

## Winning More Money versus Winning More Often

A *straight bet* is a wager in which the player must match the winning number(s) *exactly.* This type of wager has the highest payoff but also has the lowest chance of winning. A wager in which the player selects any *arrangement* of the numbers is called a *box bet.* If a player boxes a bet, then the chance of winning increases but the amount won decreases. The "gambler's rule" applies: *The higher the win, the higher the risk.*

## And the Prize Is . . .

A lottery ticket generally has a fixed price, but the prize varies with the game. The win amount may be a (pari-mutuel) function of the lottery tickets sold and the number of winners. If there are multiple winners, then the prize is shared. If there are no winners, then the payment increases as part of the next game. (The case of no winners should mandate a second drawing, but alas, this usually does not happen.)

Regardless of the win amount, the payoff amount may vary. Lottery winnings are distributed in a lump sum or by installments. The former method dispenses all the money at once (with the tax agent waiting). The latter method spreads the payments over a number of years by an annuity.

Some lottery winners have funneled their winnings into a mass purchase of more lottery tickets. One New Jersey player won the lottery twice in four months. Funneling is generally ineffective and the money won is soon lost.

## How to Win the Lottery

This discussion will focus on several common lottery forms. The principles apply to exact match and partial match number games. The specific games and names are copyrighted by the New Jersey Lottery Commission and are cited herein as instructional examples and with permission.

### The Pick-3 Model

The Pick-3 lottery involves the choice of a three-digit number. Each digit ranges from zero to nine, hence there are ten possibilities for each position. The number of possible plays is:

$$10 \times 10 \times 10 = 1,000 \text{ possible combinations}$$

The odds of winning the New Jersey Pick-3 in a straight bet are thus 1,000 to 1.

As of January 24, 2001, the average top prize for this type of bet was $275. If 1,000 tickets were purchased at fifty cents each, then the lottery brought in $500 but only paid out $275. This type of disparity is not unusual in lotteries.

Can you increase your odds of winning? Absolutely! Here are some variations:

> *The Straight Wheel* (3-way combination, 3 ways to win):
>> wins if two of the same digits match in any order
>
> *The Straight Wheel* (6-way combination, 6 ways to win):
>> wins if three different digits match in any order
>
> *The Front Pair* (10 ways to win):
>> wins if the first two digits match exactly
>
> *The Back Pair* (10 ways to win):
>> wins if the last two digits match exactly
>
> *The Split Pair* (10 ways to win):
>> wins if the first and last digit match in sequence

The cost of each type of game varies, as does the payoff. Forget ye not the gambler's rule.

## The Pick-4 Model

The Pick-4 game plays four numbers instead of three. There are ten possible choices for each digit position and four digit positions.

The odds of winning the Pick-4 on a straight bet are:

$$10 \times 10 \times 10 \times 10 = 10{,}000 \text{ possible combinations}$$

The odds of winning are 10,000 to 1.

The Pick-4 supports many hybrid games. The 24 combination box wins with any four different digits in any order. It paid $116 (not much), but the *odds of winning something* dropped from 10,000:1 to 417·1 What happened?

How many ways can there be four different digits each ranging from zero to nine? There are ten cases for position one, nine for position two, eight for position three, and seven for position four. Hence the number of different ways is:

$$10 \times 9 \times 8 \times 7 = 5{,}040 \text{ different ways to achieve four different digits}$$

These four digits, whatever they may be, have twenty-four different arrangements:

$$4 \times 3 \times 2 \times 1 = 24$$

The odds of winning are thus the probability of getting four different numbers multiplied by the probability based on the number of ways to win.

The probability of getting four different numbers $= (10 \times 9 \times 8 \times 7) / (10 \times 10 \times 10 \times 10)$. The probability of winning given there are four different digits $= 24 / (10 \times 9 \times 8 \times 7)$. The product is:

$$(5{,}040 / 10{,}000) \times (24 / 5{,}040) = 0.002398 = 427 \text{ to } 1$$

*Winning by matching two similar digits.* The number of ways of achieving two matching digits is: $10 \times 10 \times 10 = 1{,}000$. Once they have been selected, there are twelve possible rearrangements. The probability of winning by two matching digits is:

$$(1,000 / 10,000) \times (12 / 10,000) = 0.0012 = 833 \text{ to } 1$$

*Winning by two sets of two similar digits.* The first position has ten possibilities. The second position has only one, since it must match the first. The third position has nine possibilities, since it cannot use the digits already used, and the fourth position has only one, since it must match its neighbor. There are ninety cases and six arrangements. The probability of winning this game is:

$$(90 / 10,000) \times (6 / 90) = 0.0006 = 1,666 \text{ to } 1$$

*Winning by matching three digits in any order.* Using the same logic as above, position one has ten cases, position two has one, position three has one, and position four has ten. There are thus 100 ways to match three digits. Once they have been selected there are four possible rearrangements. The probability of winning this game is:

$$(100 / 10,000) \times (4 / 100) = 0.0004 = 2,500 \text{ to } 1$$

A summary of ways to win the Pick-4 game appears in table 9-14.

**Table 9-14**
Winning the Lottery: Pick-4 Game

| Type of Bet | Odds to Win | Ways to Win | Average Payoff |
|---|---|---|---|
| *Straight* (exact match) | 10,000 to 1 | 1 | $2,788 |
| *24-way combo box* (any four-digit number, all different digits in any order) | 417 to 1 | 24 | $116 |
| *12-way combo box* (any four-digit number, two digits the same in any order) | 833 to 1 | 12 | $232 |
| *6-way combo box* (any four-digit number, two sets of digits the same in any order) | 1,667 to 1 | 6 | $464 |
| *4-way combo box* (any four-digit number, three digits the same in any order) | 2,500 to 1 | 4 | $697 |

(Values courtesy of the New Jersey Lottery Commission, 2002)

## The Pick-6 Model

The Pick-6 lottery involves selecting six numbers ranging from 1 to 49. There are more positions, hence a bigger payoff, hence greater odds. The number of possible ways to select six numbers from that set is:

$$49 \times 48 \times 47 \times 46 \times 45 \times 44 = 1,006,834,752 \text{ cases}$$

These cases are subject to this number of possible arrangements:

$6 \times 5 \times 4 \times 3 \times 2 = 720$ rearrangements

The odds of winning this game on a straight bet are:

$(1,006,834,752) / (720) = 13,983,816$ to 1 (about 14 million to 1)

By comparison, the odds of being struck by lightning are about 1.5 million to 1!
A summary of ways to win the Pick-6 game appears in table 9-15.

**Table 9-15**
Winning the Lottery: Pick-6 Game

| Matching Game | Odds to Win | Average Payoff |
|---|---|---|
| 6 out of 6 numbers | 13,983,816 to 1 | $6 million |
| 5 out of 6 numbers | 54,201 to 1 | $2,700 |
| 4 out of 6 numbers | 1,032 to 1 | $56 |
| 3 out of 6 numbers | 57 to 1 | $3 |

(Values courtesy of the New Jersey Lottery Commission, 2002)

The odds of *winning something* are:

$(1 / 57) + (1 / 1,032) + (1 / 54,201) + (1 / 13,983,816) = 0.0185$ or 54 to 1

## Winning Strategies

How does one win a lottery? If you must play, then select the game that has the greatest odds of winning and forget about the Big Win. Is it possible to buy up all winning combinations so as to assure a winning bet? Yes, but the payoff will always be less than the cost. A case can be made that it is better to buy multiple tickets in one week for a straight bet game than the same number of tickets spread over separate weeks.

## *Winning at Poker*

Poker is a card game based upon a deck of 52 cards. The deck contains 9 number cards and 4 picture cards in 4 different suits. How does one win at poker?

## The Nature of Poker

The game has many variations, arguably the most common of which is straight five-card poker. The dealer distributes five cards to each player. House rules apply. The players wager, and the player with the highest hand wins the round. The game continues for a specified time or until all but one player drops out or until one player shoots the others . . .

The number of possible hands affects the wager. Assume for the sake of simplicity that everyone keeps their original hand, there are no wild cards, and every hand is drawn independently from a fresh deck.

The first card may be any of 52 cards. There are 51 choices for the second card, 50 choices for the third card, 49 choices for the fourth card, and 48 choices for the fifth and last card. The number of *possible poker hands* corresponds to the number of 5 cards dealt from a deck of 52:

$$52 \times 51 \times 50 \times 49 \times 48 = 3,118,752,000 \text{ possible hands}$$

The order of the cards is irrelevant. Given the five cards, there are five ways to arrange the first, four the second, three the third, two the second, and the last is fixed. The number of possible rearrangements of the same hand is:

$$5 \times 4 \times 3 \times 2 \times 1 = 120$$

Therefore the number of unique deals is:

$$3,118,752,000 / 120 = 2,598,960 \text{ *unique poker hands*}$$

Every poker hand has a ranked value. The hand with the highest value wins the round. Poker has the distinction over many other games that there is always a winner, unless all players agree to fold.

## Winning Hands in Poker

Table 9-16 shows poker hands and their relative value in decreasing order.

### Table 9-16
Poker Hands

| Hand | Description | Ways | Odds (approximate) |
|---|---|---|---|
| Royal flush | straight flush to ace | 4 | 649,740 to 1 |
| Straight flush | flush in numerical order | 36 | 72,193 to 1 |
| Four of a kind | same | 624 | 4,165 to 1 |
| Full house | three of one, two of another | 3,744 | 694 to 1 |
| Flush | same suit | 5,108 | 508 to 1 |
| Straight | numerical order | 10,200 | 254 to 1 |
| Three of a kind | same | 54,912 | 47 to 1 |
| Two pair | same | 123,552 | 21 to 1 |
| One pair | same | 1,098,240 | 2.36 to 1 |
| Nothing | | 1,302,540 | 2 to 1 |

(Values courtesy of Bogle 2001)

The highest-value hands are also the least likely. If in doubt, go for the straight rather than the flush. Go for the full house rather than four of a kind. Most hands are worthless. These odds explain why some house rules abandon the entire deal unless players have a pair of jacks or better.

Wild cards dramatically increase the odds. If deuces are wild, then infrequent combinations become much more likely. A wild card allows a player to have five aces (or five whatever) even though the fifth item never exists in the original deck. Multiple wild cards make the odds of a royal flush almost reasonable!

Wagers are based on many parameters. Removing cards from play affects probabilities, since the same cards cannot reappear. Some casinos routinely replace cards with a fresh deck, thereby discouraging professional card counters who monitor the odds and bet accordingly.

## Common Likelihoods

Cards come in four suits.

| | | |
|---|---|---|
| The probability of getting a particular suit: | 13 / 52 | = 4 to 1 |
| The probability of getting a particular picture card: | 4 / 52 | − 13 to 1 |
| The probability of drawing a particular card: | 1 / 52 | = 52 to 1 |

## EXERCISES AND RESEARCH QUESTIONS

### Exercises: The Abacus

E9.1   If there are two upper beads (each worth five) and five lower beads (each worth one) and a rod represents a power of ten, then express the numbers 3, 13, and 33 on an abacus.

E9.2   Do this arithmetic on an abacus: {5 + 7}, {17 − 4}.

E9.3   Why is subtracting 10 and adding 1 faster than subtracting 9 directly?

E9.4   Why can abacus addition be performed in any column order?

### Research Question 9.5

Examine how the algorist/abacist schism impacted Western scientific development.

### Exercises: Slide Rule

E9.6   If a slide rule were scaled *uniformly,* why could it do addition but not multiplication?

E9.7   Some engineers "tuned" their slide rules by loosening the slider adjustment screw or by lubricating the slide with a graphite pencil tip. The marker glided with less friction, promoting faster computation. What was the risk of having a lighter touch?

E9.8   Find the current worth of a metal and wooden slide rule.

E9.9   Follow the instructions in Meyer (1958) and build your own slide rule!

## Exercises: Casting Out Nines

E9.10  Verify: $123 + 456 = 579$ by casting out nines. Show that $135 + 284 = 418$ is incorrect.

E9.11  Verify: A number is divisible by three if and only if the sum of its digits is divisible by three. (Example: 42 is divisible by 3, and $4 + 2 = 6$, which is also divisible by 3. Find another example.) This implies the next exercise.

E9.12  Verify: A number is divisible by nine if and only if the sum of its digits is divisible by nine. (Example: 63 is divisible by 9, and $6 + 3$ equals 9, which is divisible by 9. Find another example.)

E9.13  Verify $254 + 289 + 311 + 95 = 1,649$ by hand (no calculator). Validate the answer by adding the numbers in reverse order. Validate the results using casting out nines. Which method seems faster?

## Exercises: Russian Peasant Algorithm

E9.14  Evaluate $16 \times 7 = 112$ by the Russian peasant algorithm.

E9.15  Verify $16 \times 256 = 4,096$ by hand (no calculator). Verify the result using the Russian peasant algorithm. Which method seems faster?

*Research Question 9.16*

Lattice designs often appear in the context of Hindu and Islamic art. Could this art represent arithmetic?

## Exercises: Chisenbop

E9.17  Represent the number 42 using finger-based representation.

E9.18  What is the maximum value in that representation?

*Research Question 9.19*

The "Correo 10 Centavos" postal stamp of Nicaragua shows a person doing finger counting. The stamp is part of the series celebrating *las 10 formulas mathematicas que cambiaron la faz de la tierra* ("ten formulas that changed the world"). What are the other nine formulas in the stamp series?

## Exercises: Astrology and the Delivery Room

*Research Question 9.20*

Small asteroids have passed between the Earth and the Moon. Suppose an asteroid passes halfway between the Earth and the Moon. Ask a physicist to apply the formula cited in the section and determine what mass is needed to dominate the hovering obstetrician. (Of course, if the asteroid is too big or too close, then the forces in the delivery room may not be our biggest problem . . .)

*Research Question 9.21*

Show that the Moon's gravitational force on the newborn is greater than that of the nearest star outside our solar system. Look up the mass of a nearby star using any standard library reference book. Ask a physicist to do the computation.

### Exercises: Counting Chess

*Research Question 9.22*

A chess-playing computer cannot possibly check all possible moves, yet it reaches a decision within seconds. What methods prune the enormous tree of possibilities?

### Exercises: Counting Words

*Research Question 9.23*

How many words appear in the current edition of the *Oxford English Dictionary?*

*Research Question 9.24*

How many words are in the vocabulary of an average ten-year-old, twenty-year-old, and fifty-year-old?

*Research Question 9.25*

What languages have the highest signal to-noise ratios?

### Exercises: Counting Votes

*Research Question 9.26*

Update the 1977 data to the most recent presidential election.

*Research Question 9.27*

What state currently has the highest probability of success in matching the winner? Which state has the lowest?

*Research Question 9.28*

Analyze various electoral vote strategies.

### Exercises: Counting Surnames

E9.29   What is the probability of a male heir at each generation of your family tree?

*Research Question 9.30*

Does the *-ova* ending in a traditional female Russian surname relate to the Latin word *ovum*, "eggs"?

*Research Question 9.31*

Why do some surnames seem to survive better than others?

*Research Question 9.32*

What might be an advantage of a matrilineal surname system?

### Exercises: Counting Fibonacci Rabbits

E9.33   Verify that every third term of the Fibonacci sequence is a multiple of two, every fourth term is a multiple of three, and every fifth term is a multiple of five.

*Research Question 9.34*

Identify other works of art involving the golden ratio.

### Exercises: Counting Friday the 13th

E9.35   Count the number of Friday the 13ths for this calendar year. Compare it to the occurrences of Thursday the 13ths.

*Research Question 9.36*

What is triskadekaphobia? Why is the number 13 considered unlucky in some cultures?

### Exercises: Counting the Tower of Hanoi

E9.37    Verify that the tower of Hanoi with four disks is solvable in fifteen moves.

E9.38    How many moves are necessary for a half tower of thirty-two disks?

### Exercises: Winning the Lottery

E9.39   List the possible arrangements for the box bet {3, 1, 4}.

E9.40   Why are there better odds of winning by purchasing many tickets on one lottery game than by purchasing the same number of tickets over several games?

*Research Question 9.41*

Expectation is the probability of winning multiplied by the amount of the win. Is the expectation of a lottery better or worse than that of a horse race?

CHAPTER **10** ▶ Numbering Information

God gave us the natural numbers, all else is the work of man.

—Leopold Kronecker (1823–1891)

## PRIME CUTS

### *Prime Suspects*

A natural number is a *prime* number if it has only two divisors, itself and one. If a natural number has more than two divisors, then it is called a *composite* number because it is composed of other divisors. (See table 10-1.)

These divisors in turn may be composite or prime. If they are composite, then they themselves have divisors which can also be composite or prime. The decomposition process repeats until every divisor ultimately breaks down to its prime components. *Prime numbers are thus the basic building blocks of the counting numbers.* This leads to the so-called fundamental theorem of arithmetic:

*Any positive integer greater than 1 is either prime or the product of primes*

Why is this decomposition important? *The properties of the primes control the properties of the numbers.* Special programs called "prime finders" seek out primes,

**Table 10-1**

Types of Natural Numbers

| Number | Type | Divisors |
|--------|------|----------|
| 6 | composite | 1, 2, 3, 6 |
| 7 | prime | 1, 7 |
| 60 | composite | 1, 2, 3, 4, 5, 6, 10, 12, 15, 20, 30, 60 |

providing torture tests for new computer system designs. Modern cryptography relies heavily on the identification of large primes and the difficulty of prime factorization. (See chapter 7, "Concealing Information.")

Are there enough primes to sustain all the cryptographic applications across the global Internet? More than 2,000 years ago Euclid proved *there are an infinite number of primes* (*Elements,* bk. 9, sec. 20, theorem 2). How could Euclid know this? How would anyone know if there was a larger one nearby if only they had looked a wee bit longer?

Euclid's proof is simple and elegant. It operates on a reductio ad absurdum ("reduction to the absurd") argument. The proof assumes something is true and then demonstrates that this assumption leads to a logical contradiction. The original assumption must then be false.

Here is a rough sketch of the proof. (A rigorous proof has subtleties, but this text is not intended as a math textbook.) Assume P is the absolutely largest prime. Multiply all the primes less than or equal to P together to form an even bigger number, and call it N. Then N is composite because it is divisible by many factors. Now add one. That new number N + 1 is either prime or not prime. If it were prime, then we have constructed a prime number larger than the presumably largest prime. Contradiction!

If it is not prime, then it has some prime factor that divides it. Why? The number was built from the product of all prime factors less than or equal to the largest one, so the prime factor is one of them. This number does *not* divide the number N + 1 because it has a remainder of one. So the number does and does not divide the big number N + 1. Contradiction!

There is only one way to resolve this ugly state of contradictory affairs. The original assumption must be false. There is no largest prime. There are an infinite number of primes. *Quod erat demonstrandum.* ("That which was to be shown.")

## Which Numbers Are Primes?

There are many prime numbers, but which numbers are they? Eratosthenes of Cyrene was the chief librarian at the university in Alexandria during the reign of Ptolemy III, and also the first person to accurately determine the circumference of the Earth (by measuring the shadow of sundials at two different cities a known distance apart and at the same time). He created a prime number detector known as the sieve of Eratosthenes.

Make a list of counting numbers. The sieve starts with the first prime (2). Cross out all numbers on the list that are multiples of two. The sieve goes to the next number (3). It crosses out all numbers that are multiples of three. It goes to the next number (4). Four is already crossed out. Skip to the next number (5) and cross out all multiples of five. Continue the process. *Numbers that are not crossed off are prime.*

|  |  |  |  |  |  |  |
|---|---|---|---|---|---|---|
| 2 | 3 | 4 | 5 | 6 | 7 | 8 |
| 9 | 10 | 11 | 12 | 13 | 14 | 15 |
| 16 | 17 | 18 | 19 | 20 | 21 | 22 |
| 23 | 24 | 25 | 26 | 27 | 28 | 29 |

The sieve of Eratosthenes shows that the first few prime numbers are:

$$\{2, 3, 5, 7, 11, 13, 17, 19, 23, 29, 31, 37 \ldots\}$$

The sieve is an excellent instructional exercise, but it is not commercially feasible for modern computer security applications. Centuries later Agrawal, Saxena, and Kayal (Indian Institute of Technology, Kanpur) discovered a more practical method and published their work in August 2002 (see "Outside Math," *New York Times Magazine,* December 15, 2002).

### Primal Patterns

Prime numbers show many remarkable patterns. Two is the only even prime, making it very "odd" indeed! Here are some unusual properties for your awe and delight:

> *Every prime that is greater than or equal to three has the form*
> *4N + 1 or 4N – 1*
>
>> Examples: $5 = (4 \times 1) + 1$ and $11 = (4 \times 3) - 1$

> *All odd primes greater than or equal to five have the form*
> *6N + 1 or 6N – 1*
>
>> Examples: $7 = (6 \times 1) + 1$ and $11 = (6 \times 2) - 1$

Pierre de Fermat (1601–1665) observed an even deeper pattern:

> *Every prime of the form 4N + 1 is the sum of two squares*
>
>> Example: $13 = 2^2 + 3^2$

### Prime Guesses

Mathematics folklore states that prime conjectures are discovered by amateurs but proved (with difficulty) by professionals. Power to the people. The following simple observations remain fiendishly elusive unproven conjectures:

The original Goldbach conjecture:

The even ("strong") Goldbach conjecture:

> *Every even number greater than two is the sum of two primes*

Variations on the theme:

The odd Goldbach conjecture:

> *Every odd number greater than five is the sum of three primes*

The Schinzel conjecture:

> *Every number greater than seventeen is the sum of three different primes*

The difference conjecture:

> *Every even number is the difference of two primes*

The spread conjecture:

>*There is always a prime number between N and (N + 1)²*

The twin prime conjecture:

>*There are an infinite number of twin primes*

The "weak" Goldbach conjecture:

>*Every odd number greater than seven is the sum of three odd primes*

The dual conjecture:

>*Every even number greater than six is the sum of two odd primes*

Historical footnote: Christian Goldbach (1690–1764) stated the original conjecture to Leonhard Euler in a letter dated June 7, 1742. Euler claimed that what is now known as the "odd conjecture" implied the "even (original) conjecture." There is reason to believe that René Descartes (1596–1650) and possibly others were already aware of the problem, but for reasons unknown, Goldbach received the naming credit. So much for immortality.

## Prime Facts (Things We Know)

We know that prime factorization is difficult, that there are as many primes as we need, and that primes are detectable. We also know:

The Bertrand postulate:

>*There is always a prime between N and 2N*

The prime number theorem:

>*The number of primes less than or equal to N is approximately N / log (N)*

Fermat squares:

>*Every odd prime is the difference of two squares*

Prime wastelands:

>*There are arbitrarily large gaps in the sequence of primes*

## Prime Families

*Mersenne primes* are named for Marin Mersenne, a sixteenth-century French abbot who actively promoted the study of special prime numbers. There is a fleeting degree of fame attached to the (currently) largest known prime. Many of the former record holders are Mersenne primes.

The Great Internet Mersenne Prime Search (GIMPS) harnesses the distributed computing power of the Internet. On November 14, 2001, the team of Cameron, Woltman, Kurowski, et al. calculated what they believed to be the 39th Mersenne prime:

$$2^{13,466,917} - 1$$

This monster has 4,053,946 digits and no divisors except itself and one.

*Sophie Germain primes* are named for Sophie Germain, a nineteenth-century French mathematician. Women could not enroll at the École Polytechnique when it was founded in 1794, so she obtained course notes on her own and eventually established a mathematical correspondence with J.-L. Lagrange (a developer of calculus) using the pseudonym "Antoine-August LeBlanc." She was later recommended for an honorary doctorate but died before it was awarded. The rue Sophie Germain and the École Sophie Germain are named in her honor.

*Illegal primes* are numbers that may be against the law! A computer program is a set of instructions. These instructions are expressed in binary form within a digital computer as a string of bits. Therefore, every computer program is actually a very long number. Some of these numbers are primes. One such number (program) in hexadecimal format corresponds to the decryption component of a DVD movie encryption scheme. It is illegal to distribute the source code associated with this encryption. Is it illegal to distribute this number?

> "Then there are those famous pearls
>
> That have stymied kings and earls
>
> Goldbach, twin primes and Riemann Zeta,
>
> No solution, plenty data." (Machover 2002)

## THE INTRIGUING NATURE OF PI

> *Frustra laborant quotquot se calculationibus*
> *fatigant pro inventione quadraturae circuli.*
>
> ("Futile is the labor of those who fatigue
> themselves with calculations to square the circle.")
>
> —Michael Stifel, 1544

### It's a Circle

A circle is the set of points equidistant from a given point. Divide the circumference of a circle by its diameter. *No matter how large or small the original circle, the result will always be the same.* The ratio of circumference to diameter is and will always be a special value denoted as $\pi$ (pi). This simple proportion of nature is constant and true, everywhere and for all time, producing a fundamental, universal number that is strange and mysterious.

Circles have unusual properties besides being pleasantly round. A circle has the largest area of all flat shapes with the same perimeter. It also has the smallest perimeter of all flat shapes with the same area. A circle with radius one contains an area precisely equal to pi.

### Counting Biblical Pi

The Bible cites two indirect references to pi, both of which relate to buildings.

> And he made a molten sea, ten cubits from one brim
> to another; it was round all about and the height was five cubits
> and a line of thirty cubits did compass it all about.
>
> —1 Kings 7:23; 2 Chronicles 4:2

If the sea's circumference = 30 cubits and its diameter = 10 cubits, then the biblical value is $\pi = 3.0$.

This value has two interesting cultural ramifications. First, it is a "round" number consistent with the ancient Greek concept of a rational universe. Second, it indicates that a low level of architectural precision was acceptable for the civilization of that time. Some people accept this approximate value as geometric truth because it derives from a book of Scripture. Most of them are not engineers or do not reside in a building constructed from this approximation. The Bible is not an engineering textbook.

The two verses in question have a little-known but intriguing difference. *The verses are not syntactically identical, although they are translated as such.* The word for "line" differs slightly between them. The verse from Kings uses the (here transliterated) Hebrew letters K-V-H, while the verse from Chronicles uses the transliterated letters K-V. The words are spelled differently but are read the same way because the differing letter is silent.

Hebrew letters have numerical values associated with them (Gematria). The numerical value of K-V-H is 111, while that of K-V is 106. If the biblical value of pi (= 3.0) is multiplied by the numerical ratio of the two words (111 / 106 = 1.04716), then pi = 3.1415. This value is remarkably accurate to four places. Some say this is a coincidence. Others think not.

There are two difficulties with the argument in favor of design. First, the argument is speculative. Why multiply pi as 3.0 by that specific ratio and not some other value? The fact that it works is an ex post facto justification. Second, the same differential spelling occurs in other portions of the biblical text. The word for "line" is expressed as K-V nineteen times and as K-V-H three times. There is no explanation supplied for the difference in spelling in these cases, and in neither case is there a direct or indirect reference to pi. The difference may be nothing more than an ancient transcription error or fodder for numerologists.

### A Short Chronology

The Rhind Papyrus (ca. 1650 B.C.E.) contains some of the earliest written work on the properties of pi and circles. Circles were studied by Ptolemy (ca. C.E. 150), Tsu Chung Chi (C.E. 430–501), and al-Khwarizmi (ca. 825). Al-Khwarizmi is the source of the word "algorithm." His work titled *Kitab al-jabr wa al muqabala* ("The Book of Integration and Equation") is the source of the word "algebra."

The term "pi" was first used by William Jones (1706). Leonhard Euler adopted the standard symbolic notation $\pi$ from the Greek alphabet in 1737. It has also been suggested that the word "pi" derives from the first letter of the Greek word *peripheria,* meaning "periphery."

The biblical value suggests that pi = 3.0. The Rhind Papyrus value suggests that pi = 3.16. Archimedes showed that pi lies somewhere between 3.1408 and 3.1428. Many researchers have sought the exact values of pi. J. H. Lambert (1761) proved that pi cannot be expressed as the ratio of two integers and therefore cannot be expressed exactly by *any* fraction or decimal. Persistence is futile!

Ferdinand von Lindemann (1882) showed that pi is what is known as a transcendental number. These results resolved the classical problem of antiquity known as squaring the circle, i.e., constructing a square whose area is that of a given circle. Can this be done using the construction tools of rational geometry, the compass and straightedge? The answer is unequivocally no.

## How Much Accuracy Is Too Much?

The fact that pi has a value that can never be precisely determined has not deterred so-called digit hunters. Pi has been evaluated to an enormous number of decimal places. Six-decimal accuracy in numbers suffices for the building of bridges. Twenty-decimal accuracy suffices for atomic particle calculations. A few hundred digits describes the ratio of a subatomic particle to the size of the known universe. Pi has been evaluated to more than a trillion decimal digits. (And a pattern still does not emerge . . .)

Many underutilized computers in the 1960s evaluated pi during off-peak hours. This common practice was considered less expensive than the slow process of powering down and powering up monolithic mainframes. Contemporary computers now keep busy mapping genomes, simulating fusion, forecasting weather, cracking codes, and trying to detect extraterrestrial signals.

## Mnemonics of Pi

The desire to remember the digits of pi (piphilology) has engendered several intriguing mnemonic devices. The number of letters in each word corresponds to the appropriate digit.

> May I have a large container of coffee?
>
> (3-1-4-1-5-9-2-6)
>
> How I want a drink,
>
> alcoholic of course,
>
> after the heavy lectures involving quantum mechanics!
>
> (3-1-4-1-5-9-2-6-5-3-5-8-9-7-9)

> (cited in Gephart 2002, source unknown)

The following poem is attributed to A. C. Orr (1906):

| | |
|---|---|
| Now | 3 |
| I Even I | 1-4-1 |
| Would celebrate | 5-9 |
| In Rhymes Unapt | 2-6-5 |
| The great immortal Syracusan | 3-5-8-9 |
| Rivaled nevermore | 7-9 |
| Who in his wondrous lore | 3-2-3-8-4 |
| Passed on before | 6-2-6 |
| Gave men his guidance | 4-3-3-8 |
| How to circle'd mensurate. | 3-2-7-9 |

(*Note:* The "Syracusan" refers to Archimedes.)

Brannon (cited in Gephart 2002) observed that speaking the first twenty-three digits of pi has a rhythmic meter remarkably akin to the song "America" from the musical *West Side Story* (1961).

| | |
|---|---|
| Three point one four one five nine, | 3-1-4-5-9 |
| Two six five three five eight nine, | 2-6-5-3-5-8-9 |
| Seven nine three two three eight four, | 7-9-3-2-3-8-4 |
| Six two six and a whole lot more! | 6-2-6 |

### Political Pi

The number pi is not without its politics (Beckman 1971, 175). In 1897 the Indiana state legislature sponsored House Bill Number 246 adjusting the annoying value of pi to a more convenient value, as well as dispensing with a difficult classical problem at the same time. According to various sources, the bill was authored by Edwin J. Goodwin and introduced to the Indiana House by the representative from Posey County on January 18, 1897. The bill was referred to the Committee on Canals (also known as the Committee on Swamp Lands).

A description of the bill appeared in the *Indianapolis Journal*. The article claimed that the superintendent of public instruction endorsed the new long-sought solution of the squaring the circle problem. The article also revealed an interesting hidden commercial agenda behind the bill. The author claimed a copyright for the new solution, but would allow textbooks free use if the bill were adopted.

Representative Butler submitted a report recommending that the bill be referred to the Committee on Education. On February 2 the chairman of the Education Committee recommended that the bill pass the House. The bill passed by a vote of 67–0 six days later. It was referred to the Indiana Senate on February 10, where it was sent to the Committee on Temperance(!). On February 12 Senator New recommended the passage of the bill.

By this time the bill had generated a sufficient amount of public ridicule. Senator Hubbell expressed concern that legislative resources were being wasted, and he moved that the bill be indefinitely postponed. It lies there still. (One wonders if distinguished Indiana representatives actually understood the contents of this bill that had gone so far in the legislative process!)

## Easily Stated Questions with No Easy Answers

Empirical evidence suggests that each of the ten digits appears one-tenth of the time in pi, but empirical evidence is not proof. The group known as the Friends of Pi cites table 10-2, which shows the distribution of digits in pi as evaluated to an enormous number of decimal places. An equally likely distribution would produce a value of exactly 600,000,000.

Does every given string of numbers always appear somewhere in pi? More personal perhaps, is it possible to find your birth date within the sequence of pi? Do the digits of pi contain profound messages from the cosmos or divine messages seen only by the enlightened? Not likely.

Does the number make for interesting entertainment (motion picture: *Pi,* 1998)? Does the number make for a masculine scent? ($\pi$, "The modern masculine style of the thinking man's fragrance" by Givenchy, booklet no. 832, Macy's department store, May 2002). Can the digits of pi be the basis of a secret code? Possibly. The digits could be used as an encryption key. The key could not be easily broken.

In many cases, the calculation of one digit requires a knowledge of previous digits. A single undetected mistake propagates to all future digits. In 1873 Shanks published the value of pi to 707 places, but in 1945 Ferguson discovered that the value in the 528th decimal position was incorrect, making all others following in error. Shanks achieved scientific immortality, but not the way he intended.

What value should be used for pi?

> "If inside a circle a line
> Hits the center and goes spline to spline
> And the line's length is 'd'
> The circumference will be
> 'd' times 3.14159." —Unknown

But others feel differently:

> "'Tis a favorite project of mine
> A new value of pi to assign,
> I would fix it at 3
> For it's simpler, you see,

**Table 10-2**
Distribution of Digits in Pi

| Digit | Frequency |
|-------|-------------|
| 0 | 599,963,005 |
| 1 | 600,033,260 |
| 2 | 599,999,169 |
| 3 | 600,000,243 |
| 4 | 599,957,439 |
| 5 | 600,171,176 |
| 6 | 600,016,588 |
| 7 | 600,009,044 |
| 8 | 599,987,038 |
| 9 | 600,017,038 |

(Wagon 1985; Friends of Pi 2002)

Than 3 point 1 4 1 5 9." (Baring-Gould 1967, attributed to Harvey Carter; cited in Gephart 2002)

Here are more decimal digits of pi than you will probably ever need . . .

$\pi$ = 3.14159 26535 89793 23846 26433 83279 502 . . . (approximately)

## PASCAL'S TRIANGLE

If a simple two-term expression is raised to higher powers, then the resulting coefficients produce a remarkable pattern. These values have applications to library book arrangements, birth distributions, and combinations of things.

### The Triangle

A binomial expression such as A + B has two terms. Multiply it by itself several times. The results appear in table 10-3.

If the coefficients are written separately, they form an amazing pattern:

| Level 1 | | | | 1 | 1 | | | |
| Level 2 | | | 1 | | 2 | | 1 | |
| Level 3 | | 1 | | 3 | | 3 | | 1 |
| Level 4 | 1 | | 4 | | 6 | | 4 | | 1 |
| Et cetera | | | | | | | | |

**Table 10-3**
Binomial Expansions

| Expression | Expansion |
|---|---|
| (A + B) | A + B |
| (A + B)$^2$ | A$^2$ + 2AB + B$^2$ |
| (A + B)$^3$ | A$^3$ + 3A$^2$B + 3AB$^2$ + B$^3$ |

This diagram is known as Pascal's triangle, although it was also known as the Yanghui triangle in China about 500 years earlier.

### The Triangle's Patterns

Pascal's triangle contains many fascinating and unexpected properties, some of which were discovered by amateurs.

Every row always begins and ends with a 1.

The first inner diagonal consists of the counting numbers {1, 2, 3, 4, . . .}.

The next inner diagonal consists of the triangular numbers {1, 3, 6, 10, . . .} (i.e., bowling pin rows).

The next inner diagonal consists of the sums of triangular numbers {1, 4, 10, 20, . . .}.

With the exception of the first and last elements, the value in a given position equals the sum of the left and right diagonal elements of the row above it:

4 = 1 (above left) + 3 (above right)

Every row is symmetrical. It starts with one, increases to a maximum, and then decreases.

The sum of the values in any row always equals a power of two.

If the second number in a row is a prime number, then it divides all the other numbers in that row except for the leading and ending ones:

| 1 | 4 | 6 | 4 | 1 | | | | (4 is not prime) |
|---|---|---|---|---|---|---|---|---|
| 1 | 7 | 21 | 35 | 35 | 2 | 17 | 1 | (7 is prime) |

Pascal's triangle contains thousands of intrinsic numerical patterns. What can you find?

### Pascal's Triangle and Probability

How many ways can N objects be grouped K at a time? How many ways can library books be grouped on a shelf? Or people in a room or socks in a drawer? The number depends on how you count.

A combination is a grouping in which different orderings of the same items are considered identical and counted once. It is a grouping without regard to order. If there are two colors, then {red, green} is considered the same as {green, red}.

A permutation is a grouping in which the same items in different order are distinct and are counted separately. It is a grouping with regard to order. The set {red, green} is not the same as {green, red}.

*Example 10-1*

A set of three elements {a, b, c,} has:

three combinations    (a, b), (b, c), (a, c)
six permutations      (a, b), (b, a), (b, c), (c, b), (a, c), (c, a)

The Nth row of Pascal's triangle contains the number of combinations of N objects taken one at a time, two at a time, three at a time, up to N at a time.

How many ways can four colored books on a library shelf be grouped?

one at a time?   4
two at a time?   6
three at a time?  4
four at a time?   1

How many possible boy-girl combinations are there of five children?

5 boys and no girls?    1
4 boys and 1 girl?      5
3 girls and 2 boys?    10
2 girls and 3 boys?    10

1 girl and 4 boys?          5

5 girls and no boys?        1

## EXERCISES AND RESEARCH QUESTIONS

### *Exercises: Primes*

E10.1   Why is there only one even prime?

E10.2   Find the first dozen primes using the sieve of Eratosthenes.

E10.3   Verify the even Goldbach conjecture for the first few even numbers.

E10.4   Verify the odd Goldbach conjecture for the first few odd numbers.

E10.5   A *perfect number* is a number that equals the sum of its divisors. Six is an even perfect number because one, two, and three divide six and also add to six. Even perfect numbers are related to prime numbers. What is the next even perfect number? (Hint: It is less than thirty.)

### *Research Question 10.6*

Advanced cryptography uses prime number keys. Suppose a person discovers a particularly useful prime number secret key. Can that number be patented?

### *Exercises: Pi*

E10.7   Many websites contain the value of pi evaluated to an absurdly large number of decimal places. Download one such evaluation. Use a search function and ascertain if your birth date appears as a string within pi.

E10.8   Create your own mnemonic for the first few digits of pi.

## CHAPTER 11

▶ Managing Information

## CHARACTERISTICS OF A SUCCESSFUL INFORMATION SYSTEM

Successful information systems share certain common characteristics, the presence of which improves the likelihood of success and the absence of which leads to trouble.

### Essential Mandates

An information system must serve a purpose; it must be teleological in nature. If the system does not serve a purpose, then it is not an asset and may even be a liability. If it becomes a liability or becomes *perceived as a liability,* then it will not remain long within the organization. If it serves no purpose, then it adds no value.

Measure and monitor the performance of an information system. Monitoring a system involves knowing *what* it is doing. Measuring a system involves knowing how *well* it is doing. Event logs, system logs, application logs, and static or dynamic status reports (and in the extreme case, alerts and warnings) monitor an information system.

Measures must be standard and consistent if they are to be compared. Measures must also be realistic (Ratzan 1991; Ratzan 1993). Joeckel and Winslow (1948) suggested a range of measures for the library as an information system, including input, output, and use assessments. Computer information systems have numerous productivity measures. Be aware that not all measures are relevant in all contexts. Indeed, some measures have no meaning except in very restrictive contexts. *If an information system is not monitored or measured, then it is unclear what is happening or if its performance is becoming better or worse.*

Information systems support *users* (clients). Clients are people doing their jobs or subservient machines doing their tasks. Information systems support *uses* (applications). Applications are projects.

Every information system requires support. Staff must keep it running and management must *want* to keep it running. In the absence of dedicated staff, a system flounders and performance falls. In the absence of dedicated management, funds dry up and the project decays.

Reduce the burden of continuous support by using "cloned images." A template contains standard configurations, applications, anti-virus software and data sets. The template is "stamped" onto a master copy. Each replicant is a clone of the original and can be produced (generally in minutes) without the need to install each software component individually. A clone adds value because machines are more uniform, hence fewer devices require individual support. Workstations are more interchangeable, troubleshooting takes less time, and replacements go online more quickly. If the software on a library workstation becomes corrupted, it is often easier to replace the entire hard disk with a fully working clone than to fix the individual problem.

### Some System Facts of Life

*The more complex an information system is perceived to be, the less likely it will be used.* The biggest and best information system will not be used if users perceive its operation as being too complex for their needs. Learning requires effort, but users typically take the path of least effort. If avoidance is easier than use, then the system will be avoided rather than used. An information system becomes ineffective without users.

*If information involves money or power, then it will not be willingly shared.* Information systems control information flow. *In scientia vis.* ("In knowledge there is power.") Power is not willingly shared. There is a Golden Rule of Administration: Whoever has the gold makes the rules. The flow of information controls the flow of money, and money is power.

*If it looks wrong, then it probably is.* A successful information system maintains its focus. If the focus wanders too far from its mandate, then its operation interferes with its purpose. Know your system well.

*If it looks like a duck and it quacks like a duck, then chances are it is a duck.* The attributes of an object do not change with a new name. A new label does not make a new system. Jargon and buzzwords should not disguise the nature of the system or the nature of its problems.

*If the only tool you have is a hammer, then every problem looks like a nail.* There is a tendency to see problems in terms of available methods, tools, or knowledge. Maintaining an open mind and continuously expanding your horizons offers new perspectives on problem solving.

### Two Fundamental Design Approaches

The bottom-up approach begins at the user level, with information flowing upward through levels of administration. The top-down approach begins at the top level, with information flowing downward to the user.

Information becomes distorted as it passes through levels of communication. Korzybski (1958) argued that human social knowledge progresses slower than human scientific knowledge because of the nature of language and its distortion. Information becomes altered, garbled, or distorted with each passage. The final outcome may be dramatically different than originally envisioned.

Real-life organizational structures may fold back on themselves. The overall structure may not be a balanced tree. Bureaucratic structure may not match information structure.

## The Bottom-Up Approach

*The bottom-up approach assumes that users are the most aware of organizational needs.* Users' perspective is local, not global. System development becomes a grassroots process. Users communicate their needs to the next level of management, which then passes it to the next higher level. Ideas, concepts, and actions percolate and evolve upward until receiving the blessing of corporate administration. For example, the New York City school system might be empowered for change at the school level by teachers (bottom) and not by the Board of Education (top).

Different user groups have different needs. Such needs resonate, complement, or conflict with each other. (And all of these phenomena may occur at different times!) Conflicts subvert information flow.

## The Top-Down Approach

*The top-down approach assumes that corporate leaders are the most aware of organizational needs.* This approach originates with upper management. A corporation's perspective is global, not local. Information flows downward for the benefit of the entire organization.

It is a regrettable fact that some managers become oblivious to the reality of the organization in which they serve. Their perception of corporate need may not be in alignment with true corporate need. As a result, information policy mandates from above may not address the needs of the users below.


## BUILDING A SUCCESSFUL INFORMATION SYSTEM

An information system arises from the needs of an organization and the imagination of its staff. Most successful information systems share a common set of guidelines. The sophistication of an information system is no guarantee of its success.


### The Process

*Build a prototype.* Show the system works. At the onset, effectiveness is more important than efficiency. Concepts are good, but results are better. Provide conclusive evidence of proof-of-principle.

*Do not promise all things to all people.* Too many promises form too many obligations. Be a producer, not a politician. Playing too much politics diverts personal energy from system development. Set an appropriate focus with realistic expectations.

*Let others try it.* Information system developers feel justifiably protective about their domain. Developers are consciously aware of the flaws, features, and flavors of the system. They are not the ones who will ultimately use it. Let the system evolve driven by the needs of the users.

*Get feedback.* Obtain criticism from management. Obtain criticism from users. Do not dismiss negative criticism. Do not be blinded by praise.

*Get others involved.* An embryonic information system receives more support if users perceive themselves as contributing participants in its development. Management provides more support if they have already "bought into" the project. Maintain vested interest in the information system.

*Do not be myopic.* Focus on the local needs of the information system, but do not lose sight of its global implications. Developers, users, and managers have different perspectives. A nearsighted approach blocks perspective.

*Achieve early and often.* Inform all who will listen that the system is producing and progressing. Broadcast achievements. Sometimes the perception of progress is more important than the rate of progress. Small incremental positive results maintain support more effectively than a series of delays before a big result.

*Get a budget.* A budget assures commitment of time and resources. A budget is a tangible sign of organizational support that the project shall proceed. The absence of a budget demonstrates no confidence in *future success.*

*Get an evangelist.* Identify someone who actively promotes the information system. The person must have credibility and sufficient authority that others will listen. Enthusiasm is contagious.

*Build a solid support infrastructure.* An information system requires levels of support. Users are usually oblivious of the infrastructure, but long-term growth and development relies on it, and building it takes time

### Three Fundamental Phases

In building a system, it is both easy and tempting to gloss over the core issues and dive into the fray. Know your data. Know your tools. Know their limitations. Know your results. Know if the results make sense. Know *why* the results make sense. Ask the right questions during the phases of system design, analysis, and implementation. (See table 11-1.)

**Table 11-1**

Asking the Right Questions

| Phase | Core Questions |
|---|---|
| Design | What is the problem? What are the data?<br>What are the tools and resources to get a solution? |
| Analysis | What is the solution? Is there more than one solution?<br>Is there an optimal solution? Optimal how? |
| Implementation | Make it happen!<br>Did it work? Why or why not?<br>What must change? What cannot change? |

## WHY THINGS GO WRONG

Good projects can go bad. Good plans can stumble. Common pitfalls can subvert completion. Be aware and avoid them.

### The Envious Colleague

The envious coworker or manager perceives a new project as glamorous and covets the associated recognition. They become enamored with the project after it receives favor or success, yet they have not contributed to its success, nor have they assumed any risk in its development.

At an opportune time the person claims jurisdictional or administrative control over all or part of the system. This action enables them to effectively diminish the competition, be seen as a project leader, and bask in its positive image.

The manager quickly asserts their newly imposed authority and insists on changes, claiming that they have studied the problem long and hard. In most cases the changes are poorly conceived, incomplete, or long since abandoned by the actual developers. (This would have been evident had the manager done their homework.)

The newly mandated changes display the manager's dominance and have little to do with merit. Staff who balk at such changes receive implied condemnation. Resistance is dismissed by platitudes ("You do not see the big picture," "Be a team player," etc.).

If this monster cannot be avoided, then it should be appeased. Offer an aspect of the project that seems relatively important (for their ego) but is relatively minor (for your survival). Keep them busy but isolated. If they interfere, then submit while politely making them aware that system changes are documented. Accountability may be a disincentive for further interference.

### Differences in Agenda

The project agenda should be clear. A straight path is more direct than a convoluted one. Then again, sometimes management has a different or hidden agenda.

The likelihood of a project's success increases when all parties (users, developers, and managers) share a clear and common goal. More than one agenda promotes divergence. At best there is confusion, and at worst there is conflict. Conflicts by definition work against each other.

### Insufficiencies

A project staggers if there is insufficient time, money, staff, or resources. If time runs out or money runs out, then people run out (quite literally).

Project management is an art. Spreadsheets and visual aids may help, but personal communication helps most of all. An open and honest channel of communication between parties is more effective than any project software.

Maintain realistic expectations. The fact that a supervisor *wants* a task completed within a given time within a given budget using current resources does not imply that the task *can* be completed under those constraints. Management by fiat rarely succeeds.

## COSTS AND RISKS

Information has no price, but managing information does.

### *Some Basic Costs of Information*

Most costs of information management fall within a few specific categories. The cost of infrastructure includes:

> heat, light, power, electricity
>
> telecommunications (voice and data, wired and wireless)
>
> networking (cables, hubs, routers, switches)
>
> backup power supplies
>
> renting space and leasing equipment, taxes, fees

The cost of training includes:

> staff professional development
>
> certifications and authentication
>
> newsletters, bulletins, references, vendor documentation
>
> new user orientations
>
> user application training (room, trainers, equipment, supplies, refreshments)

The cost of vendors supplying the products includes:

> software, hardware, firmware, and their upgrades
>
> warranties, maintenance contracts, service-level agreements
>
> technical support, consultants

The cost of office supplies supporting production includes:

> paper, toner, disks, envelopes, and all that mundane stuff

Securing information also has a cost:

> keys, locks, swipe cards, smart cards, biometric devices
>
> public safety, security guards, backup servers and media
>
> password management software, encryption technology
>
> authentication software, certificate servers

And never ever forget the people who do the work that keeps the system running:

> salaries, benefits, taxes, insurance

### Risks

Developing, storing, retrieving, organizing, maintaining, and managing information involves measurable and nonmeasurable risks. No operation is risk-free. There must be a dynamic (not static) balance between convenience, cost, and risk.

Hardware arrives late. It does not arrive at all. It arrives on time but does not work properly. It arrives on time but does not work at all. It works but is incompatible with other hardware or software. Software arrives late or not at all. It arrives on time but it is incompatible with preexisting versions. It is incompatible with other applications. It interferes with current operations. The budget runs out. Time runs out. Patience runs out.

Power goes out. Pipes break. Rooms flood. Telecom lines drop. Satellite links fail. Nature has a way of reminding us who is really in charge on this planet.

Never rule out sabotage. Disgruntled employees steal and spy. Insiders are the primary source of information theft.

CHAPTER **12**    ▶ The Computer as an
Information System

## HOW BIG IS AN EXABYTE?

A binary digit (bit) value ranges all the way from zero to one. If a bit has only two possible values, then representing a very large number requires a very large number of bits.

### Size and the Internet

In general, eight bits make a byte, four bits make a half-byte (nibble), and one byte represents one character. The value of one byte ranges from 00000000 to 11111111. In the binary representation system, each bit position represents an increasing power of two. The value of one byte ranges from zero to a maximum of

$$128 + 64 + 32 + 16 + 8 + 4 + 2 + 1 = 255$$

Hence there are 256 possible values for a byte.

An Internet Protocol (IP) address consists of four bytes (byte1.byte2.byte3.byte4), each of which may assume up to 256 possible values. Ignoring all other factors and based solely on this form, the Internet can support at most

$$256 \times 256 \times 256 \times 256 = 4{,}294{,}967{,}296 \text{ networked devices}$$

*Note:* The actual number is smaller because some combinations of values are reserved for special purposes.

The current Internet cannot contain more than about 4.3 billion addresses, after which there will be no more available IP addresses. Because of the continued proliferation of networked workstations, servers, printers, PDAs, and online peripherals, there are numerous schemes under development for extending the naming limitation. The Internet—in some form—should not run out of addresses for some time.

### Naming Big Bytes

Prefixes incrementing by factors of 1,024 identify successively larger numbers of bytes. Table 12-1 displays the relation between these size measures.

A kilobyte is more than a thousand bytes, a megabyte is more than one million bytes, and a gigabyte is more than a billion bytes. These labels are often confusing to an information system novice because in the metric system, "kilo" denotes one thousand, "mega" denotes one million, "giga" denotes one billion, etc. The metric system does not apply here.

**Table 12-1**
Byte Sizes

| Name | Relative Value | Absolute Value (bytes) | |
|------|----------------|------------|---|
| Kilobyte | 1,024 bytes | $2^{10}$ | 1,024 |
| Megabyte | 1,024 kilobytes | $2^{20}$ | 1,048,576 |
| Gigabyte | 1,024 megabytes | $2^{30}$ | 1,073,741,824 |
| Terabyte | 1,024 gigabytes | $2^{40}$ | |
| Petabyte | 1,024 terabytes | $2^{50}$ | |
| Exabyte | 1,024 petabytes | $2^{60}$ | |
| Zettabyte | 1,024 exabytes | $2^{70}$ | |
| Yottabyte | 1024 zettabytes | $2^{80}$ | |

## DATA COMPRESSION: REDUCING REDUNDANCY

Data compression is the process by which the representation of data is "squeezed" so that the compressed representation uses less storage space than the original. Every computer information system is limited. Most data are not needed most of the time, and data are often redundant. Redundant data take up space and eventually accumulate to the point that computer performance degrades. Data compression reduces redundancy and gives more bytes for the buck.

### Principles of Data Compression

*Lossless data compression* is a process by which the original data set can be restored *exactly.* If compression is performed such that the restored copy is "almost" the original but is good enough for practical purposes, then it is said to be *lossy data compression.* Lossless compression loses no data. Lossy compression loses less important data and is generally quicker and easier than lossless compression. It operates on the assumption that what is missing does not matter.

Image compression has some loss because the human eye does not always perceive subtle gradations in shade or hue. The loss of this information does not adversely affect the final result. By contrast, the compression of data requires zero losses. "We do not want a program that does about the same things as the one we wrote. We do not want a database that contains about the same kind of information as what we put into it" (Mertz 2000).

### Simple Compression Techniques

Whitespace compression removes unnecessary blanks. Whitespace compression has application to web design, since conventional hypertext markup language consolidates whitespace (multiple blanks resolve to a single blank).

Abbreviation compression replaces full-length terms with shorter terms. The computer associates the actual word with its abbreviation and expands it as necessary. This method has applications to long texts with multiple repeated words. (See table 12-2.)

**Table 12-2**
A Simple Abbreviation Compression in the Bible

| Word | Size (letters) | Frequency | Simple Abbreviation | Size (letters) | Savings |
|------|----------------|-----------|---------------------|----------------|---------|
| Begat | 5 | 139 | bt | 2 | 3 |
| Thou | 4 | 4,953 | tu | 2 | 2 |
| The | 3 | 28,001 | t | 1 | 2 |
| Unto | 4 | 7,391 | u | 1 | 3 |

(King James version, 1987 printing. Available at bible.gospelcom.net. Accessed 14 December 2002.)

The storage savings for this simple abbreviation is

$$3(139) + 2(4,953) + 2(28,001) + 3(7,391) = 88,498 \text{ characters!}$$

Run-length encoding (RLE) replaces a string of single bytes with a single byte followed by a repetition number. There are many variations on this theme. The method is widely used due to its robustness and speed. Huffman encoding uses a symbol table weighted by the frequency of each symbol. The Lempel-Ziv compression scheme uses a dynamic table. Fractal image compression uses self-similarity as a basis for replication. There is no single general-purpose data compression algorithm that applies well in all cases. Some file formats compress better than others. The reader may have observed that some graphics files change size dramatically when compressed, while others change very little. The reason is that some graphics formats are intrinsically already compressed. Compressing an already compressed file gains no space but does waste processor time.

Data compression has value whenever storage space is limited or at a premium. Backup systems with compression can store more bytes per component, hence reducing the cost of storage media. Infrequently used computer files utilize less space if they are compressed when dormant. Compressed sound files provide rapid downloads. Compressed archives reduce overhead.

A modem example: A modem *mo*dulates and *dem*odulates a computer signal along a telephone line. A modem can be envisioned as a pump, pushing bits back and forth along the line. Every modem has a rating capacity based on the extent of bits it can pump. Data compression can fool a modem and produce greater throughput.

Suppose a file can be compressed by 25 percent. In a sense the modem pushes only one-quarter of the original file. Therefore four times as much can be moved per unit time, resulting in faster uploads and downloads as perceived by the user. The astute reader may note that this method actually involves two additional steps, because a file must be compressed and decompressed besides being transferred. True enough, but

CPU processing time for compression/decompression is so much faster than modem processing time that the impact of the additional overhead is minimal.

## INFORMATION ISSUES IN THE BACKGROUND

Most computers have a single processor driving the interactions of the computer system. Multiprocessor computers support more than one processor, meaning that the information-processing load can potentially be distributed. Multiprocessor machines may permit enhanced parallel processing and improve overall performance.

A multitasking computer has the ability to perform more than one processing task at the same time. It is convenient to have the computer print a document at the same time the user is editing a file or reading one's e-mail. Efficient multitasking is an extremely complex internal process because the computer must constantly track which resources and memory are being used where and by what process. (*Note:* Librarians often multitask as they serve their patrons!)

A multithreading computer processes related blocks of code as a group as opposed to individual lines. Program developers often design their code in threads, taking full advantage of these increased information-processing capabilities.

Keep information cool. Computer electrical components generate heat. Too many electronic components packed into too small an area create a serious heat dissipation problem, and heat will degrade the components. Earlier low-power computers used ordinary air-venting strategies, but most contemporary computers require internal fans, which themselves draw electrical power. In fact, some ultra-high power supercomputers designed specifically for speed are literally encased in a liquid nitrogen coolant. Most modern computers now have the capability of managing their own power supplies and support "sleep" or "hibernation" modes of power conservation.

Computers enhance the communication of information but also create serious issues of security. Information should be shared, but that does not imply that information should be open. Sharing resources begs the question of who has access to what, how much, and when. File permissions assure that the computer system provides information to authorized users and no information to unauthorized users. (This is akin to the all-and-only problem of information retrieval.)

The UNIX system grants read/write/execute file permissions to the owner/group/ world as designated by an authorized user or owner. Many UNIX-based websites have been hacked because the owners maintained default settings for convenience and failed to set the correct level of file access. The Microsoft environment provides an abundance of potential file permissions that can be explicitly granted, inherited, or superseded when a file is moved or copied to a destination folder. An "Access Denied" error message is usually indicative of a conflict between the user permissions and the information permissions.

Most computer network architectures are based on either the client-server or the peer-to-peer model. In the former model, computer functionalities are allocated between the dominant server and the subservient client workstations. The server generally holds the master copy of the applications, databases, and account information. The clients fetch them as needed. This division of labor dedicates the server computer to the efficient storage, retrieval, and processing of data while the client concentrates on the effective user interface. A client-server model requires more overhead but generally performs better because special servers (web server, print server, file server, database server) focus on special tasks.

A peer-to-peer model (also known as a work group model) treats all computers as both clients and servers. Computers have no division of labor, hence all are peers to each other. A peer-to-peer network is easily set up at low cost. The primary problem of the peer-to-peer model comes with size. Each computer has its own user log-ins, access permissions, and file resources. In order for a user to access resources, he or she must have an account and access rights on every machine. Maintaining a large peer-to-peer network can easily become an administrative nightmare.

The following scenario may illustrate the difference between a peer-to-peer information-distribution model and a client-server model.

You go to a local ice cream shop for a treat. There is one person in line ahead of you. The person at the counter takes their order, fills their order, and takes their payment. You are waiting all this time. Or . . . there is one person at the counter and one additional support person. The one at the counter takes the customer orders and payments (and is not concerned with making the dish), while the one in the back prepares the order (and is not concerned about dealing with the customers).

The first scenario is analogous to peer-to-peer, the second to client-server. The former is simpler, but customers often wait for service. The second scenario is more costly to the company, but two different processes are occurring simultaneously, and customer transactions are quicker and more successful.

## EXERCISES AND RESEARCH QUESTIONS

### Exercises: How Big Is an Exabyte?

E12.1    Put the following into increasing order: one-tenth terabyte, one gigabyte, one hundred megabytes, one thousand kilobytes.

### Exercises: Data Compression

E12.2    Why might one milli-helen be the amount of beauty necessary to launch one ship? (Hint: According to legend, Helen of Troy was said to be the face that launched a thousand ships.)

E12.3    Obtain the number of words in some edition of the Bible from any standard library reference source. Assume that each word contains an average of five letters, and each letter uses one byte. Multiplying the number of words by five gives the number of bytes for that biblical edition. Does it exceed the capacity of a standard 1.44-megabyte floppy disk? Most Bible texts on disk must be stored in compressed format.

*Research Question 12.4*

Why is fractal compression especially amenable to images?

*Research Question 12.5*

How does a CODEC (*co*mpression/*dec*ompression) process work on video signals?

CHAPTER **13**  ▶  The Internet as an
Information System

There is no reason anyone would want a computer in their home.

—Ken Olsen, Digital Equipment Corporation, 1977

## BASICS OF INTERNET PROTOCOL ADDRESSING

There is a well-worn joke that the three most important factors in real estate are location, location, and location. This applies to the Internet as well. Addressing is critical to Internet operation.

### What Is an IP Address?

The Internet is a global network of public and private networks that share the common telecommunication protocol known as TCP/IP (Transmission Control Protocol/Internet Protocol). Every computer and network component physically connected to the Internet bears an Internet Protocol (IP) address. An IP address—which should not be confused with a URL, or Uniform Resource Locator—uniquely locates devices on the network.

The birth of the Internet is said to have been on January 1, 1983, when the ARPANet (Advanced Research Projects Agency) switched over to TCP/IP. The first message ever broadcast across the Internet was the word "login." The first e-mail message sent across the Internet is unknown. The Internet celebrated its twentieth anniversary in 2003. (As a point of comparison, UNIX celebrated its one-billionth-second anniversary a few months before.)

A telephone number is an address within the phone system. A phone number consists of an area code and a local exchange number. The same exchange number may exist in different area codes, but the area code–number combination is unique.

By analogy, an IP address is an address within the Internet. An IP address consists of a network component and a host component. Computers may have the same host name in different networks, or they may reside in the same network with different host names. The network-host combination is unique. The network portion is sometimes referred to as the network prefix.

The system manager of a stand-alone network may grant any computer in that network any address as desired. The computer addresses may be sequential, room number, user name, etc. This naming scheme is adequate for very small local-area networks, but arbitrary addressing becomes impractical as the network grows or connects to the Internet.

Network growth increases network complexity. Managing cable connections and addresses within a local area network of ten computers in a public computer lab is straightforward. But managing addresses across a huge corporate network is a full-time occupation. Internet connectivity requires strict adherence to a standardized address format. If standards were not enforced, then a data packet could (and would) get lost as it crossed networks.

Imagine the ensuing chaos if 10,000 computers across the globe had the same computer address "Fred." A message to "Fred" could go anywhere. Sequential addressing (Fred1, Fred2, etc.) would also induce chaos, because these addresses provide no location information. Fred314 might be a unique computer, but where is it?

An IP address identifies the network on which the computer resides and the address of the computer on that network. Most IP addresses have the form {A.B.C.D}, where each component is one byte. Recall that one byte normally consists of eight bits (i.e., an octet). *An IP address is a 32-bit numerical address composed of four bytes that uniquely identifies a computer on the Internet.* The value of one octet ranges from a minimum binary value of (00000000) to a maximum binary value of (11111111). These values correspond to a range 0–255 in decimal notation. An IP address written out consists of four consecutive numbers that are separated by periods. Conventional IP addresses thus range from (0.0.0.0) to (255.255.255.255). This format is called dotted decimal notation (DDN). It is more commonly used than its binary counterpart, since it is easier to read and speak.

The number of unique IP addresses determines the size of the Internet. Each Internet connection must have a unique IP address. If a device has multiple Internet connections (several network interface cards), then it needs multiple IP addresses. This feature is important when the same physical computer is a multifunctional server.

A telephone analogy is helpful in understanding the relationship between networked computers and multiple IP addresses. A home can have one phone with one line, one phone with multiple lines, multiple phones with one line, or multiple phones with multiple lines. A networked computer can have one Internet connection and a single IP address or it can have multiple Internet connections, each with a different IP address.

Since an IP address consists of four components, and each component has 256 possible values, the theoretical maximum number of possible IP addresses is:

$$256 \times 256 \times 256 \times 256 = 4{,}294{,}967{,}296 \text{ possible addresses}$$

The Internet may be very big, but it is nonetheless a limited network. This limitation was not foreseen as a problem during its embryonic times. Why did the original

Internet engineers use a 32-bit address? No one predicted the proliferation of online cell phones, pagers, faxes, routers, gateways, and personal computers exhausting Internet address space.

In the absence of new procedures or new design protocols, the Internet will eventually run out of addresses. What happens when the addresses run out? There is no more room at the inn. Internet real estate will become a scarce commodity.

## ADDRESSING SCHEMES

### The Class Addressing Scheme

The potential IP address space is currently divided into five classes that are determined by organizational size. (See tables 13-1 and 13-2.) The five classes are as follows:

**Table 13-1**
Internet Protocol Class Addresses

| Class | Size | Maximum Number of Networks | Maximum Hosts per Network |
|-------|--------|-----------------------------|----------------------------|
| A | large | 126 | 16,772,214 |
| B | medium | 16,384 | 65,534 |
| C | small | 2,097,152 | 254 |
| D | | reserved (applications) | |
| E | | reserved (future development) | |

An IP address consists of a network component and a host computer component. The class structure identifies the network and host component. For example, the value {131.218.23.100} is a valid IP address in a class B network (see table 13-2). In this case, 23 is the host segment number.

**Table 13-2**
IP Addresses by Class

| Class | IP Address Range (a.b.c.d) | Network Address | Host Address |
|-------|-----------------------------|------------------|---------------|
| A | 1–126.b.c.d | 1–126 | b.c.d |
| B | 128–191.b.c.d | 128–191.b | c.d |
| C | 192–223.b.c.d | 192–223.b.c | d |
| D | 224–239.b.c.d | | |
| E | 240–255.b.c.d | | |

*Application:* Suppose all computers in your network reside on segment 23. The only valid IP addresses are 130.219.23.000 to 130.219.23.255. The network administrator cannot install more than 256 networked computers on that segment.

In assigning IP addresses, the entire address and each of its two components—network address and host address—fall into specific numerical ranges. Some values are intentionally excluded from the address pool because they have special purposes. For example, the IP address 127.0.0.0 is used for local loopback testing.

### *Static versus Dynamic Addressing*

Humans typically think in terms of absolute or relative addresses. An *absolute address* is fixed in space and relevant no matter where you are (my school is located at 4 Huntington Street, New Brunswick, New Jersey). A *relative address* is shorter and located more efficiently, but only if you know your location relative to your destination (the school is the second building on the right).

An IP address may be static or dynamic. The former is set manually by the system administrator and remains constant. The latter is assigned automatically from a central server and changes from session to session. Servers typically have static IP addresses, since they are permanent fixtures on the network.

Static addressing involves a fixed IP address. This mode is practical in small networks with few computers or in large networks that rarely change. It is impractical for large networks where many computers enter/leave the system or where computers move from one network component to another.

Dynamic addressing uses a standard TCP/IP network protocol called Dynamic Host Control Protocol (DHCP). A DHCP server automatically manages IP address allocation from a pool of available IP addresses. It also releases unused IP addresses from offline computers and recycles them back into the pool.

IP addresses are "leased" from the DHCP server, and such leases expire. If an IP address lease expires, then the address is reused. DHCP reduces administrative overhead because addresses are assigned automatically and on demand. It enhances efficiency because addresses are not wasted.

Private addressing involves the assignment of specific addresses for specific machines on an ad hoc basis. These addresses are private to the organization. Private addresses can expand connectivity within a private network, but the private network may not connect to the Internet. Internet service providers do not recognize private addresses.

### *Getting to Know You*

Network administrators use a variety of hardware and software tools that monitor, gauge, and set the network environment. The casual user is generally oblivious to configuration settings and should rightfully remain so. (How many of us could or should adjust the valves in the engine of our car?)

Many common command-line utilities such as *ping, netstat, hostname, arp,* and *ipconfig* display status information to the network administrator and interested user. The invocation of these commands differs from vendor to vendor. Some commands have vendor-specific enhancements.

*Ping* is an acronym for *p*acket *I*nternet *g*roper. Given an IP address, *ping* sends out signal packets to a remote machine and displays information about their return. (This process is akin to a submarine sending out a short sonic pulse, which is also called a "ping.") If packets are returned successfully, then the device is on the network. If not, then either the device has dropped off the network or the name/address is incorrect. One format for the *ping* command is "*ping* machine name"; for example, *ping* scils.rutgers.edu.

The *ipconfig* command displays IP address, subnet mask, gateway address, and information on DHCP capabilities. *Netstat* displays the overall network status. *Hostname* shows the name of the machine in question. *Traceroute* reveals networking hops. *Arp* resolves addresses. Some commands require special privileges or permission settings.

## Problems with the Class Addressing Scheme

The class IP addressing system effectively distinguishes between networks and hosts. This scheme served well in the early Internet but has become increasingly problematic for several reasons. The pool of IP addresses is intrinsically limited; all addresses will eventually be assigned; address utilization across classes is not uniform; Class B addresses are nearly depleted; and address assignment is often wasteful.

How does one waste an IP address? Suppose a corporation maintains an entire Class B network. It is entitled to 65,534 hosts within its network and the same number of IP addresses. If the organization only needs 30,000 addresses, then the remaining numbers are in essence wasted. Recycle unused Internet addresses!

A corporate network may be cleaved into a larger number of lower Class C networks, say 20 networks with a maximum of 254 computers each. This change enhances efficiency in one regard (less waste) but reduces efficiency in another (more network routing paths).

## The Classless Addressing Scheme

Because the Internet will eventually run out of unassigned IP addresses, a classless addressing scheme known as Classless Inter-Domain Routing (CIDR) is gradually replacing the class addressing system. CIDR overcomes the problems associated with the class-full scheme by substituting a special binary representation for the previous decimal notation.

CIDR uses binary bit masks as a means of distinguishing network hosts from local hosts. A bit mask specifies the number of continuous bit values of 1. The remaining bit values are all 0's. The notation /N at the end of the CIDR address gives the length in bits of the network address. For example, if a CIDR address = 163.217.132.5/12:

> the network address is 12 bits long
>
> the host ID is 32 − 12 = 20 bits long

CIDR notation supports the efficient allocation of IP addresses. IP addresses are based on actual need, as opposed to a fixed allocation. An administrator may create a network of any arbitrary size and not necessarily a predetermined size.

There are several significant disadvantages to this addressing scheme, however. Networking routing devices must be "smart" enough to understand the new notation. Retrofitting old routers may be an expensive process. The network administrator must be fluent in both binary and decimal.

### Subnets and Supernets

Network managers often decompose existing networks into smaller subnetworks. The actual structure of the subnet can be as simple or complex as desired. It is invisible to the Internet and only visible to the local organization.

Subnet masks control the information content of the IP address. Routers can physically segment networks into subnets. Such segments reduce digital packet travel and noise across a large network. The processes of subnetting and its cousin, supernetting, involve relatively complex binary manipulation and bookkeeping.

## THE INTERNET METAPHOR PROJECT

In order to make sense of the World Wide Web, people describe the unfamiliar in terms of the familiar. They use metaphors. The preliminary results of the Internet Metaphor Project are presented here (Ratzan, "Making Sense," 2000).

### Introduction to the Problem

The vast extent of the Web makes direct user studies problematic. Representative statistical sampling tacitly assumes a homogeneous mix of users, but this is not a valid assumption in the online environment. This research study addresses two associated problems. How do people perceive the Internet and the Web? How can the Internet become an effective and efficient platform for communication about itself?

Metaphors have power, they have structure, and they are ubiquitous. The impact of computer-based metaphors is already extensive. One need only consider the paradigm of the desktop computer or such names as Netscape Navigator or Internet Explorer to view examples of metaphor penetration. Since web development is expanding, the acquisition of knowledge about the perceptions of its users by analyzing their Internet metaphors is a significant area of applied Internet research.

### Metaphors

Metaphors can be placed into several theoretical categories. (See table 13-3.) It is important to recognize that any theoretical foundation of Internet metaphors must be grounded in users' responses to the Internet in their own words. The theory of statistical self-selected sampling is appropriate for a preliminary study of Internet metaphors. It is not clear how traditional representative sampling can be accomplished in the Internet context, since there is much user variation even within the same Internet domain. A self-selected sample overcomes this difficulty because it functions as a focus group.

**Table 13-3**
Metaphor Types

| Metaphor Type | Textual Example |
|---|---|
| Spatial | I fell into a depression |
| Ontological | A mind is a terrible thing to waste |
| Personification | Life is cheating me |
| Metonymy | She is into dance |
| Synecdoche | Cars are choking our roads |
| Literal | The turnpike is very heavy this morning |
| Homonymic | I am in love |
| Poetic embellishment | "She was my English rose" (Prince Charles) |

## Related Studies

There have been only a few analytic studies of Internet metaphors in general or web metaphors in particular. Other studies have often focused on word play or general usage in regard to the Web. These initial studies suggested the existence of general topical categories from which more refined studies might be derived. Word-play studies in particular demonstrated the ubiquitous use of Internet metaphors by the online community. This in turn has applications for computer jargon as a separate and distinct linguistic form. These and other related studies showed fairly conclusively that the Internet has become a platform for the generation of information about itself.

Word-play studies, though entertaining, are intrinsically language-specific and thus have a questionable generalization value. The methodologies of prior studies were often hampered by the number of accessible participants, the associated cost of reaching them, and the difficulty of creating awareness of the study on a global Internet scale. (It is neither effective nor efficient to use a paper-based data collection technique to study users scattered across the globe.)

In addition, many data collection techniques are structured more toward the convenience of the researcher than that of the user. This is a subtle but important distinction. The single greatest weakness of most prior studies was that they did not reveal why users described the Internet as they did. In the absence of this data, prior analyses have been potentially incomplete and potentially biased by the researchers' perspective.

## Research Questions

A case can be made that a research study on Internet and web metaphors is ultimately based on two primary, associated research questions. How do users describe the online environment? Why do they describe it this way?

Many specific research questions can be posed in this regard. The unit of analysis is the individual user; the unit of data is the metaphor utilized by the user; and metaphor word-stubs identify themes. Some specific research questions addressed in the project study are listed below.

> What are the primary Internet metaphor themes expressed in users' own words?
>
> Do novices and experts differ in their descriptions of the Internet?
>
> Can a self-selecting online sampling methodology effectively study users' perceptions of the Internet?
>
> Can Bayesian conditional probabilities serve as predictors of user characteristics?

### Sampling

This study used a self-selecting sampling technique rather than a representational sampling approach. The former has the advantage that motivated users provide a response to the study. The disadvantage is that extrapolation from these results must be done with care. Traditional sampling assumes that a representation of the entire sample can be derived from a homogeneous subsample. It is highly problematic to form such a sample on an Internet scale, however.

A preliminary sample of several hundred users was collected in the first few weeks of data collection. This is small in comparison to the universe of all Internet users. It is nevertheless four times greater than any prior Internet metaphor study and the first to collect text-based data of users' perceptions and explanations in their own words.

Because it was important to collect metaphor data in the users' own words, a questionnaire format was utilized. An automated online questionnaire in the form of a web page was developed to collect demographic, categorical, and textual data.

### Results of the Study

Males tended to consider themselves as higher skilled users, while females tended to perceive themselves as lesser-skilled users. The study's data could also be broken down by the frequency of use of metaphor word-stubs. The theme of "information" dominates user perceptions of the Internet and the Web. The Internet is secondarily described as a library. The mass media phrase "information superhighway" has not penetrated deeply into users' cognitive images of the Internet.

In this data sample with normalized percentages, females were more likely to use a "highway" metaphor than were males. This held true over all age categories. Females were also more likely to use a "frontier" metaphor for the Internet than were males. This also held true over all age categories.

The metaphors of novices often bore a sense of confusion, complexity, or frustration, while expert users were much more anchored in reality. One may speculate that the former expressed novices' reactions to the unfamiliarity of the web experience. This explanation is appealing but is not consistent with the fact that intangible metaphysical metaphors were used solely by experts and never by novices. This might be indicative of a cognitive paradigm change regarding the amorphous nature of the Web. (See table 13-4.)

### Discussion

The preliminary results of this

**Table 13-4**
Internet Description by Level of Perceived Expertise

| Novices | Expert Users |
| --- | --- |
| bottomless pit | chameleon |
| maze | community |
| snaggled skein of yarn | idea processor |
| big bookstore | bookstore with a switchboard |
| locked library | void of omnipotence |

study provide empirical support to the idea that users use metaphors to describe their perceptions of the Internet and the Web. These metaphors appear to comprise a few dominant themes and may, perhaps, be verbal markers. (A verbal marker reveals in language an objective insight into what is going on in our heads.) Men and women appear to project different self-perceptions of themselves as Internet users. The results of the study are important because they suggest the existence of different cognitive images. If the way the Web is described affects perception and use, then Internet metaphors may reveal a new focus.

Our knowledge of these images may enhance future web development. For example, some researchers have suggested that men and women navigate differently when in unknown territories. Men tend to prefer absolute addressing (4 Huntington Street), while women tend to prefer relative addressing (first building on the left). The way people navigate in a foreign environment may affect online information retrieval and future web search-engine design.

Bayesian probability measures the likelihood that one event occurs given another. A preliminary Bayesian analysis suggests that it may be possible to predict the attributes of users based on their own descriptive language. This may be a significant marker, though its predictive power is currently low.

Novices tended to use finite, tangible, delimited, closed, delineated metaphors, while experts tended to use more metaphysical, intangible, open metaphors. ("Closed" is used in the sense of having a sharp boundary. A maze has a boundary of walls. Where is the boundary of a community?) This may indicate novices' discomfort at conceptualizing something amorphously vast, and the significant ability of some experts to do so. This difference in conceptual imagery may have ramifications for the development of future web services.

"Information" was the dominant theme associated with Internet and web metaphors, based on analyses of word-stub frequency. The Internet was described more often as an "information source" than as an "information conduit" or "information superhighway." The second and third most common themes were those of "library" and "network."

The Web was often described as a dysfunctional library. Users described it as a library with books scattered all over the floor or a library with its lights turned off. This suggests an image of chaotic information access.

Some user metaphors defied simple explanation. The "Internet as spaghetti" may suggest an image of entanglement, but it is unclear how to interpret the "Internet as bowl of Jello." Sweet rewards? Transparent and hence holds no secrets? Or simply amorphous, shapeless? Unfortunately, no explanations were forthcoming.

More females used "frontier" metaphors than did males, and this occurred irrespective of age distinctions. A frontier is often thought of as a pristine place (female?) as opposed to a jungle that must be conquered (male). More females thought of the Internet in terms of a highway than did males, and this was true over all ages. The use of the highway metaphor tended to decrease as experience increased.

Novice users tended to describe the Web more in terms of a place, something that is fixed in space and time. A library is a building fixed in space and associated with information. Thus it was not surprising to encounter library themes. It was surprising to see the frequency of this description decreasing consistently with higher skill levels. This may suggest that less-skilled web users need a rigid cognitive anchor to conceptualize the Web, while expert users can free themselves of this mental support and float more freely.

Metaphors appear to be a necessary component in the conceptualization of the Internet and the Web. The concepts so used manifest themselves as common themes that might be psychological markers. The metaphor images used seem to change as skill level develops.

## IS INTERNET ACCESS A PRIVILEGE OR A RIGHT?

The Internet is a computer network, but it is also a metaphorical platform for the communication of information. Is the Internet a privilege or a right?

### *The Nature of Privilege and Right*

The word "privilege" derives from the Latin terms *privus* ("separate") and *lex* (legis; "law"), forming the word-concept *privilegium*. A privilege is commonly interpreted as a benefit granted to a person, group, or organization and not to others. Membership in Congress or acceptance to a Ph.D. program are privileges because the benefits gained are only available to a chosen or qualified few. A privilege can be granted or not granted, and it can be revoked. The possession of privileges normally derives from wealth, power, ability, merit, influence, or politics.

A right is a claim to something that belongs to people by tradition or law. Governments grant rights to their citizens. Indeed, many governments expend great effort articulating the mandated rights of their citizens. Consider, for example, the Bill of Rights (United States, 1791), the Declaration of the Rights of Man and the Citizen (France, 1789), and the Universal Declaration of Human Rights (United Nations, 1948). In most countries, mandated political and civil rights cannot be removed except under extreme circumstances.

Many libraries post a Library User Bill of Rights. (The American Library Association's Library Bill of Rights was originally adopted in 1948.) Such statements set guidelines for levels of service and other duties of the library organization.

### Common Privileges and Rights

Rights and privileges vary with the culture, society, and time. A right in one social context may be a privilege in another or vice versa. A *perceived* right may or may not be a right. It might actually be a privilege. Some common examples of "rights" include the right to drive, the right to health care, the right to long-distance telephone service, nonsmokers' rights, smokers' rights, patients' rights, civil rights, human rights, the right to vote, the right to drive a gas-guzzling SUV, etc. The reader can decide which of the "rights" in this list are legitimate. *A right involves entitlement.*

Privileges can be issued, regulated, licensed, or revoked. Denying a right usually requires a concerted political effort, but denying a privilege is done by the agency that conferred it. The right to drive is really a privilege that is conferred by means of a driver's license. The word "license" derives from the Latin *licere* or *licens* (*licentis;* "to be permitted"). Typical licenses include the driver's license, marriage license, pilot license, and perhaps even a license to kill (James Bond). Privileges can assume the form of legal obligations (privileged debts, privileged witnesses, writs of privilege) or special communications (attorney-client privilege, priest-confessor privilege). President Richard Nixon invoked the principle of executive privilege as a means of preventing the release of confidential White House tape recordings during the Watergate scandal. *A privilege involves special consideration.*

### Technology Privileges and Rights

Prior to the breakup of AT&T in the 1970s, the existence in the United States of a nationwide telephone monopoly granted consumers certain protective rights. One aspect of the "universal service" doctrine assured that telephone service could not be denied by virtue of location. Telephone service became a de facto right in the United States.

In contrast, cable television service is a privilege. Cable service is not granted to all, nor is it available to all, nor is it uniform to all that receive it. The cable television provider is granted a renewable and revocable license. Cable subscribers see their channels and costs change with vendors.

Surprisingly, broadcast television service is also a privilege, even though broadcasting companies in the United States are considered public trustees and operate within the public interest. No one is entitled to or guaranteed good television reception. The television privilege model comes with a cost. The cable TV model involves payment for tiers of service. The public TV model solicits donations and governmental support. The commercial TV model relies on advertising and sponsors. The British television model involves an annual access fee.

### The Special Case of the Internet

Is access to the Internet a privilege or a right? If it is a privilege, then some have it and some do not. The privilege of Internet access in turn produces a social inequity; those with access to the Internet can exploit its resources, while those who do not have access cannot. This schism has been collectively called the "digital divide."

Internet access comes with a cost. If the Internet is a privilege, then should the privileged pay for its maintenance? Should this payment support personal usage or infrastructure overhead? If the Internet is a right, then who should fund it? The government or only wired citizens? All citizens? Software developers? Computer vendors? Telecom companies? Should the United Nations collect Internet fees from its member nations?

The issue of whether the Internet is a privilege or a right may not be a well-posed question. The Internet is a network of computer networks operating under the TCP/IP protocol. The Internet is a thing (actually many things) but not an organization. Perhaps it makes no sense to speak of the Internet as a privilege or right any more than Manhattan is a privilege or a right.

The appropriate question may be if Internet *access* is a privilege or a right. Access can be granted, bestowed, denied, restricted, and controlled. Internet access would then become a privilege. A high-bandwidth wireless connection is better than a similar wired connection, which is better than a dial-up connection, which is better than no connection to the Internet at all.

If the Internet were solely and exclusively a commercial network, then few would argue for Internet rights. The Internet provides communication and information services. Is information a right? No (regrettably). Is information access a right? Perhaps.

I can view my medical records, but you cannot see them without my explicit permission. This gives me a right and you a privilege. Insurance company clerks routinely read patient records and doctors discuss medical records. The distinction between information rights, information privileges, and information access becomes unclear.

There is an older but venerable model of information service that provides insight into this problem. The public library provides a range of information services to the general population. *Is the public library a privilege or a right?*

### The Public Library as an Information Access Model

If a public library is a privilege, then some towns will have good libraries, some will have mediocre libraries, and some will have no libraries at all. Libraries are intertwined with the community education process. The right to an education is conspicuously absent from the U.S. Constitution's mandates of political rights and civil liberties. Nevertheless, in most states children have a derived right to public education up to a certain age. How does this position libraries as an educational and information privilege or right?

O'Connor (1990) provides an excellent characterization of the issues regarding library privilege versus library right. The status of libraries has legal, social, and economic ramifications whose resolution determines the means and methods of supporting the public good. Suppose libraries are a citizen's right. Then citizens may insist (demand!) minimum levels of service. This kind of outcry is in the spirit of Joeckel (1935, 1948). If the library and school are considered educational institutions, then library rights parallel educational mandates.

The state of New Jersey, for example, considers public libraries as educational institutions, but libraries are often considered a privilege. A case can be made that in this state libraries are a de facto right based on the historical precedent of the New Jersey Entitlement Act of 1879 and its updates. The act created a library fund with the mandate that "every library . . . established under this act shall be forever free to the use of the inhabitants of the city . . ." O'Connor (1990, 48) claims that this "implies a right of access to library collections and services."

By contrast, the case for public libraries in New Jersey being a privilege rather than a right uses an educational system argument. Small and poorly funded communities provide schooling via local schools or contracted services. They do not necessarily provide library access or services. Therefore libraries are a privilege, since some populations receive services and others do not.

O'Connor counters the logic of the preceding argument on two grounds. First, the argument is built upon the behavior of a few communities that have no library. This is an ex post facto argument. Second, "on the basis . . . of many of the laws governing New Jersey's libraries . . . the public library is [not] an optional privilege of the community; instead, like the schools, it is a community obligation" (O'Connor 1990, 51). If it is an obligation, there is a need that must be fulfilled.

### Resolution

If the mandate of the public library involves informing citizens, promoting the democratic process, providing literacy, and training citizens to interact in government and commerce, then there is a strong case for the public library being a citizen right. The reality, however, is that public libraries are often *optional* community obligations and hence a privilege, not a right.

In an ideal wired world, Internet access would offer immediate information and communication services to all. Internet access should be a right, not a privilege, but the world is not yet ideal. Internet access requires a complex and reliable infrastructure that is not yet available in most of the world. (Some estimates suggest that 80 percent of the world's population does not yet have access to reliable telephone service.) If we assume there are five billion people on the planet and 500 million Internet users, then only 10 percent of the world's population has access to the Internet. Ninety percent does not. Internet access is currently a privilege, not a right.

## OTHER INTERNET ISSUES

The Internet is simultaneously a forum and a medium. If the reader will forgive a play on words, the Internet is a very large medium. The nature of the Internet poses some intriguing questions.

*In what respect did the Internet evolve rather than grow in a planned manner?*

The original conception of the Internet as *inter*connected *net*works bore a framework with regard to addressing, protocols, authentication, formats, and layers. Much of this structure remains. On the other hand, the original engineers did not conceive of applications such as mass music downloads or the World Wide Web. As a result, the Internet now has many social issues warranting discussion.

### Who pays for e-mail?

Conventional message transmission has a cost associated with size (or weight), distance, and duration. A package costs more to mail than a letter. A phone call to France costs more than a call across the street. A long phone call to Japan costs more than a short call.

Try the following experiment: Simulate the Internet by issuing each student some form of address. Randomly distribute sheets of paper to the students, with each sheet containing the address of where it will be sent. Simulate networking by asking the students to pass the papers to the designated address such that papers may only be passed to other students whom they can physically reach (connect). Simulate bandwidth by placing a limit on how many papers may pass through a given person (server) at a time. Simulate network traffic by forced pausing when papers collide at some student at the same time. Simulate disruptions by having dead spots (bounceback) where anything arriving must be rerouted. At a common signal, let the papers (e-mail) move and watch the traffic flow. After a predetermined time stop the exercise.

If your e-mail message was sent from a New Jersey server, passed through multiple nodes, and was received by someone at an Alaska server, then who paid for it? In a sense, everyone paid for it and no one paid for it. Those who paid for it did so only within the confines of their own network environment.

### What is an appropriate economic model for the Internet?

| | |
|---|---|
| The commercial television model | Funded by commercial sponsors<br>Policy decisions based on popularity or sales |
| The British television model | Funded by sponsors, government, and an annual license fee<br>Many of the same aspects as commercial TV model |
| The public television model | Funded by tax dollars and donations<br>Selective development |
| The cable television model | Funded by monthly usage fees<br>Not all services (channels) available in all areas<br>Different levels of service, depending on fees |
| The telephone model | Pay per use, cost depends on duration and use<br>Special plans for subscribers |
| The ISP model | Monthly fee, varies with provider<br>Competition for limited ports (busy signals) |

The public library model

> Most services are free
> Public location but no after-hours access
> Possible filtering by community standards

The government model

> Funded by tax revenue
> Subsidized but also legislated

What about the newspaper model? The motion picture model? The radio model?

### Who should run the Internet?

Should the Internet be run by a collection of local agencies, a national agency, an international agency, a commission, or a commercial corporation? Or no one at all? Internet management could be a mighty edifice spanning the globe or an assortment of little feudal kingdoms. It could be run as a form of organized anarchy or by an evolving set of protocols. People, corporations, and other organizations run their individual networks, but no one runs the Internet, a network of networks.

### Should the Internet be public, private, or democratic?

*The case for being public:* Based on governmental mandate, and designed for the common public good, hence politically driven; major changes performed through legislation; subsidized fees; protective laws enforced by the judiciary; governmental standards.

*The case for being private:* Someone is in charge; only a few major technologies dominate; it is more in the interest of the private companies to cooperate on standards than to compete with each other; greater interoperability and uniformity; smoother transfer of data between platforms; able to assume large investment risks; market driven; intellectual property rights sustained.

*The case for being democratic:* No monopolies; the Internet becomes a worldwide forum; opposing interests balance by policing each other; elected regulators adjudicate disputes; no official gatekeeping; anyone can make an impact; minimal governmental interference.

*The case for a tiered approach:* Each layer is independent of all other layers; users utilize each layer as they wish subject to the restrictions of each; no special hierarchies; services vary.

## EXERCISES AND RESEARCH QUESTIONS

### Exercises: IP Addressing

E13.1   Is DHCP running on your network?

E13.2   Does the *ping* command change a network value?

E13.3   What might happen if a server had a dynamic IP address?

E13.4   Determine the name or IP address of a local server. What is its class?

E13.5    Which of the following values are legitimate IP addresses?
(130.219.23.100) (300.300.300.300) (130.220.6.275)

## Exercises: Internet Issues

*Research Question 13.6*

Should the United Nations run the Internet for the benefit of the global environment? The UN is a political entity and not an engineering agency. To what extent should or could the UN set and enforce standards?

*Research Question 13.7*

What are the current statistics on global Internet access?

*Research Question 13.8*

Should a government impose an "Internet tax" on its citizens whose revenues would subsidize Internet access costs? Should these subsidies go directly to individuals or to public agencies such as schools and libraries?

*Research Question 13.9*

It can be argued that the cause of rapid global Internet growth was the *absence* of special privileges. Anyone could send e-mail or develop applications. Should *anyone* have a say in how the Internet is run?

*Research Question 13.10*

The Internet did not grow according to a structured long-range plan. It evolved. Examine the evolution of the Internet in terms of privilege and right.

CHAPTER **14**  ▶ Music as an Information System

Music contains *tonal* data organized in a particular way that has meaning *to the composer* and *listener.* In the spirit of previous chapters, this discussion of music information systems progresses from the description of music (sound) to the representation of music (tonal tuning), the organization and construction of music (melody machines), and the nature of music information retrieval.


## THE NATURE OF MUSIC AND SOUND

The physics of a single sonic note are extraordinarily complex. The speed of sound varies with the medium, and the nature of sound varies with the method of its production. J. S. Bach's *Third Brandenburg Concerto* and a traditional cowboy song are entirely different musical forms, yet both are music.

Music originates from sound. Sound originates from a sonic energy wave vibrating through a medium. There is no sound in outer space for lack of a vibrating medium. (The universe is a very violent place. Would the impact of colliding galaxies and the thunder of supernova explosions overwhelm us if we could hear them?)

Hearing is a primary sense that is fundamental to hominid survival. It tends to be the last sense to dissolve upon sleep and is often the first to reappear while awaking. Surgeons tell tales of anesthetized patients recalling what they overheard in the operating room!

The human ear can distinguish approximately 1,400 different frequencies. Human hearing ranges from a low 12 cycles/second to a moderately high 15,000 cycles/second (Olson 1967). (See table 14-1.) Elephants chant at frequencies below our level of perception, while bats sing above it. Acoustic analysis of more than 100,000 human speech samples has revealed ten frequency peaks that match significant intervals of the musical scale. The roots of music may thus lie in the human voice itself (Farley 2003). There is indeed music all around us.

**Table 14-1**
Typical Tunings

| Tone | Cycles per Second | Ratios |
|------|-------------------|--------|
| A above middle C | 440 | |
| Major third at C-sharp | 550 | (5:4 ratio to A) |
| Perfect fifth at E above C | 660 | (3:2 ratio to A) |
| Two octaves above A | 1,760 | (4:1 ratio to A) |

A sine wave models a sound wave. *Wavelength* measures the distance between one wave crest and another. *Amplitude* measures wave height. *Frequency* measures the number of wave cycles per second.

The sine function is well understood. It is usually first encountered in high school (as trigonometry), then in college (as special functions), and perhaps in graduate school (as solutions to differential equations). In fact, these definitions are equivalent. The sine has a counterpart function (cosine) with similar properties but ninety degrees out of phase.

We experience waves in radio, television, pagers, cell phones, sonar, radar, microwaves, light, color, music, sound, and perhaps even gravity. FM radio uses frequency-modulated waves. AM radio uses amplitude-modulated waves. Amplitude and frequency are different physical attributes, and hence AM and FM radio have different characteristics.

Conventional musical instruments produce different frequencies of sound imposed on each other. The value of a wave at a point in time depends on the mechanics of the instrument, acoustics, and the performer. If a musician plays *portamento,* then a tone glides continuously between frequencies; if *tremolo,* then the tone's intensity pulsates.

The *fundamental frequency* is the most prominent sound in a tone. *Harmonics* are integral multiples of the fundamental frequency (F, 2F, 3F, . . . where F is the fundamental frequency). Harmonics determine the quality of the instrumental sound. Electronically generated music sounds strange and unnatural because it has few harmonics.

*Pitch* may be loosely defined as the frequency of sound corresponding to an entry of a musical scale. A *note* involves pitch and duration. The relative strengths of the harmonics determine the *timbre* of the sound. A trumpet and a violin do not sound the same when playing the same note because each has a different timbre.

Joseph Fourier (1768–1830) initially developed the theory of harmonic analysis as applied to the transmission of heat, not the propagation of sound. The resulting mathematical expressions (Fourier series) describe the decomposition of a periodic function into the sum of individual wave components. Harmonic analysis is used extensively in the signal processing of music, nuclear fusion, the prediction of earthquakes, and the detection of submarines. (Submarines leave a characteristic signature waveform in their wake.)

An *interval* is the ratio of two pitches. An *octave* is the interval corresponding to the 2:1 ratio interval. Two notes played an octave apart sound the same yet different. The sounds blend and enhance each other.

An interval is simple (less than one octave) or compound (an octave plus a simple interval). A *scale* is a series of sounds from low frequency to high frequency within an interval. A classical octave contains eight steps (some forms of music do not use the eight-step octave but retain the 2:1 ratio nonetheless).

*Consonance* involves harmonious sounds whose frequencies blend. *Dissonance* involves sounds that do not blend. *Unison* is perfect consonance involving the play of two identical notes. Arguably the most important forms of consonance occur at the fifth and the octave. The *extent* of consonance depends primarily on lower harmonics, because harmonic strength decreases as the multiple of the fundamental frequency increases. Consonant harmonies dominated earlier musical forms. Much twentieth-century music involves dissonant tonalities.

## TUNING INFORMATION SYSTEMS

There must be a consistent association between notes written and heard. Music as conceived by the composer should match that of the performer and be consistent from performance to performance. Tuning a musical instrument to the tones within an octave is problematic because scaled notes do not always fit well. *Tuning systems provide tonal information, building the foundation of all composed music.*

### Pythagorean Tuning

The Pythagorean system is based on the *dominance of the musical fifth*. According to one version of the legend, Pythagoras (the man or the Pythagorean academy) received divine inspiration on the relationship between music and mathematics after hearing the sounds of striking hammers and plucked strings. (The Chinese version of this story relates to the phoenix bird assisting in the discovery.)

There is a simple numerical relationship between this type of harmonious sound and whole number ratios. The basic Pythagorean scale contains the following relationship between notes and numbers: the octave bears a 2:1 ratio to the fundamental tone, while the fifth bears a 3:2 relationship and the fourth bears a 4:3 relationship. (See table 14-2.)

The Greeks celebrated the discovery that their music was built upon numbers and simple ratios. The fifth and octave relationships were so highly prized that they served as the basis for the entire tuning system.

The musical fifth (3:2 ratio) dominates the tuning process in the Pythagorean system. Here is an example: extrapolate forward five full steps, making notes appropriate powers of 3/2 (the "circle of fifths"). If the original octave is exceeded, then transpose up and down the octave by multiplying or dividing by two as appropriate. The difference between the fourth and the fifth is considered a "whole" tone and is given the 9:8 ratio (9/8 = 3/2 × 3/2 × 1/2). Fill in any resulting gaps with consistent ratios. (Pythagorean tuning is complicated!)

**Table 14-2**
Pythagorean Tuning Scale

| Tone in scale | 1 | 2 | 3 | 4 | 5 | 6 | 7 | 8 |
|---|---|---|---|---|---|---|---|---|
| Tonal ratio | 1 | 9:8 | 81:64 | 4:3 | 3:2 | 27:16 | 243:128 | 2:1 |

(Fekete and Denyer [1984, 28] express this table in terms of the lengths of violin strings.)

Tonal fifths always remain in tune in the Pythagorean music information system. The method was in common use until the end of the sixteenth century. Its longevity may be due to constrained musical formats, numerological elegance, or organized religion. The fourteenth-century French academy at Notre Dame in Paris decreed that all scales should be based on 3/2 in deference to the Trinity.

Pythagorean tuning has two major flaws, one of which was known at the time. An octave has a ratio 2:1 and the fifth has a 3:2 ratio, but no power of 3/2 is ever exactly a power of 2. The circle of fifths never closes properly and never exactly repeats. (Equivalently, the logarithm of three divided by the logarithm of two is irrational.) This problem caused much consternation to a Greek society seeking rational explanations of the universe.

Musical fifths remain in tune, but other tones become progressively worse. Music composed in Pythagorean tuning avoids undesirable tones. The error is called the Pythagorean comma (Greek, "cut" or "crack").

The second flaw relates to the use of musical key signatures. A change in musical key requires a change in musical tuning because the ratios no longer apply properly. The same musical information system that assures precisely correct consonant fifths creates progressive creeping errors. Music must either remain in a single key or musicians must retune from one key to another. An impatient audience would find the latter eminently impractical.

A Pythagorean scale may contain more than eight tones, but the relationships of tones are no longer obvious. Elegance is lost. The tonal ratio of C-sharp (2,187:2,048) seems unnatural and disturbs the simplicity of the 3/2 ratio.

### Just Tuning

The Just musical system is based on *whole number ratio intervals*. The Pythagorean approach is a special case of the Just intonation scale motivated by preserving the power of the fifth. One variation of the scale (see table 14-3) is credited to the father of Galileo Galilei.

Note that tones 1, 3, 5 and tones 4, 6, 8 have the ratio 4:5:6 to each other. This intonation scale supports traditional 4:5:6 "barbershop quartet" harmonies better than the Pythagorean scale. (The ancient Greeks may not have appreciated this musical attribute.)

**Table 14-3**
Galilei (Just) Tuning Scale

| Tone in scale | 1 | 2 | 3 | 4 | 5 | 6 | 7 | 8 |
|---|---|---|---|---|---|---|---|---|
| Tonal ratio | 1 | 9/8 | 5/4 | 4/3 | 3/2 | 5/3 | 15/8 | 2 |
| Whole number scale | 24 | 27 | 30 | 32 | 36 | 40 | 45 | 48 |
| | | | | | Fifth | | | Octave |

(Tomes 2002)

The Pythagorean system contains intervals strictly based on the prime numbers two and three. (Numerologists find rich fodder here.) The Just intonation scale permits freedom of design; intervals are not restricted to exponential powers of 3/2. Some microtonal scales base their intervals on the prime numbers 13 and 19. Pentatonic (five-tone) scales appear in Andean, Chinese, Javanese, Balinese gamelan, and early American minstrel music. Heptatonic (seven-tone) scales appear in Gregorian chants.

Such freedom (or disarray) results in musical compositions sounding better or worse depending on the tuning! If composers changed ratios, then some instrument makers created new instruments for these new ratios. The Tanaka Enharmonium supported 312 steps to the octave (Hall and Josic 2000, citing Barbour 1953). Most such instruments are now musical artifacts.

Minor frequency changes are not significant, because the human ear adjusts for small consonant discrepancies. The whole number ratio 301/200 sounds consonant to 3/2. The human voice adapts easily to music of whole number ratios. Singing often uses a Just intoned scale.

Major frequency differences *are* significant, and changes of key remain a problem. Complex music progresses slowly.

### Meantone Systems

The meantone information system places *emphasis on musical thirds rather than fifths.* Composers could experiment with triads. New tunings provide new sounds. Interval values are formed by the average (mean) of the tones, hence the name. This convention sacrifices the "true" value of a tone for a "smoothing" of a tone. (Some might say smoothing is closer to smearing.) Arithmetic elegance shifts from powers of 3/2 to even intervals.

### Golden Meantone

Tuning systems address the problem of where to place the tones. The tuning process involves selecting fixed points in the scale and filling in the gaps with an appropriate ratio. Tonal placement affects compositional style.

The golden meantone system uses an interval ratio approaching the *special value from the Fibonacci sequence.* The ratio sequence is 3:2, 5:3, 8:5, converging ever closer to the value of the golden Fibonacci ratio (1.618033 . . . ). Does a ratio harmonious to the eye apply to a ratio harmonious to the ear? Perhaps so.

Golden meantone tuning lends itself to variously sized scales. The tuning system retains the elegance between music and mathematics, though based upon a different arithmetic principle.

### Equal-Tempered Tuning

The equal-tempered approach uses *a constant music interval.* Equal tempering spreads tonal error uniformly across the scale. It sounds natural and is the contemporary norm. We are used to it. In fact, *no tone is technically correct.*

The idea that every note was tonally incorrect shocked musicians of the past. Equal temperament was then known, but only as a theoretical and impure construct rarely used in compositional practice.

Equal tempering maintains the same frequency ratio of an interval across keys, so changing keys does not require retuning. Composers thus acquire a consistent range of standard tonal qualities on which to create their music. The Pythagorean and Just intoned systems have long since been abandoned.

## HOW MANY TONES BELONG IN A SCALE?

A one-note scale is not very interesting, notwithstanding songs such as "Johnny One Note" (Rogers and Hart) and "One Note Samba" (Jobim and Mendonca). The concept of musical fourths and fifths does not make sense for scales of two or three tones. In theory, any scale can have any number of tones. However . . .

Suppose a composer retains the musical fifth (3:2), musical fourth (4:3), and octave (2:1) ratios *as closely as possible* while still maintaining freedom of key modulation. What possibilities are available? The problem returns to the fundamental flaw, the Pythagorean comma. The solution involves rational approximations to irrational numbers.

Scales with 7, 12, or 19 tones produce acceptable tonal characteristics. A twelve-tone scale is really a consolidation of a seven-tone scale (whole tones) and a five-tone scale (semitones). The piano represents this as an octave with seven white keys and five black keys. The absence of piano keys between B and C and between E and F is a by-product of this approximation and avoidance of the comma.

If the scale has N tones and an octave has the 2:1 ratio, then each equal-tempered interval has length $2^{(1/N)}$. Table 14-4 provides a quick comparison between a seven- and a twelve-tone scale.

### Table 14-4
Comparison of Seven- and Twelve-Tone Equal-Tempered Scales

|  | Seven Tone | Twelve Tone |  |
|---|---|---|---|
| Interval size (exact) | $2^{(1/7)}$ | $2^{(1/12)}$ |  |
| Interval size (approx.) | 1.10408 | 1.05094 |  |
| Location of third | $2^{(3/7)}$ | $2^{(5/12)}$ |  |
| Value of third | 1.3458 | 1.3348 | (exact = ⅓ = 1.3333) |
| Location of fifth | $2^{(5/7)}$ | $2^{(7/12)}$ |  |
| Value of fifth | 1.6406 | 1.4982 | (exact = ½ = 1.5000) |

A twelve-tone equal-tempered scale is the scale with the *least number of tones that maintains a high level of approximation* to the musical fifths and fourths and also allows freedom of key modulation.

## MAKING CENTS OF IT ALL

Each step of a twelve-tone scale can be decomposed into 100 units called cents (Ellis, 1875). This system has been universally adopted in the theory of tuning systems. For a twelve-toned equal-tempered tuning system:

> one semitone = 100 cents
>
> 1,200 cents   = 12 semitones = 1 octave

Cents are more easily compared than frequencies or ratios. The following are several illustrative examples of cent manipulations courtesy of Tyler (2002):

*Example 14-1* (pitch comparisons)

> It is clear that 3/2 is a higher pitch than 4/3.
>
> Is 6,561/4,096 a higher pitch than 729/512?
>
> The former tone is G-sharp and is higher than the latter tone, F-sharp. Cents make the fractional relationship more apparent.

*Example 14-2* (complex manipulations)

> What is the size of the major second?
>
> "The size of the major second is formed by going up a major sixth (5/3), descending a fifth (3/2), working out the difference between that value and the equivalent major second formed by going up a fifth (3/2) and down a fourth (4/3)" (Tyler 2002).
>
> The solution (1/72) is obtained after much effort. The solution by cents is much easier:
>
> > 884 − 702 = 182
> >
> > 702 − 498 = 204
> >
> > 204 − 182 = 22 cents

Cents relate to intervals, and intervals relate to frequency ratio. (See table 14-5.) Since an octave corresponds to a 2:1 ratio, a cent can also be defined in terms of base-two logarithms (ugh):

> cents = 1,200 × [logarithm (ratio)]

The cent measure permits the quantification of many elusive measures. The infamous Pythagorean comma is expressible as an error of about 24 cents. It makes sense to speak

**Table 14-5**
Tones, Ratios, and Cents

| Tone | Name | Ratio | Cents (rounded) |
|------|------|-------|-----------------|
| C | unison | 1/1 | 0 |
| E-flat | minor third | 6/5 | 316 |
| E | major third | 5/4 | 386 |
| F | fourth | 4/3 | 498 |
| G | fifth | 3/2 | 702 |
| A | major sixth | 5/3 | 884 |
| C | octave | 2/1 | 1200 |

(Values and examples courtesy of Tyler 2002)

of the "distance" between the tones of a specific scale as being 204 cents wide. Cents make sense of tuning systems and hence the theory of musical composition.

## MELODY MACHINES

Music consists of more than structured sounds punctuated by silence. Musical composition involves control and organization and rules. If each individual sound is a wave and each wave has fundamental waveforms, then manipulating these waves composes music. A much more intriguing task is *composing music by manipulating representational rules*.

### Composing by Tone

How many musical compositions are there? The simplest music is the sound of silence. Mystical, perhaps even enlightening, but lacking in tonality. The next simplest composition is one long sustained note. This musical work has tonality, but it is dull. Slightly more colorful is music consisting of two long notes (or three long notes, etc.). Generalizing this enumeration for every combination of tone, duration, and format within human hearing generates an enormous number of musical possibilities.

Suppose an octave consists of eight whole tones. How many possible musical compositions eight tones long can be constructed with the same duration from eight tones played in any order? Each tone can be any one of eight choices. The number of arrangements yields:

$$8^8 = 16,777,216 \text{ musical compositions}$$

If such music is a song, then there are over sixteen million different songs possible.

Suppose the same tone cannot be used more than once. There are eight choices for the first tone, seven choices for the second tone, etc. The number of arrangements yields:

$$8 \times 7 \times 6 \times 5 \times 4 \times 3 \times 2 \times 1 = 40,320 \text{ musical compositions}$$

There are about 40,000 different possible songs consisting of eight tones with none repeated.

Music composed in this manner contains much repetition. The method includes do-do-do-do-do-do-do-do and re-re-re-re-re-re-re-re and other musical gems. None of these cases accounts for notes of different duration. If one considers quarter notes, half notes, whole notes, eighth notes, and sixteenth notes, then every tone above has one of five possible attributes. *The count explodes but melodies emerge.*

All of the previous counts relate to a single instrument. Compositions involving duets, trios, quartets, ensembles, and orchestra expand the repertoire. Note that genre, volume, and mood have not yet been incorporated into the model!

This successive enumeration produces every piece of music that *has* been composed. It also produces every piece of music that *will* ever be composed. It also produces an enormous amount of junk.

### Composing by Machine

A less chaotic solution to the question of automated musical composition uses randomized preexisting musical fragments. These fragments are constructed in such a way that they are always consistent with respect to beats and harmonics. The arrangements of these fragments can result in a musical composition.

This automated process has appeared in several forms. Kirnberger (1757) suggested the use of dice as a means of selecting randomized musical fragments in his book *The Ever-Ready Composer of Polonaises and Minuets* (Gardner 1988, 87). Some musicologists claim that Mozart invented a similar musical dice game called Musikalisches Wurfelspiel. It produced short six-bar waltzes and was published a year after his death.

The game is also known as the Mozart Melody Machine. Each composition consisted of 176 measures of random music selected from two specially constructed tables controlled by throws of the dice. A modern version of the game appeared in 1974 under the name of the Melody Dicer (Carousel Publishing Corporation in Brighton, Massachusetts; see Gardner 1988, 89). A later variation called the Scott Joplin Melody Dicer generated jazz compositions.

### A Musical Bias?

A toss of two standard dice does not produce equally likely values. Some values (like seven) appear more often than other values. The method of composition by dice toss skews the appearance of tonal elements and hence the frequency of musical fragments. Was Mozart aware of this bias?

### How Much Music?

How many waltzes can the Mozart Melody Machine produce? There are a total of eleven columns in the two tables, each of which generates sixteen measures of music. The total potential number of waltzes is:

$$11^{16} = 45,949,729,863,572,161 \text{ musical compositions}$$

(almost 46,000 trillion compositions)

This number is so great that *it is likely that every time the game is played it produces a waltz never before heard in the history of the world.*

## Variations

A simplified version of the game has two identical columns in the music matrix. The player chooses a column based solely on the value of the toss being odd or even. The total number of possible waltzes is:

> 2,518,999,334,332,964 musical compositions
>
> (more than 2,500 trillion compositions)

Calegari (1801) developed a compositional device avoiding the use of dice. Potential composers selected a bar from column A, another from column B, etc. The Kaleidacousticon (1822) used card shuffling as the source of its random musical choices, producing more than 200 million possible waltzes. The Quadrille Melodist (1865) randomized values using pre-marked cards, producing over 400 million possible quadrilles.

## Capturing the Spirit of the Great Composers

Can music information systems simulate the style of a given composer? Sophisticated algorithms can ascertain the likelihood that note A follows note B based on analyzing the works of the composer. The computer selects notes weighted by these probabilities. The result is automated music with a style presumably similar to that of the original composer.

## *A Simple Method of Musical Representation*

Parsons (1975) proposes a novel and simple form of musical information representation. The method identifies tonal music solely upon the relative (up/down) positions of the notes. (The book is often referred to as the "up-down" book for that reason.)

Mark the first tone with an asterisk. Mark the second note with a U (up) if the second note is higher than the first. Mark it D (down) if it is lower. Repeat the process with the next sixteen notes. The text cites different sets of sequences and their musical associations. For example, Parsons claims the following compact representations:

> *UDDUUUU   ("White Christmas," Irving Berlin, 1941)
>
> *DDUUDUU  ("El Salon Mexico," Aaron Copland, 1935)

Non-contextual musical representation may have intriguing applications to music cataloging and music information retrieval but has never been researched in depth. Additional sample representations are available in Fogwall (2001).

## FUNDAMENTALS OF MUSIC INFORMATION RETRIEVAL

A quiz show asks contestants to name a tune after hearing a few notes. Musicians retain thousands of tonal themes in their repertoire. Jazz artists can improvise around a musical fragment without ever losing its identity. A patron asks a music librarian for the name of the musical composition that sounds like "da-da-da-dah," while another seeks the historical impact of unusual time signatures. Music information retrieval manifests itself in strange, beautiful, and mysterious ways.

Music information retrieval (MIR) is the process of identifying, locating, and accessing structured auditory information or its representations. MIR involves a traditional text retrieval component with regard to printed scores, though with a dynamic symbolic versus a static alphabetic notation. Music information can be said to transcend language information in the sense that directly or indirectly music relates to absolute physical phenomena.

## The Nature and Principles of Music Information Retrieval

Music information retrieval differs significantly from conventional text retrieval. Music contains levels of highly structured multidimensional information including pitch, rhythm, tonality, and harmony.

Music provides auditory information. Music can be read, but music is meant to be heard. A basic unit of text is the word, but what is the basic unit of music? Music does not start and stop in discrete units within a measure. Music flows.

## MIR Systems

Libraries catalog musical works by composer, title, or genre. Librarians index scores, recordings, and interpretative texts. This simple first-order retrieval method is crude but surprisingly effective. It has worked well for a long time.

Musical notation is a form of text, but "a musical work is an intellectual sonic conception" (Smiraglia 2001). Hence, every arrangement, every instrumentation, every tuning, every performance of a musical work produces a different manifestation of the same music. Two performances of the same work may differ in duration or embellishment. Two different performances of the same musical work will probably not overlap exactly if played simultaneously and indeed may not even contain the same number of notes.

Music librarians catalog different recordings or performances of a single musical work, while in contrast, public libraries have multiple identical copies of the same work of text. Library patrons may identify a musical work, but they can also identify (and request) *specific instances* of a given work according to their arrangements, performers, conductors, and performances.

A patron hums a tune ("query by humming"). A musician plays notes. A researcher selects themes. The user may seek *portions* of a musical work or the entire work itself.

The best way to classify musical characteristics depends on need. The needs of an academic musician differ from those of a film score developer. The needs of a music distributor differ from those of a songwriter. Some users seek an *exact musical match* to a musical fragment. Other users want a *similar musical match*. For example, a music historian asks why many of Sir Noel Coward's songs are in the key of E-flat. A composer seeks a precise chord used by Dvorak in the *allegro con fuoco* movement of his

*Symphony No. 9 in E Minor,* opus 95 (*New World*). A jazz artist wants similar recordings of the same music by different performers.

## Music Databases

Music has expanded beyond the tribe, clan, church, salon, and music hall to phonograph records, radio, television, DVDs, and the Internet. Music propagates easily over the Internet. Collectors can and do create individual, private musical databases for their own research or entertainment. The corpus of world music is vast and diverse, and so are the forms of musical storage.

An effective music database service such as exists in libraries or commercial collections must classify its musical works. A (very) short list of categories includes composer, title, arrangement, form, genre, instrument, and mood. Categories can be qualitative or quantitative. The term "staccato" is a definitive statement by the composer, while "soft rock" is a subjective perception of the listener.

Keywords act as representative summary terms of a text, and this also applies to musical texts, although a keyword takes on a different meaning here. Summary terms carry less information content than the totality (and in this case, tonality) of the piece to which they correspond. MIR keyword searching is sadly limited. Keywords might be adequate for a low-level general query identifying *musical works* (e.g., a particular symphony). They might be inadequate for a high-level specific query identifying *musical structures* (e.g., a particular harmony). Bibliographic music retrieval is a variation on traditional text retrieval well developed by librarians. Structured music retrieval is more an art than a science, relying much on the background and experience of the seekers.

### MIR User Interfaces

Online keywords are terse, while music is rich in color and texture. How does one coalesce a tune into keywords? A trained musician and a trained music librarian might together resolve the identity of a musical piece. What of the casual user who knows not the articulation except in their own head? No single uniform user query or user interface fits all needs, and in fact every need involves a complex user interface.

### MIR: Meaning and Aboutness

An effective text-based information retrieval system satisfies the all-and-only problem, retrieving *all* relevant items and retrieving *only* relevant items. Relevance involves "about-ness," yet it is often surprisingly difficult to articulate what a document is about.

What is music about? Is *Le Sacre du Printemps* (*Rite of Spring,* Stravinsky, 1913) about primitive pagan dances, as envisioned by the composer, or is it about dinosaurs as envisioned by Walt Disney (*Fantasia,* 1940)? What is abstract music like Bach's *Toccata and Fugue in D Minor* about?

One possibility is that music is all about structure. A vocal duet is easily distinguished from a string quartet. This concept provides a useful structural organizing scheme. Or perhaps musical works should be classified because they are "about" the same idea, even though they may differ in format. For example, Tchaikovsky, Berlioz, and Bernstein all composed works based on Shakespeare's play *Romeo and Juliet*.

## MIR Queries

Many musical queries are based on one or more of the parameters listed below.

| | | |
|---|---|---|
| title | composer | genre |
| pitch | major/minor interval | phrasing |
| up/down trend | conductor | tempo |
| rhythm | note sequence | key signature |
| melody | theme | arrangement |
| instrumentation | variation | harmony |
| performer | performance | tuning system |
| chord structure | initial or final tones | |

*Bibliographic MIR.* A "query by identifier" is a traditional text query applied to a cataloged musical object. The relevant information lies in static bibliographic data pertaining to the musical work; for example, a title such as *Brandenburg Concerto no. 2,* first movement.

*Sonic MIR..* This is the process of scanning a musical recording for tonal structure using a sufficiently highly sophisticated audio examiner, supplying an exact query, and performing a high-speed matching process. *In practice,* its retrieval effectiveness is quite limited. High effectiveness is too often restricted to small, specialized collections in standardized formats with relatively simple queries.

*Content MIR.* A "query by content" retrieves tonal quality and structure; for example, a recognizable stylistic musical trait. A frequency analyzer might identify a middle C quarter note in the seventh measure, but probably could not distinguish a sonata from an overture. A structural analyzer might identify a symphony composed in the Italian versus the French style but could not detect the nuances of jazz.

*Variational MIR.* A "query by variation" targets the differences between the same music. Users seek a *specific variation* of given music; for example, the same work performed by different artists or in different formats.

Monophonic (single-tone) music is fundamentally simpler than polyphonic (multi-tone) music. It is also less interesting. Chords provide emphasis, harmonies blend, and polyphonic music has coloration. Few MIR systems can handle the intricacies and complexity of polyphonic sound.

Some MIR queries do not deal with harmony, theme, melody, title, or composer. A pitch list, for example, sometimes reveals folk song origins. Final phrasing may be more indicative of style than initial phrasing.

Traditional music queries are based on exact or inexact matches. But MIR queries can also be based on probabilities. *A probabilistic query is a likelihood match.* MIR becomes a screening tool: eliminate candidates that are least likely to fit a given criterion, and identify candidates that are most likely to fit that same criterion. This method has been shown to be useful for generating statistically similar musical fragments.

MIR may also involve transformation. Different arrangements can transform the same music into different forms. Consider a Bach concerto played on period instruments versus a contemporary rendition. Imagine an Elvis Presley love ballad sung in rock-and-roll style or in classical Latin. (Such recordings actually exist!) This device is occasionally used for entertainment, such as performing the "Happy Birthday" song in the style of Mozart. The musical comedians Victor Borge and Peter Schickele mastered the art of merging diverse musical styles into a single composition.

This process has research applications beyond entertainment because it allows the detailed analysis of composer and performer styles. Great performers often make significant changes to a musical text. The cellist Yo-Yo Ma once described the extensive artistic stylistic changes performed by violinist Isaac Stern as "leaving no tone unSterned."

## MIR Objects

For generations of musicians, MIR meant retrieving a relevant musical score. Trained musical professionals "read" and "hear" a score. Amateurs think of the score as the music itself. *The score is not the music.* It is only a *representation* of the music.

A score contains musical objects. It can thus be modeled as a container whose objects include notes, clefs, key signatures, rests, measures, chords, and other components. Musical container models are not completely satisfactory (music is not a bucket), but some simple cases are amenable to this concept.

A score is also a sequence of notes. More generally, a score is a collection of sonic events. An auto-correlation pitch tracker can be used to analyze sonic events. Musical drama is lost in this process, but musical retrieval might be enhanced from this perspective.

Computer-readable music files serve as tokens of exchange for electronic music interchange. Digitized formats are eminently suitable for online distribution, but are not always suitable for content-based retrieval. A computer audio file contains information on the tone and duration of notes, but it is usually not a full and faithful replica of the original. It is usually a very low-information replica.

## Machine-Readable Music Notation

A score is a musical object with a standardized notation, but a score is not amenable to automated information retrieval. Automated score-based MIR requires a specialized notation, such as GUIDO, which is a score-based musical language (Hoos, Renz, and Gorg 2001). The name originates from Guido d'Arezzo (992–1050), a founder of modern musical notation. The GUIDO musical language is readable by both computers and humans. Simple musical concepts are expressible by simple linguistic terms.

The World Wide Web has become a forum for mass-media music. Extensible Markup Language (XML) provides another potential musical representation language. XML is human-readable and has the additional benefit of being independent of the computer platform. XML supports metadata structures that describe information about information. To date, XML has not been overly successful as a musical retrieval language, however.

### MIR and Intellectual Property

In April 2002 the International Organization for Standardization issued a document entitled *Information and Documentation: International Standard Musical Work Code* (ISO 15707). The document provides a means of identifying musical works within the computer databases used by music publishers, record companies, and copyright agencies. The ISWC number is similar in function to an ISBN book number. It applies to any musical form, from symphonies to songs. It transcends political and national boundaries (much like the Internet!). Query by ISWC number may become a new component of MIR systems.

Some Native American tribes associate rights and obligations with the singing of songs. The right to sing a particular song belongs to a designated group or individual as an honor or cultural obligation. Such a song is not a public commodity, and unauthorized singing violates cultural tradition. A music retrieval system might allow the indiscriminate distribution of such songs, posing social and ethical questions (UNESCO 1989).

### Number-Based MIR

There are many techniques for converting music to text. Notes have pitch, duration, and harmony. Let's assume that pitch intervals dominate music identification. This is a simplifying assumption, but a very useful one. Let's also ignore tonal duration and silence (rests).

A "unigram" is a string of numbers representing the rise and fall of pitch of contiguous notes and is expressed in terms of increments. For example,

[+5, +7, –9, +9, –7 . . . ]

represents the first five notes in the song "Lucy in the Sky with Diamonds" (Lennon and McCartney, 1967). If this vector is scaled, then the rock-and-roll hit is expressed by

[30 32 16 34 18 . . . ]

"Bigrams" use the same principle, except that they are based on multiple contiguous notes.

Numerical representation takes the magic out of music, but it provides expedient pattern recognition. If longer musical passages are assumed to be more representative than shorter musical passages, then bigrams (or n-length fragments called "n-grams") can improve musical retrieval precision.

### Musical Abstracts

An abstract summarizes the contents of a document. Scanning abstracts is faster and more efficient than scanning full text. What is the musical equivalent of an abstract?

One likely candidate consists of the first few seconds of auditory information (incipit) of a musical work. "The Star Spangled Banner" and the first movement of Beethoven's *Fifth Symphony* are served well by incipits.

The incipit is not always a good identifier, however. The most recognizable portion of a musical piece may not occur at the onset or might be preceded by equally important themes. The most popular theme (used as the theme music to the television program *The Lone Ranger*) only appears at the end of Rossini's *William Tell Overture*.

A more useful variation on the incipit is the musical thumbnail, a short musical fragment extracted from the score. A thumbnail contains relevant, significant, or easily recognizable portions of the musical work and so may be a better identifier. Incipits are easily generated automatically, while thumbnails require careful planning.

## Musical Style Recognition

The music of Bach does not sound like that of Brahms. The style of Vivaldi is rarely confused with that of Rimsky-Korsakov. Composers have a compositional style. *Style is recognizable to the trained ear even if it is not easily articulated in words.*

Musical notation is a highly structured form of text. Notational parameters should indicate compositional style in the same way that words and phraseology indicate writing style. Musical style recognition has research and forensic applications. The automatic detection of score characteristics may resolve issues of compositional authenticity, for example. Ordinary computer compression software has been successfully used to identify musical works by unknown composers (Muir 2003).

Stylistic parameters include composer preferences, idiosyncrasies, and tonal distribution statistics. Individual musical events within a piece receive an individual weight factor quantifying the composer (hence every score has a score!). The frequency of note occurrence, key signatures, and modulations offer stylistic markers.

A symphony or other large musical work contains an enormous number of notes. Full documentation of these is quite impractical for most library environments. One possible solution involves reducing information resolution by eliminating notes shorter than a specific duration. (For example, drop all notes shorter than 32nd notes). Lower information content means faster processing.

Music identification may rely more on psychological imprints and aural perception than on statistical measures. Do we hear music metaphorically? How does a composer "turn single-note-at-a-time passages into perceptual streams" (Byrd and Crawford 2002)?

## Theme-Based MIR

A musical work may contain a recognizable theme. If the theme is identified and indexed, then the musical work can be efficiently and effectively retrieved. This logic is appealing but flawed. A musical work may have no themes, one theme, or many themes. A theme may be long or short and may occur anywhere in the score.

The theory of theme searching is similar to the theory of text-string matching, but the implementation is much more difficult. The query may not be an accurate representation of the theme because it could be off-key or off-tempo. The theme may not even be a melody; harmony may be more important than a specific string of thematic notes. Moreover, theme searching requires extensive signal processing. Theme searching by note alone sometimes produces false positive results because the same set of tones forming the theme might appear elsewhere yet not be the theme in question.

The essential problem of musical information retrieval systems returns to the problem of defining the unit of music, the metaphorical musical word. This unit could be melodic contours as a function of pitch versus time. *This MIR approach does not use notes explicitly, as do other MIR methods.*

A broader application of thematic-based searching involves genre searching. How does one distinguish country and western, rock and roll, Baroque, Renaissance, reggae, calypso, Gregorian chant, and the myriad forms of jazz? *Genre identification is a problem in music similarity.*

### Melody-Based MIR

What is a melody? A melody is "a succession of tones with rhythmic and tonal organization" (Olson 1967, 56). Tonal arrangement defines a melodic contour. This definition does not incorporate the subjective criteria of joy, humor, sadness, anger, or other emotions associated with a melody. How does a composer create a melody?

Do listeners recognize melodic contours more effectively than incipits? How far can a composer stretch a melody before it becomes a different melody? When are melodies similar? Similarity depends on the concept of closeness, and this requires a metric. When are melodies close, and what is the appropriate measure of such closeness? Traditional metrics do not work. How does a young child recognize a favorite melody?

### EXERCISES AND RESEARCH QUESTIONS

### Exercises: Music and Sound

E14.1   Listen to the same musical composition played in different keys. Then listen to the same composition in different tuning systems.

E14.2   Compare a musical work played on period instruments with a performance of the same work on contemporary instruments and then on electronic instruments.

E14.3   If the frequency of tone A above middle C is 440, then what is the frequency of the tone A one octave higher? One octave lower?

E14.4   How do you know if a bad musician is knocking at the door? (Read backwards: ni emoc ot nehw wonk ton seod dna yek eht evah ton seod eH) (Cohl 1997)

E14.5   Musical compositions utilize an organizational framework. Identify ten structured musical formats.

E14.6    Sound waves travel at approximately 1,100 feet per second at sea level. Lightning and thunder occur simultaneously, but lightning is seen before the thunder is heard. Why does counting the number of seconds between lightning and thunder and dividing that value by five approximate one's distance in miles from the lightning strike?

E14.7    A piano uses hammers to strike its strings. Is the piano considered a member of the string or the percussion family of instruments?

### *Research Question 14.8*

Why do the London Symphony Orchestra and New York Philharmonic use different terms for their respective musical organizations?

### *Research Question 14.9*

Identify ten different musical styles (Baroque, calypso, etc.).

### *Research Question 14.10*

The ancient Greeks sought order and logic in the universe by the application of rational ideals. The interplay of simple mathematical principles with music reinforced a cosmic perspective called the "music of the spheres." By contrast, the Newtonian view of the universe was not sublime music but an intricate clockwork mechanism. Discuss the impact of the specific metaphor on the musical style of the period. Does the Einsteinian view of the universe have an impact on contemporary music?

### *Research Question 14.11*

Barbershop quartet harmony (4:5:6 ratio) is an American musical form. It is now more a musical novelty than a mainstay. Did the advent of mass-media music promote the demise of local barbershop quartets?

### *Research Question 14.12*

A chord is a series of simultaneous musical notes. Does the music of Mozart appear "light" due to a minimal use of chords, while the music of Wagner seems "heavy" because of too many chords?

### *Exercises: Melody Machines*

E14.13    Why is seven the most likely value for a toss of the dice? Why are two and twelve the least likely?

### *Research Question 14.14*

Identify other random music generators. How popular were they for their time?

CHAPTER **15**    ▶ Interpreting Information

*Numbers as Meanings*

Numbers measure values. Words have meanings. But sometimes numbers also have meanings.

## GEMATRIA

Gematria [pronounced geh-MAH-tree-ah] is an ancient form of numerology. The word derives from the Greek word *geometria* ("earth-measure"). The less common terms "isopsephia" or "arithmography" are also occasionally encountered. The process of Gematria substitutes the letters of a word with their numerical associations in the hopes of deriving insight, interpretation, or deeper meaning from writings. There are several variations on this idea. *Notarikon* involves the first (or middle or last) letters combined to form a new word. *Temurah* uses numerical tables for letter organization.

Many ancient cultures showed a reverence for numbers. Mesopotamian documents contain numerical references to the Assyrian Tree of Life. The Pythagorean cult considered odd numbers as having male attributes and even numbers as having female attributes (possibly based on creation rituals). The first recorded use of Gematria may have been by the Assyrian king Sargon II (705 B.C.E.), who constructed a wall at Khorsabad of 16,283 cubits corresponding to the numerical value of his name.

Hebrew Gematria probably originated from the Greek. Hebrew and Greek have a strong history of Gematria usage because both cultures used their alphabet to represent both letters and numbers. This discussion focuses on Hebrew Gematria.

The Hebrew alphabet (or more properly the *aleph-bet*, named after the first two letters) consists of twenty-two letters and five dual letters. Dual letters assume a different form when appearing at the end of a word. The letter symbols may have derived from earlier Semitic cultures. Hebrew is written right to left, contrary to most European languages, which are written left to right. The Hebrew language has no formal vowels, although vowel sounds appear as diacritical marks (*nikkudim,* "points") above/below/

inside a letter so as not to disturb its relative spacing. A dot within a letter (*dagesh*) changes the pronunciation of the letter itself (e.g., the sound of the second letter of the Hebrew alphabet changes from V to B). Cantillation marks (*teamim*) provide accents for singing.

All of the above aspects create difficulties for the process of transliteration, where a letter in one alphabet is substituted for another in a different alphabet. Since the Roman and Hebrew alphabets do not correspond, one commonly sees the Hebrew word for the "Festival of Lights" expressed as either "Hanukah" or "Chanukah" in English.

In Gematria, the absolute value of a Hebrew letter depends on its position within the alphabet. The first nine letters represent multiples of one (1–9). The next nine letters are multiples of ten (10–90). The final four are multiples of one hundred (100–400). This method is called a triple ennead system. If a letter appears at the end of a word, it assumes a higher value. (See tables 15-1 and 15-2.)

**Table 15-1**
Gematria Letter Values:
Ragil Method

| Letter Name | Absolute Value | Ordinal Value |
|---|---|---|
| aleph | 1 | 1 |
| bet | 2 | 2 |
| gimmel | 3 | 3 |
| dalet | 4 | 4 |
| hei | 5 | 5 |
| vov | 6 | 6 |
| zayin | 7 | 7 |
| chet | 8 | 8 |
| tet | 9 | 9 |
| yud | 10 | 10 |
| kaf | 20 | 11 |
| lamed | 30 | 12 |
| mem | 40 | 13 |
| nun | 50 | 14 |
| samech | 60 | 15 |
| ayin | 70 | 16 |
| pei | 80 | 17 |
| tzadik | 90 | 18 |
| kuf | 100 | 19 |
| raysh | 200 | 20 |
| shin | 300 | 21 |
| tav | 400 | 22 |

**Table 15-2**
Gematria Letter Values:
Mispar Godol Method

| Letter | Absolute Value | Ordinal Value | Name |
|--------|----------------|---------------|------|
| Final kaf | 500 | 23 | kaf sofit |
| Final mem | 600 | 24 | mem sofit |
| Final nun | 700 | 25 | nun sofit |
| Final pei | 800 | 26 | pei sofit |
| Final tzadik | 900 | 27 | tzadik sofit |

(The Millui method differs from these two traditional enumerations. The value of a letter is the value of the letters that make up the name of the letter. An example appears later in the text.)

The order of the letters in a word is irrelevant to a letter's numerical value. Spaces and vowel signs are ignored. For example, the number 11 can be represented as:

$$11 \quad = \text{yod} + \text{aleph} = 10 + 1$$
$$= \text{aleph} + \text{yod} = 1 + 10$$
$$= \text{heh} + \text{vov} = 5 + 6$$
$$= \text{dalet} + \text{dalet} + \text{gimel} - 4 + 4 + 3$$

Devout believers in Gematria avoid certain numerical combinations because they "spell" special words. For example:

$$15 \quad = \text{tet} + \text{vov} = 9 + 6 \qquad \text{(used)}$$
$$= \text{yod} + \text{heh} = 10 + 5 \qquad \text{(not used)}$$

$$16 \quad = \text{tet} + \text{zayin} = 9 + 7 \qquad \text{(used)}$$
$$= \text{yod} + \text{vov} = 10 + 6 \qquad \text{(not used)}$$

The letters not used are part of the Tetragrammaton, the four-letter biblical name of God variously transliterated as Yahweh or Jehovah. It should be noted for the sake of this discussion's completeness that normal decimal number representation is also commonly used.

*Example 15.1* (Ragil method)

The Hebrew word *shalom* translates as "peace." It is used as the greeting "hello" (come in peace). The word is composed of the letters shin (300), lamed (30), vov (6), and mem (40). The word *shalom* has the number value 376.

*Example 15.2* (Millui method)

The name of the first Hebrew letter is spelled using the letters: aleph-lamed-pei (aleph = 1, lamed = 30, pei = 80). Hence the letter aleph has the number value 111.

*Example 15.3*

The Hebrew word *chaiyim* means "life." It has the numerical value 18. Many Jewish congregations often receive donations in increments of $18. Twice 18 is 36. There are folklore stories of "Thirty-Six Just Men" (Lamedvavniks, from the Hebrew letters adding to 36) who quietly save the world during every generation.

Gematria is often invoked as a theological premise. Words with the same numerical value are associated with each other in the Bible, and this association is believed to happen by design, not by coincidence. Gematria may also be used to affirm preexisting knowledge or beliefs. It never denies a dogmatic principle. In this sense, Gematria "adds spice" to the interpretation of a biblical text. The following is a sample of such "spice" based on a discussion in Potok (1967, 136–37):

> "The Talmudic commentary called the *Mishnah* (Avot 4:16) states 'Prepare thyself in the vestibule, that thou mayest enter the hall.' The hall is metaphorically the World-To-Come (*Olam Habah*) and the vestibule is This-World (*Olam Hazeh*). The difference between the numerical values of the two Hebrew expressions is nine. Nine is half of eighteen and eighteen is *chayim,* life. Therefore we are only half-alive in this world!"

*Example 15.4*

The biblical name of God (Tetragrammaton) is expressed by the Hebrew letters yud-hey-vov-hey. The numerical value of this word equals 26. The word for "love" (*ahavah*) has a numerical value of 13, as does the word for "one" (*achad*). To the devout, this is sufficient evidence that love and oneness are the essence of God.

These numbers have power in Jewish folklore. For example, the Golem was a pre-Frankenstein monster who was animated to do good but was banished or destroyed when it went out of control. Some variations of this tale explain the Golem's animating process by mystical Gematria incantations. The word *emet* ("truth") was emblazoned on the monster's forehead and it became alive. When the word was changed to *met* ("death"), the numerical value was destroyed and the monster lost its power.

## Logical Flaws of Gematria

The order of the letters in a word is irrelevant for numerical value purposes in Gematria. There are thus an enormous number of possible arrangements for any given value. It should not be surprising that some arrangements spell words.

Numerology is a pseudoscience. Mathematical symbol manipulation is not mathematical logic and it is not even science. Science must be replicable, where conclusions follow by logical and correct steps that are subject to critical review. Many numerological arguments evaporate when applied to different number systems or contexts. This shows that the presumed meaning is tied to symbols and not to underlying concepts.

The rules are often applied selectively in Gematria. Different representations produce different results. Numerical values are assigned to letters arbitrarily. Mathematical operations are not relevant to word forms. Contrary word forms that oppose "evidence" are ignored.

The use of arithmetical methods does not imply mathematical reasoning. Conclusions are often determined based on serendipitous evidence taken as truth. Strictly speaking, Gematria is only relevant to Hebrew by virtue of the associated cultural system. The use of any other language is symbolic word play. It may be fun, but it is not information.

Because there are an infinite number of numbers and the human mind strives for order out of chaos, there is no lack of associated meanings between numbers and letters. Many of these "associations" are made after the fact. It is very easy to predict or find meaning after the fact in much the same way that Epimetheus, the brother of Prometheus, foretold the future after it had happened. Whether such meanings are artifacts of the number system or bear deeper insight is left for the reader to decide.

### Deconstructing Gematria Arguments

The folly of Gematria as a misuse of numbers is often revealed when special numerical values must be assigned in order to generate a special reverent or meaningful value. This is effectively trying to prove a result after the fact. It is highly likely that *any* word has *some* special meaning in *some* counting basis. Observe the following pseudo-analysis:

If A = 36, B = 37, etc., then "SUPERSTITIOUS" = 666

And perhaps that says it all . . .

The following are several Gematria arguments (and their rebuttals) for the entertainment of the reader (Tenuta 1997).

*Argument 15.1*

Assign the natural ordering (A = 1, B = 2, . . .). Fold the letters back on themselves so that A folds with Z, B with Y, etc. Add the matched pairs of numbers. Every matched pair adds to the value of 27! The digits of 27 add up to 9, so the number 9 is encoded within the Roman alphabet! Amazingly, the value of the word CODE equals 27! Coincidence?

The folding operation works on an alphabet with an even number of letters. If the alphabet contained 28 letters, then the magic sum would be 29. The pseudo-justification of the word CODE would no longer work and would be irrelevant. The results are language-dependent. It is easily proven that if a number is divisible by three, then so is the sum of its digits. The result generalizes to the number nine. There is no magic here.

*Argument 15.2*

There are 22 letters and 5 final forms (22 + 5 = 27) in the Hebrew alphabet. The number 27 was shown to be mysterious by the previous example. Therefore Gematria is valid in English!

Not so. It is only a case of word and number play.

*Argument 15.3*

The number 13 has importance to the Mayan calendar. The value of THIRTEEN is 99. The sum of the digits of 99 is 18. The sum of the digits of 18 is 9. Twice 13 is 26. The value of TWENTY-SIX is 159. The sum of its digits is 15.

The sum of the digits of 15 is 6. The word MAYAN has the value 54, which equals 9 × 6! Coincidence?

Gematria derives from Greek and Hebrew. There is a great cultural distance and many centuries between Hebrew and English. An already questionable numerical value does not validate this association.

*Argument 15.4*

Quetzalcoatl was an Aztec/Toltec deity. The word sums to 153. English has a special use of 13 and 27. Observe that 13 × 27 = 351, which is a mirror image of the numerical value of the deity! In fact, the sum of all letters in the English alphabet tallies to 351! Coincidence?

The conclusion, if there is one, is vacuous.

## Numerology and Music

Numerology extends into music. The eminent conductor Leonard Bernstein (1918–1990) noted that the baroque composer Johann Sebastian Bach was a numerologist. This should not be surprising, since the art of the fugue lies in its numerically enunciated patterns, and numerical mysticism was common in seventeenth-century Europe. Bernstein (1967) suggested the following patterns that might have been known to the composer.

If the value of each letter is its position in the alphabet, then B-A-C-H adds to 14. Fourteen is expressed as 1-4. One is the Unity and four is the Gospel. Four minus one is three, representing the Trinity. In old German B-A-C-H adds to 41, which is 14 reversed. The last work of Bach contained 14 notes in a phrase and 41 notes in a melody.

Is it coincidence? The coincidence may seem strong, but the argument is weak. A particular alphabetic ordering is used because it works. Any other ordering (Z = 1, Y = 2, etc.) is equally valid and produces different results. Such combinations make interesting data but not useful information.

## Chinese Numerology

Some numbers in Chinese culture bear special significance due to *auditory* similarity. Numbers have meaning because they *sound* like other words (as opposed to *count* like other words). The number four is "unlucky" because its *pronunciation* is similar to the words for "death," "dead," or "die." Even numbers connote affairs going smoothly, while odd numbers imply the opposite.

Only the Chinese emperor could use the number 999. This was because the number nine uses the same pronunciation as the word for "forever." Three nines in sequence meant a lack of imperfection. The emperor should live forever.

The numbers six and eight suggest a successful career or a rich future, respectively. The number 888 represents fortune. Hence price tags in China often end in .88 (as opposed to .99 in the United States). It has been claimed that some Chinese pay a premium to their local telecom company for a phone number containing multiple 4s, 6s, and 8s. (There are only a limited number of ways these digits may appear in a phone number, so competition must be high!)

A legend claims that before Buddha departed Earth he summoned every animal to bid him farewell. Twelve animals arrived. He named each year after them as a reward for their loyalty. Each birth year thus has animal associations and admonitions. These cycles are repeated every twelve years (see table 15-3). Add or subtract twelve as appropriate if your birth year does not appear. (*Caveat:* The admonitions are subject to interpretation!)

**Table 15-3**
Chinese Numerology Years

| Animal | Admonition | Applies to These Birth Years (+12) |
|---|---|---|
| rabbit | avoid the rooster | 1939, 1951, 1963, 1975 |
| dragon | avoid the dog | 1940, 1952, 1964, 1976 |
| snake | avoid the boar | 1941, 1953, 1965, 1977 |
| horse | avoid the rat | 1942, 1954, 1966, 1978 |
| goat/ram/sheep | avoid the ox | 1943, 1955, 1967, 1979 |
| monkey | avoid the tiger | 1944, 1956, 1968, 1980 |
| rooster | avoid the rabbit | 1945, 1957, 1969, 1981 |
| dog | avoid the dragon | 1946, 1958, 1970, 1982 |
| boar/pig | avoid other boars | 1947, 1959, 1971, 1983 |
| rat | avoid the horse | 1948, 1960, 1972, 1984 |
| ox | avoid the sheep | 1949, 1961, 1973, 1985 |
| tiger | avoid the monkey | 1950, 1962, 1974, 1986 |

*Note:* The Chinese and Western calendar years begin and end on different dates.

## THE NUMEROLOGY OF 666

In Chinese culture the number six has an association with affairs going well. The number 666 represents events going very smoothly, hence the number 666 has a positive and welcome image. In contrast, many Christians consider 666 as the Number of the Beast or by implication the sign of the Devil. This interpretation derives from the following biblical text:

> "Here is the wisdom: Let him that hath understanding count the number of the beast for it is the number of a man: and his number is six hundred three score and six" (Revelations 13:18).

Scholars disagree on the basis for this specific number, and the text does not explain its reference. It may derive from an obscure political reference, a long-lost symbol, some quantity, or a coded clue. It could be an inside joke, contemporary event, or a long-forgotten transcription error.

If the choice of the number was politically motivated, then could the biblical warning associated with 666 be an adverse sociopolitical reaction against impinging foreign (Asian) cultural influence? Might it be an exhortation against competing religious forms recognized by their common and liberal use of 666? As far as this author knows, this Asian cultural explanation for the biblical reference to the number 666 has never been explored.

Scheifler (citing Anderson 1974, 125) suggests that Revelations' 666 refers to pagan priests wearing amulets bearing the seal of the Sun (*sigilla solis*). These amulets had the numbers 1 through 36 inscribed on them in such a way that each column added to 111. Six such columns added to 666. Numerologists refer to this configuration as the "magic square of the sun." Pagan priests could certainly be construed as competitors for the early Christian congregations.

### 666 of the World Wide Web

The popular abbreviation for the World Wide Web is WWW. Suppose one converts these English characters into their Hebrew equivalents to make a formal Gematria analysis. The letter w transliterates to vov. Vov is the sixth letter of the Hebrew alphabet.

Does this mean WWW = W − W − W = 666? Is the World Wide Web the long-sought and mysterious biblical reference? Is the Web the sign of impending doom?

Not really . . .

First of all, WWW is an abbreviation, not a word. Secondly, purists note that the number as cited in the biblical text must *count* to 666. The physical appearance of three six symbols in a row is not sufficient. The count of vov-vov-vov is $6 + 6 + 6 = 18$, so whatever the World Wide Web is, we can be reasonably sure that it is not the Mark of the Beast. (*Note:* vov-vov-vov counts to 18. The number 18 has the same value as the word *chaiyim,* meaning "life." Words with the same numerical value presumably have an association. Does this imply that the Web is life-affirming?)

### The Arithmetic of 666

The number 666 has many remarkable arithmetic properties in and of itself. Some of these were surely known to ancient pagan or competing mystics. Could this be the source of its numerological significance?

Consider these facts:

$$666 = 1^6 − 2^6 + 3^6 \qquad \text{(alternating powers)}$$
$$666 = (6^3 + 6^3 + 6^3) + (6 + 6 + 6) \qquad \text{(three cubes plus three values)}$$
$$666 = 1 + 2 + 3 + 4 + 567 + 89 \qquad \text{(sequential digits)}$$
$$666 = 123 + 456 + 78 + 9 \qquad \text{(sequential digits another way)}$$
$$666 = 9 + 87 + 6 + 543 + 21 \qquad \text{(reverse sequence of digits)}$$

$$666 = (6 + 6 + 6) \times (6^2 + 1) \qquad \text{(product sums)}$$

$$666 = 2^2 + 3^2 + 5^2 + 7^2 + 11^2 + 13^2 + 17^2 \qquad \text{(prime squares)}$$

The number appears in other intriguing and unexpected ways, as shown in the following examples.

*Example 15.5* (triangular numbers)

If numbers are expressed in a diagram akin to successive rows of bowling pins, the cumulative total for each row forms a sequence of triangular numbers (e.g., 1, 3, 6, 10, . . .). The Nth triangular number is $N \times (N + 1) / 2$. The 36th triangular number is 666.

*Example 15.6* (digits of the number pi)

Note that $(6 + 6) \times (6 + 6) = 144$

Do the first 144 digits of pi add to 666?

*Example 15.7* (right triangles)

A Pythagorean triple is a set of three numbers satisfying $(a^2) + (b^2) = (c^2)$.

These values constitute the lengths of the sides of a right triangle.

The triad (216, 630, 666) is a Pythagorean triple.

This example might seem contrived until one notices that

$$(216)^2 + (630)^2 = (666)^2 = (6 \times 6 \times 6)^2 + (666 - (6 \times 6))^2 = (666)^2$$

*Example 15.8* (regular triangles)

sine (666 degrees) = cosine ($6 \times 6 \times 6$ degrees)

*Example 15.9* (Roman numerals)

666 = sum of the first six Roman numerals in decreasing order
(D + C + L + X + V + I)

### Some Politics of Numerology

Numerology even influences affairs of state. Political pundits cite the Zero Factor. *No U.S. president elected after 1840 in a year ending with a zero ever lived out his term:* Lincoln, 1860; Garfield, 1880; McKinley, 1900; Harding, 1920; Roosevelt, 1940; and Kennedy, 1960 (Wallechinsky and Wallace 1975, 126). Some astrologers attribute the significance of the Zero Factor to the Jupiter solar cycle of 12 years and the Saturn solar cycle of 28 years overlapping on the same degree of the zodiac every 20 years.

The United States is a relatively new nation, and thus the sample size for presidents is quite low. U.S. presidential elections occur every four years. Decade-year elections occur relatively infrequently, since four does not divide evenly into ten. Should a presidential candidate run against the Zero Factor or let the opponent take the hit? The presumed significance of the Zero Factor evaporated when Ronald Reagan was elected president in 1980 and retired gracefully from office in 1989.

### Numerological Miscellany

Was 1961 a special year because it reads the same upside down?

Was 1998 a bad year because 1998 equals 666 + 666 + 666?

Was 8:02 p.m. on February 20, 2002, auspicious because it can be represented as 2002-2002-2002? (= 20:02, 20/02, 2002)?

Was 10:01 a.m. on October 1, 1001, an auspicious date for the same reason?

## EXERCISES AND RESEARCH QUESTIONS

### Exercises: Gematria

E15.1   Verify the arithmetic properties of 666 as cited in the text.

### Research Question 15.2

How prominent was the male/odd and female/even principle among early human cultures? Are there any male/even and female/odd cultures?

### Research Question 15.3

One sociological explanation for the difference in directional writing lies in the nature of writing materials. Early Semitic writing used stone as a medium. Since most people are right-handed the hammer would be in the right hand and chisel in the left. If writing were performed left to right, then the chisel hand would obscure the letters (error correction is difficult on a stone tablet). Asian cultures use vertical letter placement because bamboo was abundant and provided a vertical surface when sliced. Europeans used paper from abundant trees, providing a disposable flat surface. Discuss the validity of these ideas.

### Research Question 15.4

Are the symbols for Hebrew letters remnants of stylistic renderings of common ancient physical objects?

CHAPTER **16**    ▶ Counterintuitive Information

## NOT QUITE PARADOXES

Information is not always intuitive or consistent. If information is inconsistent, then it makes nonsense. Good logic should never lead to nonsense. If a logical conclusion is nonsense, then check the logic.

### Counterintuitive Statements

The assertions and problems given below are not quite paradoxes. They demonstrate intriguing perspectives on the use, misuse, interpretation, misinterpretation, and manipulation of information. Is something wrong? If so, what and why?

#### The Opposite of False May Not Be True

Consider the following statement:

> This sentence contains seven words.

Is this statement true or false? The statement is false because the sentence contains five words.

The opposite of the statement is:

> This sentence does not contain seven words.

Is this statement true or false? The sentence has seven words, so the statement is false.

Here is the rub. If the first sentence is false, then its negation should be true. The second sentence is the negation of the first, so it should be true. But it is false. The statement and its opposite are both false (Gardner 1982, 8).

## Information Being Both True and False

*This sentence is a lie.* Is the sentence true or false?

If the sentence is true, then the sentence is a lie and therefore false.

If the sentence is false, the sentence is not a lie and so it is true. This type of logical conundrum is called undecidability. The sentence is both true and false AND neither true nor false. Here is an ancient Greek example:

> All Cretans are liars
>
> I am a Cretan
>
> Therefore I am a liar

## The Lower Half of the Class

A superintendent decries the fact that 50 percent of the students in the school are in the bottom half of the class. A politician stands before a commission and insists on a larger budget allocation because 50 percent of the citizenry are in the lower half of the income levels. What shall be done to overcome this terrible injustice?

The problem lies in the misapplication of mean and median. The mean is the statistical average. The median is the halfway value when data points are sorted. By definition, half of a sample must be above or below the median. The mean is generally not the median.

## Happiness or a Sandwich

Which is better, complete happiness or a peanut butter and jelly sandwich?

Nothing is better than complete happiness . . . but a sandwich is better than nothing.

The information is perverted because "nothing" is improperly used as a synonym for the expression "no thing."

## Tacit Assumptions

Two people play chess. Each person plays six games. Each wins four games. How?

The brevity of the text leaves out information. Most people make sense of missing information by filling in the gaps. Sometimes our gap-filling assumptions are wrong. How can this scenario be possible? The people are not playing each other.

## One Equals Two

This arithmetic chestnut misuses simple algebra and obtains an unexpected result. Math-phobics can skip this section secure in the knowledge that 1 does not equal 2.

> Let $a = b$   Choose any number and denote both by a and b
>
> Then $ab = b^2$   Multiply both sides by the same number b
>
> Then $ab - a^2 = b^2 - a^2$   Subtract $a^2$ from both sides
>
> Factor $a(b - a) = (b + a)(b - a)$   Factor both sides

> Cancel  $a = b + a$   Cancel out both sides by the common factor $(b - a)$
>
> But     $a = b$   From line 1
>
> So      $a = b + a = a + a = 2a$   Simple substitution and addition
>
> If      $a = 2a$   then $1 = 2$   Divide by the number a
>
> Therefore one equals two   *Quod erat demonstrandum!*

If a series of logical steps yields an illogical result, then check the logic. Where did this logic go awry? Determine *the first time* an aberrant result appears. Go back one step. In many cases the error occurs *in the transition*.

In this case, the error occurs when the common quantity $(b - a)$ is canceled from both sides. Cancellation simplifies the arithmetic. Look carefully. If $a = b$ from line 1, then what is the value $b - a$? It is zero. Dividing by $(b - a)$ is dividing by zero, something we were sternly admonished about in elementary school. Dividing by zero yields logical contradictions (like this example) and so must be avoided.

### The Paradoxes of Zeno

The Greek philosopher Zeno of Elea (ca. 450 B.C.E.) posed a series of problems demonstrating the impossibility of motion and indivisibility. A few references to these problems survive in the writings of Aristotle and Simplicius. Some examples follow.

### The Impossibility of Crossing a Room

A fly is located at one end of a room. Traversing the room involves traveling halfway across, then traveling half the remaining distance, then half of that remaining distance, then half of that remaining distance, etc. After any finite time there still remains a distance to go. Therefore a fly cannot cross a room. (A variation on this theme shows there is no sense in asking why did the chicken cross the road, because it cannot.)

The easy resolution of the room-crossing problem lies in the physical impossibility of sustaining the halving rule. The traversal distance is eventually smaller than the traveler can navigate because the distance is smaller than their foot or wing. The rule is violated and so its accompanying logical contradiction disappears.

The more subtle solution lies in *the validity of representing a continuum by a series of finite intervals*. The model for room traversal is the infinite sum

$$\tfrac{1}{2} + \tfrac{1}{4} + \tfrac{1}{8} + \tfrac{1}{16} + \text{etc.}$$

Add as many terms as you like. The sum will approach but never reach the value one (the other side of the room).

### Achilles and the Tortoise

Swift-footed Achilles can never win a race with a slow-footed tortoise if the tortoise is given a head start. Both start moving at the same moment, but the tortoise is ahead at the start of the race. By the time Achilles has reached the point where the tortoise started, the tortoise has moved forward, even if it is only by so much as a millimeter.

By the time Achilles has moved ahead to this point, the tortoise has also moved ahead by another small increment, and so on. No matter how fast Achilles runs, there is always some small difference between them. Achilles can never catch the tortoise.

### Space amidst Space

If everything is in space, then space must be in space. That space must be in space. The process continues without end.

### The Sum of Its Parts

A bushel of corn makes a loud sound when it spills on the floor. A bushel of corn consists of individual pieces of corn. Pieces of corn barely make a sound when they hit the floor. How can this be?

### The Moving Arrow

An arrow shot from a bow takes up a position in space. At any moment of flight it is in a fixed static position of space. This applies at every moment of its flight. Therefore an arrow will never be in motion.

### All Things Finite and Infinite

There must be a finite number of things in the universe because there are as many things as there are. There must be an infinite number of things in the universe because in order to separate two things, there must be something between them. And something between them. And something between them . . .

Zeno's paradoxes involve the continuity of time and of space. Expressing time/space as the infinite sum of finite discrete steps produces logical inconsistencies. An arrow moves, a fly crosses the room, and Achilles wins the race.

## *Counterintuitive Situations*

### The Stopped Clock

Which is more accurate, a clock that has stopped or a clock that runs five minutes fast? The stopped clock is more accurate because it displays the correct time twice a day.

This question is relevant to traditional twelve-hour clocks. A stopped clock displays the correct time when the correct a.m. and p.m. time occurs because the clock face makes no distinction between them. A clock that runs fast is always wrong.

### The Mystery of the Missing Day

There are 52 weeks in a year. There are 7 days in a week.

$$52 \times 7 = 364 \text{ days in a year}$$

What happened to day 365?

The terrestrial day, lunar month, and solar year are time units based on the natural phenomenon of one celestial body rotating about another. The concept of a week has no such basis, however, and is totally arbitrary. A week could be 3 or 16 days long. Hence it is not necessarily true that there are precisely 52 weeks in a year. If a week has 7 days, then there are 365 / 7 = 52 weeks plus one day left over. But if there are 5 days in a week, then there are 73 weeks in a year, and there is no missing day.

### Too Many Fingers

You may have more fingers than you think. Place both hands before you, palms facing down. Count fingers starting from the left hand and count down. Ten, nine, eight, seven, six. Now count the fingers on the right hand. One, two, three, four, five. Since six plus five equals eleven, you must have eleven fingers.

If you count down starting from the left hand going to the right hand, then the numbering properly goes from ten to one. The apparent contradiction occurs because of a change in the counting reference point. The finger labeled six (on the left hand) is not the sixth counted finger. Counting begins with one and it is on the right hand. The label six and the count of six are confused.

### Whenever Shall We Wed?

The following sweetheart problem is paraphrased from a comedy routine performed by Abbott and Costello. A complete version appears in *Buck Privates* (1941):

You are 40 years old. Your girlfriend is 10, so you are four times as old as she. You wait 5 years. Now you are 45 and she is 15. You are only three times as old as she. You give her 15 years to catch up. Now you are 60 and she is 30. You are now only twice as old. How long should you wait until both of you are the same age?

Give up. The absolute difference between their ages remains constant (30 years), although the relative difference becomes smaller. Absolute and relative differences do not measure the same quantities and are being confused.

### The Pseudo-Raise

Rising and falling do not always cancel each other. The boss informs the staff that everyone must take a mandatory 10-percent salary reduction. The following year the same boss announces that happy days are here again and grants a 10-percent salary increase. The new paycheck is smaller than the old one despite the equivalent reduction and increase. What happened?

The percentage decrease and the percentage increase are applied to different baselines. If you made $1,000/week and took a 10-percent cut, you would make $900/week. If you then received a 10-percent raise on that, you would make $990/week and that is less than the original $1,000. Loss and gain do not cancel unless they are relative to the same reference data.

### Numbers of Interest

*Theorem:* All numbers are interesting.

Divide all numbers into two categories where one set contains "interesting" numbers and the other "uninteresting" numbers. Use whatever criterion you choose to define interesting and uninteresting. Examine the least interesting of all uninteresting numbers. That is a very interesting number because it is the least interesting of all uninteresting numbers! If the *least* uninteresting number is interesting, then all others must be even more interesting. Therefore all numbers are interesting.

Bechenbach (1945) first proposed this unorthodox logic. It subtly manipulates the qualitative property of interest (interesting/uninteresting) with the quantitative property of ranking (least/more).

## Red Cars

More red cars in New Jersey receive speeding tickets than cars of any other color.

This information appears absurd. Vehicle color is unrelated to the position of the gas pedal.

And yet . . . Bright colors attract attention. Red is a bright color. Red cars attract attention. Police check speeding cars that attract their attention.

## Impossible Paper Folding

A square sheet of paper cannot be folded in half eight times.

This example is not quite counterintuitive, although it is sufficiently difficult as to make it seem impossible. Every fold in half doubles the paper's thickness. Eight folds increase the overall thickness by a factor of 256. The average thickness of one sheet of standard printer paper is approximately $\frac{1}{250}$ of an inch, so the eighth folding creates a wad slightly more than one inch thick. Most people cannot generate sufficient force to make the final fold.

## Lost Items

Why are so many lost items found in the last place you look?
Once you find them you stop looking!

## *The Birthday Paradox*

In a random group of 30 people there is a 70-percent chance that two will share the same birthday. The odds increase to 90 percent for a group of 40 people.

Suppose a room contains N people. What is the chance that two will share the same birthday? One might expect a very small likelihood, since there are 365 (or 366) days in a year. But the answer may surprise you.

For the sake of simplicity, let's assume there are 365 days in a year and any birth date is equally likely. (In fact, birth dates are not uniformly distributed. April is a particularly busy month for many obstetricians.) Suppose there are N people in a group and none have the same birthday. The first person can be born on any of 365 days, the next person any of 364, etc. The number decreases because once a date is selected, it cannot be used again, since by assumption no one has the same birthday. This can be expressed as the probability of *no* birthday matches for N people being

$$P = [(365 \times 364 \times 363 \times \ldots (365 - N + 1)] / [(365N)]$$

The probability of at least one match with the same birthday is:

1 − (probability of no birthday matches)

Some empirical results of this formula appear in table 16-1.

The table confirms that the likelihood of two matching birthdays is about 50 percent for 23 people, a 70-percent chance for 30 people, and a better than 95-percent chance for 50 people. Make a bet and amaze your friends! (*Caveat:* These numbers are probabilities. It is always possible, though unlikely, that everyone or no one has the same birthday.)

There is a famous anecdote about Woodrow Wilson and the birthday paradox. Wilson spon-

**Table 16-1**

Probability of Two People Chosen at Random Sharing the Same Birthday

| Number of People | Probability of Sharing a Birthday | |
|---|---|---|
| 23 | 0.507 | approximately 50% |
| 25 | 0.569 | |
| 30 | 0.706 | approximately 70% |
| 35 | 0.814 | |
| 40 | 0.891 | approximately 90% |
| 50 | 0.970 | |

(Goodman and Ratti 1971, 140)

sored a gala reception at Princeton University. As parlor entertainment he predicted that two guests out of thirty would share the same birthday. The guests proffered their dates and there was no match. Wilson was very embarrassed. He realized that only twenty-nine people were present in the room. A waitress entered. Her birthday made the match!

The same logic that derives the birthday distribution has many practical real-life applications. The following examples come from Feller (1968).

*Congressional committees.* Every U.S. state has two senators. If fifty senators are chosen at random for a committee, what is the likelihood that a given state is represented? What is the likelihood that all states are represented? (p. 35)

*Parking tickets.* A librarian receives twelve illegal overnight parking tickets, all of which occur on Tuesday or Thursday. Does it pay to rent a garage on those days? (p. 55)

*Book misprints.* A book contains 500 pages and 50 misprints. What is the likelihood that pages 1 through N contain a given number of misprints? (p. 57)

*Blood screening.* Suppose N people must take a blood-screening test. If everyone takes the test, then it requires N screenings. If fewer people (K) take the test, the results are pooled, and the result is negative, then one test suffices for those K people. If K people take the test and the results are positive, then K + 1 blood tests are necessary (each person is screened separately plus the original pooled test). Pooled tests can achieve an 80-percent cost savings! (p. 239)

## THE TROUBLE WITH INFINITY

The word "infinity" evokes powerful images of the everlasting, eternal, omniscient, omnipotent, omnipresent, cosmic, and profound, or just something very very big. Vague concepts of infinity are problematic and often paradoxical. There is a context in which infinity is meaningful, however. There are levels of infinity and they can be counted.

### A Very Short History of Infinity

Humans looked to the stars and saw the vastness of space beyond all measure of time. The oceans were filled with water beyond measure. That which could be measured was finite (Latin *finis,* "end"). That which could not be measured was infinite.

The ellipsis symbol (. . .) occurs as a shorthand for a never-ending list. Calculus manipulates infinitesimals as infinitely small units of time. John Wallis (*Arithmetica Infinitorum,* 1665) is credited with being the first to use the tilted-eight or love-knot symbol for infinity. Georg Cantor developed innovative ideas on the nature of infinite sets. Some of these ideas are still controversial. Infinity is not what it used to be.

### Theological Infinity

The theological aspects of infinity engender paradoxical consequences. Can an all-powerful deity create a stone so large that the deity cannot move it? If a deity is all knowing, then have we no free will because everything is predetermined? How can a deity be omnipresent at every possible moment at every possible time? *Infinity as All* is a problematic concept with regard to space, time, and power.

### Infinity and the Real World

The concept of infinity applied to the real world is equally elusive but somewhat more palatable, possibly because of human language limitations. Linguistic misuse takes the edge off logical paradoxes. Infinity becomes a figure of speech.

Physicists speak of an "infinite singularity" at the origin of the Big Bang when they really mean an entity so small that it disregards currently known principles of interaction. Computer programmers avoid "infinite loops" in their code structure. Astronomers wonder if the universe is "infinitely expanding" (into what?).

The term "infinity" is occasionally misused as an inaccurate synonym for a very big number. The known universe does not contain an infinite number of atoms. The speed of light is not infinite; if the Sun exploded as you read this text, no one on Earth would detect the blast traveling at the speed of light until about eight minutes later.

### What Infinity Is

Does there exist a context in which the concept of infinity makes logical sense? Yes. It even makes sense to speak of transfinite arithmetic. The following concepts and definitions describe the nature of infinity in the context of sets. The concepts are simplified for the benefit of the non-technical reader while hopefully retaining much of the spirit and elegance of the core ideas.

### Some Preliminary Working Definitions

A set is a collection of objects. Examples of a set include library patrons or cars on a road. A proper subset is a set entirely contained within a given set. For example, newspapers are a subset of all periodicals.

A function is a mapping from one set (called the domain) to another set (called the range) such that every element in the domain is assigned a unique value in the range. For example, there is a functional mapping between students and their final grade. Is there is a functional mapping between a set of books and their titles?

A function may or may not be a simple formula, but a function maps one input into one output. The mapping of titles to books is not a function. A book has only one title, but the same title may correspond to many books.

There is a functional mapping between students and grades. Every student has a final grade, some students may have the same grade, and some grades have no students (none of my students receives a D).

### Mappings Have Properties

A mapping is called *one-to-one* (injective) if no two domain elements map to the same range element. If there is a one-to-one mapping between students and grades, then different students receive different grades.

A mapping is called *onto* (surjective) if for every element in the range there is a corresponding element in the domain. If there is an onto mapping between students and grades, then every grade is achieved by some student.

A mapping can be both *one-to-one and onto* (bijective). This type of mapping is also called a one-to-one correspondence. Both sets "match up" element by element. Bergamini (1963, 171) compares this to a Noah's Ark two-by-two or closing the teeth of a zipper. In a vague sense, the sets have the same number of elements. (It can be shown that the "same number of elements" is not meaningful in an infinite context.)

### What Is Counting?

The concept of a one-to-one correspondence is intimately related to the ordinary act of counting. Early humans associated the concept of one with a single object, perhaps a pebble. The concept of two was associated with a single pebble and another pebble. The process continues, numbers associating themselves with tangible quantities. The process of counting associates numbers with objects.

Every object has a mapping with a unique number, and every number has a mapping back to a unique object. Counting N items in a list is essentially making a one-to-one correspondence with a subset of positive integers $\{1, 2, 3, 4, \ldots N\}$.

Consider the last time you had difficulty counting something. The items (like chess moves) probably could not be clearly enumerated. Forming a one-to-one correspondence was not a straightforward process.

## Making Sense of the Infinite

The following working definitions offer a testable condition for the finite and the infinite.

A set is finite if there is a number N such that the elements of the set can be placed into one-to-one correspondence with the set $\{1, 2, 3 \ldots N\}$. The set then contains N elements. This is the ordinary sense of counting.

A set is infinite if no such N exists. This test works whether the set contains six elements or six million billion elements. There is no largest natural number N, so the set of natural numbers is infinite. This result is known as the Archimedian principle.

Assume there are a finite number of natural numbers. Suppose N is the largest. Add one. Then $N + 1$ is bigger than N. By assumption, N is the largest. Contradiction! The largest natural number N does not exist.

If a set can be placed into one-to-one correspondence with the set of positive integers, then it is said to be countably (denumerably) infinite. The cardinality of this set is called aleph-0 (pronounced aleph-null).

There is a subtle idea afoot here. Counting establishes a one-to-one correspondence, and hence enables comparison and pairing off. Counting in this sense does not require knowing the number of elements, only that one set matches up with another. The cardinality of a set is determined *without the logical pitfall of knowing how many elements it contains*.

The set of all even positive numbers is countably infinite.

> The even numbers are in the set $\{2, 4, 6, 8, \ldots\}$. The positive integers are in the set $\{1, 2, 3, 4, \ldots\}$. Match each even number with a positive integer. The two sets "match up" element by element. The two sets have the same cardinality.

The set of all odd positive numbers is countably infinite.
> The previous argument applies. Match every odd number with its integer counterpart.

The set of all fractions (rational numbers) is countably infinite.
> Fractions take the form A/B where A and B are integers and B is not zero. There is a way to enumerate fractions and associate them with positive integers.

The numbers between zero and one are not countably infinite.
> This set cannot be enumerated (Kaplansky 1972). The mapping will *always* leave out values. There is *no* one-to-one correspondence. The cardinality must thus exceed countable infinity! This value is denoted by aleph-1 (pronounced aleph-one).

*Until the late nineteenth century, infinity was infinity and there was only one infinity.* Cantor showed that there are at least two levels of infinity. How much "bigger" is the next level of infinity? How much "larger" is aleph-one than aleph-null? Are there more levels of infinity? Are there an infinite number of levels of infinity? The concepts are mind-boggling.

## Playing with Transfinite Arithmetic

The arithmetic of infinite quantities is called transfinite arithmetic. Transfinite arithmetic follows rules, but the results are often surprising.

Adding a finite number to a countably infinite set gives a countably infinite set. Taking away a finite number from a countably infinite set gives a countably infinite set.

If a set is infinite and a finite number of elements are removed, then the set remains infinite. Therefore, an infinite set need not contain all items in order to remain infinite.

Contrast this with the theological concept of infinity that requires an all-knowing, all-powerful, and all-present deity. The prefix "all" mandates that nothing is excluded. *An infinite deity cannot lose its powers and remain infinite, but an infinite set can lose some of its elements and still be infinite.* (Weird, huh?)

Some authors use the preceding property as an alternative definition of infinity: a set is infinite if some of its elements can be removed with no change in cardinality.

Natural numbers are either even or odd. The parity (oddness or evenness) changes every other term. It seems that half of all natural numbers are even and half are odd. This is a fallacy. It is not always meaningful to speak of the number of numbers in an infinite set.

Why is the statement a fallacy? The set of odd numbers (or set of even numbers) "contains" the same number of elements because they can be placed in one-to-one correspondence with each other and also in one-to-one correspondence with all natural numbers. *Containment has a different meaning in an infinite context.* Many apparent logical contradictions subtly exploit this ambiguity.

This sense of containment offers another definition of the infinity mentioned previously. It is sometimes called the Galileo paradox: an infinite set is a set that is in one-to-one correspondence with a proper subset of itself.

## What Infinity Is Not

Zero is a conventional number. Infinity is an unconventional number. Infinity is not the evil twin of zero, despite the oft-repeated but incorrect assertion that

$$1 / 0 = \text{infinity} \quad \text{(This is inaccurate because it is meaningless)}$$

The justification for this statement is that the value of $1/N$ becomes larger as $N$ becomes smaller. If $N$ becomes "infinitely big," then $1/N$ becomes "infinitely small," hence zero. The empirical observation is correct, but the logic is flawed. Infinity is not a number, and division by zero is undefined. (See any algebra text for details.)

### Using Infinity

The preceding discussion on the nature of infinity has hopefully intrigued the mind and enlightened the soul. An ambiguous concept of infinity is fraught with problematic contradictions. Does infinity actually have an impact on our daily lives?

Physicists, engineers, and researchers use infinity. An infinite Fourier series describes the signals emitted by radio and cell phones. Telephone companies manage message loads knowing that calls are approximated in the infinite limit by a Poisson statistical distribution. Satellite and medical equilibrium are described by infinite limits.

> "Only two things are infinite: The universe and human stupidity.
> And I am not so sure about the former." —Albert Einstein

## EXERCISES AND RESEARCH QUESTIONS

### Exercises: Not Quite Paradoxes

E16.1  Why is the probability of two people sharing *some* birthday different than two people sharing a *specific* birthday?

E16.2  Try the birthday paradox as a means of soliciting two class volunteers. (Announce that the instructor is omniscient and knows that two students have the same birth dates. The matching students are the volunteers.)

*Research Question 16.3*

Speculate why April might be a busy month for obstetricians.

### Exercises: Infinity

*Research Question 16.4*

How many atoms would it take to fill up the known universe? The universe is big but not infinite. Estimate the number using the following values. The universe is a ball whose radius is five billion light years. One light year is six trillion miles. One mile is one and a half kilometers. One kilometer is one thousand meters. One atom is a ball with a radius of $10^{-15}$ meters (a thousand-trillionth of a meter).

APPENDIX A  ▶ Which Librarian
Has the Server?

Information requires a structured framework. The following exercise demonstrates the difficulty of retrieving a simple answer to a simple question with simple rules if the information is not well structured.

*Which librarian has the SERVER?*

| | |
|---|---|
| There are 5 library services: | circulation, youth, reference, media, administration |
| There are 5 foods: | cookies, chips, pretzels, pizza, cake |
| There are 5 desks: | red, blue, green, ivory, yellow |
| There are 5 computers: | laptop, PC clone, Unix, SERVER, dumb terminal |
| There are 5 drinks: | tea, coffee, milk, water, orange juice |

*Here are the clues:*

The reference librarian has a red desk

The media librarian has Unix

Coffee is drunk at the green desk

The youth librarian drinks tea

The green desk is to the right of the ivory desk

The librarian who eats pizza has a dumb terminal

Pretzels are eaten at the yellow desk

Milk is drunk at the middle desk

The circulation librarian works at the first desk on the left

The librarian who eats chips works next to the one with the laptop

Pretzels are eaten at the desk next to the one with the PC clone

The librarian who eats cake also drinks orange juice

The administrative librarian eats cookies

The circulation librarian works next to the blue desk

---

*Note:* There are at least two solutions to the exercise, because one clue is ambiguous. See the "Answers to Selected Exercises" section for the solutions.

# APPENDIX B ▶ The Square Root of Two Is Irrational

The easy proof that follows reveals the power of indirect thinking. It is a proof by contradiction. It also proves a mathematical fact with very little algebra.

Let's assume that the square root of two *is* a rational number. If so, then it can be expressed as the ratio of two natural numbers. Call them A and B. Without loss of generality, assume that the fraction A/B has already been reduced to its lowest terms, so any common factors have already been canceled out.

If A/B = square root of two

Then by definition $(A / B)^2 = 2$

Thus $A^2 = 2B^2$

The right side is divisible by two, so it is even

If the right side is even, then the left side is even

If the left side is even, then A is even

If A is even, then it is two times some number. Call that number C

So $A = 2 \times C$

Substitute back in to get

$(2 \times C)^2 = 2B^2$

This is equivalent to

$4C^2 = 2B^2$

Both sides are divisible by two. Cancel it out, obtaining

$2C^2 = B^2$

The left side is even because it has a factor of two

By the same argument as before, the right side is even, so B is even

Thus A and B are both even

By assumption, A and B have no common factor and cannot both be divisible by two

CONTRADICTION!

The only way to resolve this is by denying the original assumption. Therefore, the square root of two *cannot* be expressed as the ratio between two integer values. It must be an irrational number.

The square root of two can never be calculated exactly. Some numbers can only be approximated.

# APPENDIX C ▶ Who's on First?

The same words at the same time can represent different meanings, and hence different information. Communicating such information often results in chaos (and in this case, humor).

| | |
|---|---|
| ABBOTT: | Well Costello, the team manager gave me a job as coach for as long as you are on the team. |
| COSTELLO: | Look Abbott, if you are the coach, you must know all the players. |
| ABBOTT: | I certainly do. |
| COSTELLO: | Tell me their names and then I'll know who's playing on the team. |
| ABBOTT: | Oh, I'll tell you their names, but you know it seems to me they give these ball players nowadays very peculiar names. |
| COSTELLO: | You mean funny names? |
| ABBOTT: | Well, let's see, we have Who's on first, What's on second, I Don't Know is on third . . . |
| COSTELLO: | That's what I want to find out. |
| ABBOTT: | I say Who's on first, What's on second, I Don't Know's on third. |
| COSTELLO: | Are you the manager? |
| ABBOTT: | Yes. |
| COSTELLO: | And you don't know the fellows' names? |
| ABBOTT: | Well I should. |
| COSTELLO: | Well then who's on first? |
| ABBOTT: | Who. |
| COSTELLO: | The guy on first. |
| ABBOTT: | Who. |
| COSTELLO: | The first baseman. |

---

(Text courtesy of the National Baseball Hall of Fame and Museum, Cooperstown, N.Y.)

ABBOTT:     Who.

COSTELLO:   The guy playing . . .

ABBOTT:     Who is on first!

COSTELLO:   I'm asking you who's on first.

ABBOTT:     That's the man's name.

COSTELLO:   That's who's name?

ABBOTT:     Yes.

COSTELLO:   Well go ahead and tell me.

ABBOTT:     That's it.

COSTELLO:   That's who?

ABBOTT:     Yes.

COSTELLO:   *(Pausing)* Look, you got a first baseman?

ABBOTT:     Certainly.

COSTELLO:   Who's playing first?

ABBOTT:     That's right.

COSTELLO:   When you pay off the first baseman every month, who gets the money?

ABBOTT:     Every dollar of it.

COSTELLO:   All I'm trying to find out is the fellow's name on first base.

ABBOTT:     Who.

COSTELLO:   Who gets the money . . .

ABBOTT:     He does, every dollar of it. Sometimes his wife comes down and collects it.

COSTELLO:   Who's wife?

ABBOTT:     Yes.

ABBOTT:     What's wrong with that?

COSTELLO:   I want to know when you sign up the first baseman, how does he sign his name?

ABBOTT:     Who.

COSTELLO:   The guy.

ABBOTT:     Who.

ABBOTT:     That's how he signs it.

COSTELLO:   Who?

ABBOTT:     Yes.

COSTELLO:   *(Pauses)* All I'm trying to find out is what's the guy's name on first base.

ABBOTT:     No. What is on second base.

| | |
|---|---|
| COSTELLO: | I'm not asking you who's on second. |
| ABBOTT: | Who's on first. |
| COSTELLO: | I'm not changing nobody! |
| ABBOTT: | Take it easy, buddy. |
| COSTELLO: | I'm only asking you, who's the guy on first base? |
| ABBOTT: | That's right. |
| COSTELLO: | OK. |
| ABBOTT: | Alright. |
| COSTELLO: | What's the guy's name on first base? |
| ABBOTT: | No. What is on second. |
| COSTELLO: | I'm not asking you who's on second. |
| ABBOTT: | Who's on first. |
| COSTELLO: | I don't know. |
| ABBOTT: | He's on third, we're not talking about him. |
| COSTELLO: | Now how did I get on third base? |
| ABBOTT: | You mentioned his name! |
| COSTELLO: | If I mentioned the third baseman's name, who did I say is playing third? |
| ABBOTT: | No. Who's playing first. |
| COSTELLO: | What's on first? |
| ABBOTT: | What's on second. |
| COSTELLO: | I don't know. |
| ABBOTT: | He's on third. |
| COSTELLO: | There I go, back on third again! |
| COSTELLO: | Would you just stay on third base and don't go off it. |
| ABBOTT: | Alright, what do you want to know? |
| COSTELLO: | Now who's playing third base? |
| ABBOTT: | Why do you insist on putting Who on third base? |
| COSTELLO: | What am I putting on third? |
| ABBOTT: | No. What is on second. |
| COSTELLO: | You don't want who on second? |
| ABBOTT: | Who is on first. |
| COSTELLO: | I don't know. |
| TOGETHER: | Third base! |
| COSTELLO: | Look, you got a outfield? |
| ABBOTT: | Sure. |

| | |
|---|---|
| COSTELLO: | The left fielder's name? |
| ABBOTT: | Why. |
| COSTELLO: | I just thought I'd ask you. |
| ABBOTT: | Well, I just thought I'd tell you. |
| COSTELLO: | Then tell me who's playing left field. |
| ABBOTT: | Who's playing first. |
| COSTELLO: | Stay out of the infield!!! I want to know what's the guy's name in left field? |
| ABBOTT: | No, What is on second. |
| COSTELLO: | I'm not asking you who's on second. |
| ABBOTT: | Who's on first! |
| COSTELLO: | I don't know. |
| TOGETHER: | Third base! |
| COSTELLO: | The left fielder's name? |
| ABBOTT: | Why. |
| COSTELLO: | Because! |
| ABBOTT: | Oh, he's center field. |
| COSTELLO: | Look, You got a pitcher on this team? |
| ABBOTT: | Sure. |
| COSTELLO: | The pitcher's name? |
| ABBOTT: | Tomorrow. |
| COSTELLO: | You don't want to tell me today? |
| ABBOTT: | I'm telling you now. |
| COSTELLO: | Then go ahead. |
| ABBOTT: | Tomorrow! |
| COSTELLO: | What time? |
| ABBOTT: | What time what? |
| COSTELLO: | What time tomorrow are you gonna tell me who's pitching? |
| ABBOTT: | Now listen. Who is not pitching. |
| COSTELLO: | I'll break your arm if you say who's on first!!! I want to know, what's the pitcher's name? |
| ABBOTT: | What's on second. |
| COSTELLO: | I don't know. |
| TOGETHER: | Third base! |
| COSTELLO: | Got a catcher? |
| ABBOTT: | Certainly. |

| | |
|---|---|
| COSTELLO: | The catcher's name? |
| ABBOTT: | Today. |
| COSTELLO: | Today, and tomorrow's pitching. |
| ABBOTT: | Now you've got it. |
| COSTELLO: | All we got is a couple of days on the team. |
| COSTELLO: | You know I'm a catcher too. |
| ABBOTT: | So they tell me. |
| COSTELLO: | I get behind the plate to do some fancy catching, Tomorrow's pitching on my team and a heavy hitter gets up. Now the heavy hitter bunts the ball. When he bunts the ball, me, being a good catcher, I'm gonna throw the guy out at first. So I pick up the ball and throw it to who? |
| ABBOTT: | Now that's the first thing you've said right. |
| COSTELLO: | I don't even know what I'm talking about! |
| ABBOTT: | That's all you have to do. |
| COSTELLO: | Is to throw the ball to first base. |
| ABBOTT: | Yes! |
| COSTELLO: | Now who's got it? |
| ABBOTT: | Naturally. |
| COSTELLO: | Look, if I throw the ball to first base, somebody's got to get it. Now who has it? |
| ABBOTT: | Naturally. |
| COSTELLO: | Who? |
| ABBOTT: | Naturally. |
| COSTELLO: | Naturally? |
| ABBOTT: | Naturally. |
| COSTELLO: | So I pick up the ball and I throw it to Naturally. |
| ABBOTT: | No you don't, you throw the ball to Who. |
| COSTELLO: | Naturally. |
| ABBOTT: | That's different. |
| COSTELLO: | That's what I said. |
| ABBOTT: | You're not saying it . . . |
| COSTELLO: | I throw the ball to Naturally. |
| ABBOTT: | You throw it to Who. |
| COSTELLO: | Naturally. |
| ABBOTT: | That's it. |

| | |
|---|---|
| COSTELLO: | That's what I said! |
| ABBOTT: | You ask me. |
| COSTELLO: | I throw the ball to who? |
| ABBOTT: | Naturally. |
| COSTELLO: | Now you ask me. |
| ABBOTT: | You throw the ball to Who? |
| COSTELLO: | Naturally. |
| ABBOTT: | That's it. |
| COSTELLO: | I throw the ball to Who.<br>Whoever it is drops the ball and the guy runs to second.<br>Who picks up the ball and throws it to What.<br>What throws it to I Don't Know.<br>I Don't Know throws it back to Tomorrow, triple play.<br>Another guy gets up and hits a long fly ball to Because.<br>Why? I don't know!<br>He's on third and I don't give a darn! |
| ABBOTT: | What? |
| COSTELLO: | I said, I don't give a darn! |
| ABBOTT: | Oh, that's our shortstop . . . |

# ▶ Answers to Selected Exercises

## Chapter 1

E1.1 A tree is an information system because it provides information on how all trees interact with their environment or how trees differ from one another. A museum is an information system because it provides information on the context, function, significance, or meaning of objects.

E1.2 A person is an information system because he or she provides information on how people interact with their environment or how people differ from each other.

E1.3 Not really. The meanings of the phrases are important, not the fidelity transmission of their signals.

E1.4 Read the sentence as: Show that *one word* can be formed from the letters OEDONWR. (Rearrange the letters to form ONE WORD.)

E1.5  hiccough  thOUGH  PTomaine  nEIghbor  deBT  burEAU
            P      O      T         A      T      O

## Chapter 2

E2.1 The word INFORMATION contains:

| | | | | | |
|---|---|---|---|---|---|
| inform | formation | riot | roof | moan | train |
| form | matron | fiat | morn | foam | rain |
| nation | moor | fort | torn | roam | main |
| atom | room | rant | font | mint | faint |
| trim | tram | iron | moat | moot | format |
| from | trio | firm | fair | motion | front |

E2.2

$$
\begin{array}{rl}
61 & \text{L X I} \\
+\ 39 & \text{XX X  IX} \\
\hline
100 & \text{(LXX) (XXX)}
\end{array}
$$

E2.3a   Proof 1: The seven must be placed in the tens column, not the units column. Proof 2: Carry just the value of two to the tens column, not the full value twenty-one.

E2.4   An even number is divisible by two (remainder of zero). An odd number is not divisible by two (remainder of one).

E2.10   If each square increases by sixteen times, then there are more than one million grains by the sixth square.

## Chapter 3

E3.1   One CD-ROM contains 800 megabytes

> $= 800 \times 1,024 \times 1,024 \times 8$ bits
>
> $= 6.7$ billion bits (approximately)
>
> 200 billion bits per brain / 6.7 billion bits per CD $= 29.8$ CDs

A complete brain dump could be accomplished by thirty CDs (rather humbling . . .)

E3.3   Lee and Robert are first cousins.

E3.4   Aaron and Evan are first cousins.

E3.5   Viewing 200 million pages

> divided by 1 page per second
>
> divided by (60 seconds per minute $\times$ 60 minutes per hour)
>
> divided by (16 hours per day $\times$ 5 days per week $\times$ 52 weeks per year)

requires 13.35 years (assuming the Web has not grown in the meantime!).

E3.6   Calendar, dictionary, telephone directory, radio station display, newspaper sections, television station program guide, restaurant menu, television station display, house numbers.

## Chapter 4

E4.1   None. Moses did not have the Ark. Noah did.

E4.2   None. The president cannot declare war. Only Congress can declare war (United States Constitution, article 1, section 8).

E4.3   The lion. A lion that has not eaten in three months is dead.

E4.4    Any current former president who is still living.

E4.5    The gender subsets are mutually exclusive because no one is in both the male and female set at the same time. The hair/eye coloring sets are not mutually exclusive because eye color is (usually) independent of hair color. A person with any color eyes may have any color hair.

E4.8    A OR {B AND C} contains {circulation, administration, youth, music}.
{A OR B} AND C contains just {music}.

The two query expressions are not the same.

## Chapter 6

E6.2    The sixth position has twenty-six cases, as does the seventh. The number of possibilities is $26 \times 26 = 676$.

E6.4    These strings of characters are lines along the keyboard in plain sight.

## Chapter 7

E7.1    Dots and dashes replace letters. It is a cipher, not a code.

E7.2    The Roman alphabet contains 26 letters. A Rot-13 encryption shifts a letter 13 letters down the alphabet. Applying it a second time shifts the letter another 13 letters back to its original position.

E7.3    The text of the first verse in the poem "Jabberwocky" reads:

Twas brillig, and the slithy toves

Did gyre and gimble in the wabe:

All mimsy were the borogroves,

And the mome raths outgrabe.

E7.4    The common letter E is entirely absent!

E7.5    The following guidelines are useful:

There are three single-letter words (A, I, O).

Contractions typically end in S or T, the latter often preceded by N.

The most frequently used letters are {E, T, A, I, S, O, N, H, R, D, U} (varies with text).

A repeated vowel may be {ee, oo, uu}.

A repeated consonant may be {bb, dd, ff, gg, kk, ll, mm, nn, pp, rr, ss, tt}.

THE is a common three-letter word that begins a sentence.

The letter U always follows Q.

Two-letter words are either vowel-consonant or consonant-vowel.

Common plurals end in S or ES.

"I before E except after C" or when sounded like "A," as in neighbor and weigh (but weird is weird).

E7.6    $100 = 2 \times 2 \times 5 \times 5$    $30,030 = 2 \times 3 \times 5 \times 7 \times 11 \times 13$
Factoring is easy for small numbers but difficult for large numbers.


## Chapter 8

E8.1    Assuming a simple version of Lotka's law applies, then one-fourth of the authors will have two papers, one-ninth will have three papers, one-sixteenth will have four papers, and one twenty-fifth will have five papers. One thousand divided by 25 is 40, so 40 authors will have five papers.

E8.12    Multiple people could be using the same computer over different times. The same IP address would register in each case. If the local network were running dynamic host control protocol (DHCP), then different computers could use the same IP address at different times. In either case, there is no specific connection between web use and IP address for any individual.

E8.13    A patron could write a script that continually accesses the same website, thus artificially raising its hit rate. One web author could arrange (conspire?) with another to each refer to the other's site more than a normal number of times. A person might have a poor connection and access the site multiple times, but only because the connection is not stable.


## Chapter 9

E9.1

|  |  |
|---|---|
| Three | 3 beads up |
| Thirteen | 1 bead up (tens column) and 3 beads up (units column) |
| Thirty-three | 3 beads up (tens column) and 3 beads up (units column) |

E9.3    The process of subtracting 10 and adding 1 involves only one bead motion in the tens and units columns, respectively (total of two bead moves). Subtracting 9 involves nine bead moves.

E9.4    Beads will move differently along the abacus depending on how the operator pairs off numerical values. Only the final position of the beads matters.

E9.6    Appending the length of one rule to another models addition, but only if both use the same scale.

E9.7    Not enough friction could result in slippage and reading the wrong values!

E9.10 Casting out nines

| Numbers | | Digit Sums |
|---|---|---|
| 123 | → | 6 |
| 456 | → | 6 |
| 579 | → | 12 |
| 12 | → | 12 |

Casting out nines

| Numbers | | Digit Sums |
|---|---|---|
| 135 | → | 0 |
| 284 | → | 14 |
| 418 | → | 14 |
| 4 | → | 5 |

E9.14 Russian peasant algorithm applied to $16 \times 7 = 112$

| Bowls (column 1) | Bowls (column 2) | |
|---|---|---|
| 16 | 7 | |
| 32 | 3 | |
| 64 | 1 | Stop! |
| 112 | | |

E9.15 Russian peasant algorithm applied to $16 \times 256 = 4{,}096$

| Bowls (column 1) | Bowls (column 2) | |
|---|---|---|
| 16 | 256 | even values, cross off and ignore |
| 32 | 128 | same |
| 64 | 64 | same |
| 128 | 32 | same |
| 256 | 16 | same |
| 512 | 8 | same |
| 1,024 | 4 | same |
| 2,048 | 2 | same |
| 4,096 | 1 | Stop! |
| 4,096 | | |

E9.17 Forty-two is represented by left pinky finger (40) and right index finger (2).

E9.18 The maximum value for the standard form is $90 + 9 = 99$.

E9.38 There are $2^{32} - 1 = 4{,}294{,}967{,}295$ movements. It depends on how long each movement takes!

E9.39 Three digits, six arrangements: 3-1-4  3-4-1  1-3-4

1-4-3  4-1-3  4-3-1

E9.40 Suppose there are 1,000 possible values in a game, and each game is independent of the others. If you buy 100 tickets for a game, then the odds of winning are $100/1{,}000 = 1{:}10$. If you buy 100 tickets and apply each one once to a separate game, then the odds of winning each game are 1,000 to 1, since each game is independent of the others.

## Chapter 10

E10.1   Every even number is divisible by two and hence not prime, except for the first.

E10.5   The number is 28. The divisors of 28 are 1, 2, 4, 7, and 14, which add to 28.

## Chapter 12

E12.1   One thousand kilobytes are less than one hundred megabytes, which are less than one gigabyte, which is less than one-tenth of a terabyte. Do not let the small coefficients fool you!

E12.2   According to legend, Helen of Troy was the woman whose face launched a thousand ships. One milli-helen (one-thousandth of a helen) must therefore be the amount of beauty necessary to launch one ship.

## Chapter 13

E13.2   The *ping* command checks connectivity but does not alter any values.

E13.3   If an information system application or client expects to find its server at a specific address and the address changes, then the server might not be found!

E13.5   The IP address (130.219.23.100) is legitimate. The others contain a value exceeding 255 and are hence out of range.

## Chapter 14

E14.3   One octave above doubles, so the value is 880. One octave below halves, so the value is 220.

E14.5   Symphony, concerto, oratorio, fugue, march, waltz, string quartet, minuet, overture, opera.

E14.6   Sound travels at approximately one-fifth of a mile per second. Dividing the time value by five gives the approximate distance in miles.

E14.7   A piano is considered a percussion instrument.

E14.13  There are six different ways to roll a seven using two dice. There is only one way to roll a two or a twelve.

## Chapter 16

E16.1   Matching a specific birthday involves a fixed date. Matching *some* birthday offers flexibility.

### Solution: Which Librarian Has the Server?

*Solution 1* (most common)

| Circulation | Youth | Reference | Media | Administration |
|---|---|---|---|---|
| pretzels | chips | pizza | cake | cookies |
| yellow | blue | red | ivory | green |
| laptop | clone | dumb terminal | Unix | SERVER |
| water | tea | milk | juice | coffee |

*Solution 2* (discovered by Jill Ratzan, September 2000)

A second solution is possible because "The green desk is to the right of the ivory desk" is ambiguous. Most people automatically assume that the green desk is to the *immediate* right of the ivory desk, but this need not be the case.

| Circulation | Media | Reference | Administration | Youth |
|---|---|---|---|---|
| cake | chips | pizza | cookies | pretzels |
| ivory | blue | red | green | yellow |
| laptop | Unix | dumb terminal | clone | SERVER |
| juice | water | milk | coffee | tea |

# ▶ *References*

Abell, George. 1969. *Exploration of the Universe.* 2d ed. New York: Holt, Reinhart and Winston.

Adair, Robert. 1994. *The Physics of Baseball.* 2d ed. New York: Harper Perennial.

Albert, Jim. 1994. "Exploring Baseball Hitting Data: What about Those Breakdown Statistics?" *Journal of the American Statistical Association* 89:1066–74. Available at www. math.bgsu.edu/~albert/papers/saber. html. Accessed 14 December 2002.

Alemanni, Jean-Bernard. 2002. Private communication. At jean-bernard. alemanni@wanadoo.fr.

Allen, Julia. 2001. *The CERT Guide to System and Network Security Practices.* New York: Addison-Wesley.

Anderson, Roy Allan. 1974. *Unfolding the Revelation.* Ontario: Pacific.

Bailey, Nathan. 1964. *The Elements of Stochastic Processes with Applications to the Natural Sciences.* New York: John Wiley and Sons.

Barbour, J. M. 1953. *Tuning and Temperament.* East Lansing: Michigan State College Press.

Baring-Gould, William. 1967. *The Lure of the Limerick.* New York: C. N. Potter (distributed by Crown Publishers).

Baxter, S. R. 1969. "To Prove That the Thirteenth Day of the Month Is More Likely to Be a Friday Than Any Other Day of the Week." *Mathematical Gazette* 3:127–29, 383.

Bechenbach, Edwin. 1945. "Interesting Integers." *American Mathematical Monthly* 52 (April): 211.

Beckman, Peter. 1971. *A Short History of Pi.* New York: Barnes and Noble.

Belkin, Nicholas. 1978. "Information Concepts of Information Science." *Journal of Documentation* 34, no. 1 (March): 55–85.

Belkin, Nicholas, and Bruce Croft. 1987. "Retrieval Techniques." *Annual Review of Information Science and Technology* 22:109–47.

Bellman, Richard, and M. Giertz. 1973. "On the Analytic Formalism of the Theory of Fuzzy Sets." *Information Sciences* 5:149–56.

Bennett, J., and J. Flueck. 1984. "Player Game Percentage." *Proceedings of the 1984 Social Sciences Section, American Statistical Association.*

Bergamini, David, and the Editors of *Life.* 1963. *Mathematics.* New York: Time Incorporated.

237

Berkowitz, Rose, and Howard Berkowitz. 2000. Private communication. At rmberkowitz@att.net.

Bernstein, Leonard. *The Joy of Music.* 1967. New York: New American Library.

Blair, D., and M. Maron. 1985. "An Evaluation of Retrieval Effectiveness for a Full-Text Document Retrieval System." *Communications of the ACM* 28, no. 3:289–99.

Bogle, Dave. 2001. "The Hands of Poker." Available at www.bogle-dw.freeserve.co.uk/mtpk01.htm. Accessed 14 December 2002.

Bontempo, Charles. 1987. *Introduction to Database Management: Lecture Notes.* Atlanta: Association for Media-Based Continuing Education for Engineers.

Bookstein, Abraham. 1980. "Fuzzy Requests." *Journal of the American Society for Information Science* 31, no. 14:240–47.

———. 1985. "Probability and Fuzzy Set Applications to Information Retrieval." *Annual Review of Information Science and Technology* 20:117–54.

Booth, A. 1969. "On the Geometry of Libraries." *Journal of Documentation* 25, no. 1 (March): 113–19.

Brooks, Michael. 2000. "Fooled Again." *New Scientist* 168, no. 2268 (9 December): 24.

Buckland, Michael. 1991. *Information and Information Systems.* New York: Praeger.

Budd, Richard, and Brent Ruben. 1972. *Approaches to Human Communication.* New York: Spartan.

———. 1979. *Beyond Media: New Approaches to Mass Communication.* New Brunswick: Transaction.

———, eds. 1979. *Interdisciplinary Approaches to Human Communication.* Rochelle Park: Hayden.

Bukiet, Bruce, Elliot Harold, and Jose Palacios. 1997. "A Markov Chain Approach to Baseball." *Operations Research* 45, no. 1 (January): 14–23.

Bush, Vannevar. 1945. "As We May Think." *Atlantic Monthly* 176:101–7.

Byrd, D., and Tim Crawford. 2002. "Problems of Music Information Retrieval in the Real World." *Information Processing and Management* 38, no. 2 (March): 249–72.

CENDI. At www.dtic.mil/cendi. Accessed 14 December 2002.

Clarke, Arthur C. 1987. "The Nine Billion Names of God." In *The Nine Billion Names of God.* New York: New American Library.

Cleverdon, C. 1972. "On the Inverse Relationship between Recall and Precision." *Journal of Documentation* 28, no. 3 (September): 195–201.

———. 1974. "User Evaluation of Information Retrieval Systems." *Journal of Documentation* 30, no. 2 (June): 170–80.

Cohl, Aaron, ed. 1997. *The Friars Club Encyclopedia of Jokes.* New York: Black Dog and Leventhal.

Cooper, W. 1973. "On Selecting a Measure of Retrieval Effectiveness," pts. 1 and 2. *Journal of the*

*American Society for Information Science* 24, no. 2:87–100, 413–24.

Crume, Jeff. 2000. *Inside Internet Security.* New York: Addison-Wesley.

Date, C. 1986. *An Introduction to Database Systems.* 4th ed. New York: Addison-Wesley.

Dearing, Bill. 2002. "Lineup Construction for Maximum Run Production." Available at www.geocities. com/statplanetweekly/170.html. Accessed 14 December 2002.

Dehaene, Stanislas. 1997. *The Number Sense.* New York: Oxford University Press.

Dickson, Leonard Eugene. 1957. *Introduction to the Theory of Numbers.* New York: Dover.

Doyle, Sir Arthur Conan. 1997. *The Adventure of the Dancing Men and Other Sherlock Holmes Stories.* New York: Dover.

Dreyfus, Harold. 1972. *What Computers Can't Do.* New York: Harper and Row.

Drosnin, Michael. 1997. *The Bible Code.* New York: Simon and Schuster.

Eves, Howard. 1976. *An Introduction to the History of Mathematics.* New York: Holt, Reinhart and Winston.

Farley, Peter. 2003. "Musical Roots May Be in the Human Voice." Available at www.newscientist.com (6 August 2003).

Fekete, Irene, and Jasmine Denyer. 1984. *Mathematics.* London: Orbis.

Feller, William. 1968. *An Introduction to Probability Theory and Its Applications.* Vol. 1. 3d ed. New York: John Wiley and Sons.

*Fibonacci Quarterly.* Department of Mathematics and Computer Science, Central Missouri State University, Warrensburg, Missouri.

Fleming, Ian. 1962. *Dr. No.* New York: New American Library.

Fogwall, Niclas. 2001. Available at www.af.lu.se/~fogwall/notation.html and niclas@fogwall.com. Accessed 14 December 2002.

Freeze, R. 1974. "An Analysis of Baseball Hitting Order by Monte Carlo Simulation." *Operations Research* 22:728–35.

Friends of Pi. Vienna, Austria. At 3.14159@astro.univie.ac.at. Available at www.astro.univie. ac.at/~wasi,PI/pi_club.html. Accessed 14 December 2002.

Galton, F., and H. Watson. 1874. "On the Probability of the Extinction of Families." *Royal Anthropological Institute* 4:138–44. Also in Smith, David, and Nathan Keyfitz. 1977. *Mathematical Demography: Selected Papers.* New York: Springer.

Gardner, Martin. 1977. "A New Kind of Cipher That Would Take Millions of Years to Break." *Scientific American,* August.

———. 1982. *Gotcha!* New York: W. H. Freeman.

———. 1988. *Time Travel and Other Mathematical Bewilderments.* New York: W. H. Freeman.

Gephart, John. 2002. "The Useless Pages." Available at www.go2net. com/useless/useless/pi.html. Accessed 14 December 2002.

Goodman, A., and J. Ratti. 1971. *Finite Mathematics with Applications.* New York: Macmillan.

Greenberg, Robert. 2002. *How to Listen to and Understand Great Music.* Courseno. 700. The Teaching Company. Available at www.teach12.com. Accessed 14 December 2002.

Grosswald, Emil. 1966. *Topics from the Theory of Numbers.* New York: Macmillan.

*Guide, The.* 2002. New Jersey Public Television. August, 3.

*Guinness Book of World Records 2002.* 2002. Barcelona: Guinness World Records.

Hall, Rachael, and Kresimir Josic. 2000. "The Mathematics of Musical Instruments." Available at www.sju.edu/~rhall/newton/mathandmusic.pdf. Accessed 14 December 2002.

Hardy, G. H., and E. M. Wright. 1960. *An Introduction to the Theory of Numbers.* 4th ed. New York: Oxford University Press.

Hayes, Brian. 2002. "Eureka." *The Sciences,* November/December.

Hoos, H., K. Renz, and M. Gorg. 2001. "GUIDO/MIR: An Experimental Musical Information Retrieval System Based on GUIDO Notation." Presentation at the Second Annual International Symposium on Music Information Retrieval 2001. Indiana University, Bloomington, Ind., 15–17 October. Available at ismir2001.indiana.edu/papers.html. Accessed 14 December 2002.

James, Bill. 1982–88. *The Bill James Baseball Abstract.* New York: Ballantine.

Joeckel, Carleton. 1935. *The Government of the American Public Library.* Chicago: University of Chicago Press.

Joeckel, Carleton, and Amy Winslow. 1948. *A National Plan for Public Library Service.* Chicago: American Library Association.

Johnson-Laird, P., et al. 2000. "Illusions in Reasonings about Consistency." *Science* 288 (21 April): 531–32.

Joyner, David, ed. 2000. *Coding Theory and Cryptography.* New York: Springer.

Kahn, David. 1983. *Kahn on Codes.* New York: Macmillan.

Kaplan, Robert. 1999. *The Nothing That Is.* New York: Oxford University Press.

Kaplansky, Irving. 1972. *Set Theory and Metric Spaces.* Boston: Allyn and Bacon.

Kasner, Edward, and James Roy Newman. 1940. *Mathematics and the Imagination.* New York: Dover.

Kaufman, James, and Alan Kaufman. 1993. *The Worst Baseball Pitchers of All Time.* Jefferson: McFarland.

Kent, A., et al. 1954. "Machine Literature Searching," pt. 6. *American Documentation* 5:238–44.

———. 1955. "Machine Literature Searching," pt. 8. *American Documentation* 6:93–101.

Keyfitz, Nathan. 1968. *Introduction to the Mathematics of Population.* Reading: Addison-Wesley.

———. 1977. *Applied Mathematical Demography.* New York: John Wiley and Sons.

Kleber, Michael. 2002. "The Best Card Trick." *Mathematical Intelligencer* 24, no. 1 (winter).

Knott, R. 2001. "Fibonacci Numbers and Nature." Available at www.mcs.surrey.ac.uk/Personnel/R.Knott/Fibonacci/fibnat.html. Accessed 14 December 2002.

Knuth, Donald. 1973. *The Art of Computer Programming*. Vol. 3, *Sorting and Searching*. Boston: Addison-Wesley.

Kolodzie, Will. 2002. "Building the Best Lineup." Available at www.sportplanet.com/som/articles/kolo32.htm. Accessed 14 December 2002.

Korzybski, Alfred. 1958. *Science and Sanity: An Introduction to Non-Aristotelian Systems and General Semantics*. Lakeville: Non-Aristotelian Library Publishing.

Kraft, D., and D. Buell. 1983. "Fuzzy Sets and Generalized Boolean Information Retrieval Systems." *International Journal of Man-Machine Studies* 19:45–56.

Lancaster, F. Wilfrid. 1979. *Information Retrieval Systems: Characteristics, Testing and Evaluation*. New York: John Wiley and Sons.

Lee, W. 1950. *Math Miracles*. Durham: Seeman Printery.

Lehrer, Tom. 1965. "New Math." In *That Was the Year That Was*. Audio recording. Reprise Records. Lyrics available at www.emba.uvm.edu/~mdebowsk/newmath.html. Accessed 14 December 2002.

Lieberthal, Edwin. 1983. *The Complete Book of Fingermath*. New York: McGraw-Hill.

Lindsey, G. 1963. "An Investigation of Strategies in Baseball." *Operations Research* 11:447–501.

Livio, Mario. 2002. *The Golden Ratio: The Story of Phi, the World's Most Astonishing Number*. New York: Broadway.

Lubotsky, Alex. 1997. Review of *The Bible Code*, by Michael Drosnin. Available at cs.anu.edu.au/~bdm/dilugim/opinions/lubotsky.html. Accessed 14 December 2002.

Machlup, Fritz. 1980. *Knowledge: Its Creation, Distribution and Economic Significance*. Princeton: Princeton University Press.

———. 1980. *Knowledge and Knowledge Production*. Princeton: Princeton University Press.

———, ed. 1983. "Semantic Quirks in the Study of Information." In *The Study of Information*. New York: John Wiley and Sons.

Machlup, Fritz, and Una Mansfield. 1983. *The Study of Information: Interdisciplinary Messages*. New York: John Wiley and Sons.

Machover, Maurice. 2002. Fermat's Last Theorem Poetry Contest. St. John's University, New York. Available at raphael.math.uic.edu/~jeremy/poetry.htm. Accessed 14 December 2002.

*Masters of the Universe*. 1987. Motion picture. Cannon Films. Directed by Gary Goddard.

McLeish, John. 1991. *Number*. New York: Fawcett.

Mertz, David. 2000. "A Data Compression Primer." Gnosis Software, April. Available at www.gnosis.cx/publish/programming/compression_primer.html. Accessed 14 December 2002.

Meyer, Jerome. 1958. *Fun with Mathematics.* New York: Crest.

Microsoft Corporation. 2000. "Cryptography and PKI Basics." Available at www.microsoft.com. Accessed 14 December 2002.

———. 2000. "Cryptography for Network and Information Security." Chap. 14 in *Microsoft Windows 2000 Server Distributed Systems Guide.* Redmond, Wash.: Microsoft. Also available at www.microsoft. com. Accessed 14 December 2002.

———. 2000. *Microsoft Windows 2000 Network and Operating System Essentials.* Redmond, Wash.: Microsoft.

Morrison, Phillip, et al. 1982. *Powers of Ten: About the Relative Sizes of Things in the Universe.* New York: Scientific American.

Muir, Hazel. 2003. "Software to Unzip Identity of Unknown Composers." Available at www.newscientist.com. Accessed 9 July 2003.

New Jersey Lottery Commission. Available at www.njlottery.net. Accessed 14 December 2002.

Newman, James R. 1956. *The World of Mathematics.* Vols. 1–4. 9th ed. New York: Simon and Schuster.

Niven, Ivan, and Herbert Zuckerman. 1966. *An Introduction to the Theory of Numbers.* New York: John Wiley and Sons.

O'Connor, Daniel. 1990. "Public Libraries as a Right of Citizens." In *Library Education and Leadership: Essays in Honor of Jane Anne Hannigan,* edited by Sheila Intner and Kay E. Vandergrift. Metuchen, N.J.: Scarecrow.

Olson, Harry. 1967. *Music, Physics and Engineering.* 2d ed. New York: Dover.

Orr, A. C. 1906. Poem. *Literary Digest* 32:84.

Palmquist, Ruth. 2002. "Bibliometrics." Course notes. Available at www. gslis.utexas.edu/~palmquist/courses/ biblio.html. Accessed 14 December 2002.

Parsons, Denys. 1975. *Dictionary of Tunes and Musical Themes.* Cambridge, Eng.: C. Brown.

Paulos, John Allen. 1998. *Once Upon a Number: The Hidden Mathematical Logic of Stories.* New York: Basic Books.

Penniman, W. David. 1988. Private communication. At penniman@ buffalo.edu.

*Pi.* 1998. Motion picture. Artisan Entertainment. Directed by David Aronofsky.

Poe, Edgar Allan. 1965. "The Gold Bug." In *Eighteen Best Stories by Edgar Allan Poe.* New York: Doubleday.

Potok, Chaim. 1967. *The Chosen.* New York: Simon and Schuster.

Potter, William Gray. 1988. "Of Making Many Books There Is No End: Bibliometrics and Libraries." *Journal of Academic Librarianship* 14 (September): 238a–c.

Ratzan, Lee. 1975. "The Astrology of the Delivery Room." *The Humanist,* November/December, 27.

———. 1977. "Some Mathematics of the Electoral College." Hearings before the Subcommittee on the Constitution of the Senate

Committee on the Judiciary. *The Electoral College and Direct Election of the President and Vice President,* 95th Cong., 1st sess., 1977. Washington, D.C.: U.S. Government Printing Office.

———. 1991. "Some Novel Non-Traditional Measures of Library Effectiveness." *Unabashed Librarian* 79:15–16.

———. 1992. "Fatal Retraction." *Wilson Library Bulletin* 66, no. 7 (March): 30.

———. 1993. "L'Homme Moyen (The Canonical Man)." *Chance* 6, no. 2:15.

———. 1995. "Just a Two-Bit Genie." *Wilson Library Bulletin* 69, no. 8 (April): 48. Available at www2. umdnj.edu/~ratzan/genie.html. Accessed 14 December 2002.

———. 2000. "I Know Why the Computer Hums." *Byte Magazine,* 29 March. Available at www. byte.com. Accessed 14 December 2002.

———. 2000. "Making Sense of the Web: A Metaphorical Approach." *Information Research* 6, no. 1 (October). Available at http:// informationr.net/ir/6-1/paper85.html. Accessed 14 December 2002.

———. 2000. "Two Digits." *Byte Magazine,* 20 August. Available at www.byte.com. Accessed 14 December 2002.

———. 2001. "Network Jumping Leaves No Trail." *Linux Journal,* 14 February. Available at www. linuxjournal.com. Accessed 14 December 2002.

———. 2001. "While True Do." *Unix Review,* 1 July. Available at www. unixreview.com. Accessed 14 December 2002.

Roberts, D., and M. Roberts. 1983. "Surnames and Relationships: An Orkney Study." *Human Biology* 55:341–47.

Robertson, S. 1978. "On the Nature of Fuzz: A Diatribe." *Journal of the American Society for Information Science* 29, no. 6:305–6.

Rowling, J. K. 1997. *Harry Potter and the Sorcerer's Stone.* New York: Scholastic.

Ruben, Brent. 1988. *Communication and Information Behavior.* New York: Prentice-Hall.

Sagan, Carl. 1975. *Other Worlds.* New York: Bantam.

Sage, Andrew, ed. 1990. *Concise Encyclopedia of Information Processing in Systems and Organizations.* New York: Pergamon.

Salton, Gerald. 1986. "Another Look at Automatic Text Retrieval Systems." *Communications of the ACM* 29, no. 7:648–56.

———. 1987. "Historical Note: The Past Thirty Years in Information Retrieval." *Journal of the American Society for Information Science* 38, no. 5:375–80.

Saracevic, Tefko. 1971. "Selected Results from an Inquiry into Testing of Information Retrieval Systems." *Journal of the American Society for Information Science* 22, no. 2:126–39.

———. 1975. "Relevance: A Review." *Journal of the American Society for Information Science* 26, no. 6:321–43.

Scheifler, Michael. 2002. "666: The Number of the Beast." Available at www.aloha.net/~mikesch/666.htm. Accessed 14 December 2002.

Schickele, Peter. 2002. *Schickele Mix.* Public Radio International. Available at www.schickele.com. Accessed 14 December 2002.

Schiffman, Mike. 2001. *Hacker's Challenge.* Berkeley: Osborne.

Schneider, Harold. 2002. Private communication. At hjq50@aol.com.

Scott, Norman. 1985. *Computer Number Systems and Arithmetic.* Englewood Cliffs, N.J.: Prentice-Hall.

Shannon, Claude. 1950. "Programming a Computer for Playing Chess." *Philosophical Magazine* 41:256–75.

Shannon, Claude, and Warren Weaver. 1948. *The Mathematical Theory of Communication.* Chicago: University of Illinois Press.

Simonson, Shai, and Tara Holm. 2002. "A Combinatorial Card Trick." Available at shai@stonehill.edu and tsh@mit.edu. Accessed 14 December 2002.

Singh, Simon. 1999. *The Code Book.* New York: Doubleday.

Smiraglia, Richard. 2001. "Musical Works as Information Retrieval Entities: Epistemological Perspectives." Presentation at the Second Annual International Symposium on Music Information Retrieval 2001. Indiana University, Bloomington, Ind., 15–17 October. Available at ismir2001.indiana.edu/papers.html. Accessed 14 December 2002.

Smith, Daniel, and Nathan Keyfitz. 1977. *Mathematical Demography.* New York: Springer.

Society for American Baseball Research. At www.sabr.org. Accessed 14 December 2002.

Society for the Preservation and Encouragement of Barbershop Quartet Singing in America. Available at www.spebsqsa.org. Accessed 14 December 2002.

Spalding, George. 2000. *Windows 2000 Administration.* New York: Osborne/McGraw-Hill.

Stallings, William. 1985. *Communication Networks.* Atlanta: Association for Media-Based Continuing Education for Engineers.

———. 1985. *Fundamentals of Data Communication: Study Guide.* Atlanta: Association for Media-Based Continuing Education for Engineers.

———. 1988. *Data and Computer Communication.* 2d ed. New York: Macmillan.

State of New Jersey. 1879. *Laws of New Jersey, 1879: Acts of the One Hundred and Third Legislature of the State of New Jersey and Thirty Fifth under the New Constitution.* Morristown, N.J.: Vance and Stiles. Chap. 163, pp. 262–65.

Stefik, Mark. 1997. *Internet Dreams: Archetypes, Myths and Metaphors.* Cambridge, Mass.: MIT Press.

Steig, William. 1968. *CDB!* New York: Windmill Paperbacks.

———. 1984. *CDC?* New York: Farrar, Straus and Giroux.

Stewart, Ian. 1971. "The Number of Possible Games of Chess." *Journal of Recreational Mathematics* 4, no. 1 (January): 50.

Stoll, Clifford. 1989. *The Cuckoo's Egg: Tracking a Spy through the Maze of Computer Espionage.* New York: Doubleday.

———. 1995. *Silicon Snake Oil: Other Thoughts on the Information Super-highway.* New York: Doubleday.

Swanson, D. 1977. "Information Retrieval as a Trial and Error Process." *Library Quarterly* 47, no. 2:128–49.

———. 1988. "Historical Note: Information Retrieval and the Future of an Illusion." *Journal of the American Society for Information Science* 39, no. 2:92–98.

Tenuta, Gary. 1997. "Alphanumeric Patterns Discovered within the English Alphabet." Available at members.aol.com/ccodeufo/gematria-l.html. Accessed 14 December 2002.

Thorn, J., and P. Palmer. 1993. *Total Baseball.* New York: HarperCollins.

Tobin, Jacqueline. 1999. *Hidden in Plain View: The Secret Story of Quilts and the Underground Railroad.* New York: Doubleday.

Tomes, Ray. 2002. At www.tardyon.de/mirror/tomes/alex-ha.htm and rtomes@kcbbs.gen.nz. Accessed 30 December 2002.

Trappe, Wade, and Lawrence Washington. 2002. *Introduction to Cryptography with Coding Theory.* Upper Saddle River, N.J.: Prentice-Hall.

Tyler, Chris. 2002. "Ratios and Cents." Available at www.ppexpressivo.wyenet.co.uk. Accessed 14 December 2002.

UNESCO. 1989. "Recommendation on the Safeguarding of Traditional Culture and Folklore." Available at www.unesco.org/webworld/com/compendium/5414.html. Accessed 14 December 2002.

Verne, Jules. 1965. *A Journey to the Center of the Earth.* New York: Airmont.

Voos, Henry. 1974. "Lotka and Information Science." *Journal of the American Society for Information Science* 25, no. 4:270–73.

Wagon, Stan. 1985. "Is Pi Normal?" *Mathematical Intelligencer* 7:65–67. Available at www.astro.univie.ac.at/~wasi/PI/pi_normal.html. Accessed 14 December 2002.

Wallechinsky, David, and Irving Wallace. 1975. *The People's Almanac.* New York: Doubleday.

Wilson, Meredith. 1962. Song lyrics. "Ya Got Trouble," from *The Music Man.*

Witztum, Doron, Eliyahu Rips, and Yoav Rosenberg. 1994. "Equidistant Letter Sequences in the Book of Genesis." *Statistical Science* 9, no. 3:429–38.

Young, Neville. 1973. *A Complete Slide Rule Manual.* New York: Drake.

Zadeh, Lofti. 1965. "Fuzzy Sets." *Information and Control* 8:338–53.

Zhang, Qian. 2002. "Last Glimpse of a Disappearing Tradesman." *Shanghai Star,* 1 March.

# ► *Index*

666 in numerology, 203–5

**A**
abacus, 14, 105–7
Abbott and Costello
    aging sweethearts paradox, 211
    "Who's on First?" routine, 10, 222–27
abbreviation compression, 159
"about-ness" in music, 190–91
abstracts, musical, 193–94
"access denied" errors, 160
access rights to data, 63. *See also* Authentication
    of access
access to information, right of, 174–75
Achilles and the tortoise, 209–10
adaptive systems, 1
addressing schemes, 165–68
Adelman, Leonard, 85, 86–87
ad-hoc sort, 35
agendas, hidden, 154
aging sweethearts paradox, 211
all-and-only problem
    music retrieval, 190
    in precision *vs.* recall, 41
amplitude, definition, 180
arp command, 167
assumptions, tacit, 208
astrology, 111–12
asymmetric cryptography, 77, 82–84
authentication of access, 66
authentication of messages, 83
averages, misuse of, 208
Aztec abacus, 106

**B**
backups, 63–66
baseball statistics, 96–101
Bateson, 4

batting averages, 97–98
Beckett, Samuel, 3
bees and Fibonacci sequence, 124
Bellovin, Steven, 71
Berra, Yogi, 97
Bertrand postulate, 141
betting strategies
    lottery, 128–31
    poker, 131–33
Bible
    and Gematria, 199–200
    hidden messages in, 90
    pi in measurements, 143
bibliometrics, 92–96
binary system, 14–18
binary tree model of organization, 26–27
birthday paradox, 212–13
bits, 157
Boolean logic, 42–47
boot sector viruses, 69
Borge, Victor, 7, 20–21, 192
boundaries
    and fuzzy sets, 51
    of systems, 1–2
box bets, 128
Bradford's Law, 95–96
bridges, network, 61
bubble sort, 34–35, 36
Buckley, Lord, 8
budget for system design, 153
bus topology, 57–58
bytes
    definition, 157
    names for, 158

**C**
cable television as privilege, 173
Caesar substitution cipher, 78

Calegari (musician), 188
calendar
    Chinese, 203
    and Friday the 13th, 125–26
    missing day mystery, 210–11
Cantor, Georg, 8
case sensitivity in UNIX, 28
casting out nines method, 108–9
CENDI, 102
checkers, 116–17
chess, 112–16
Chinese abacus, 106
Chinese numerology, 202–3
chisenbop, 110–11
ciphers, 77, 78
circles and pi, 142
citation analysis, 93–94
Clarke, Arthur C., 127
class addressing scheme, 165–67
classless addressing scheme, 167–68
Classless Interdomain Routing (CIDR), 167–68
client-server model of computer networks, 160–61
clock paradox, 210
"cloned images," 151
Cocks, Clifford, 87
codes, 77
collection development and Bradford's Law, 95–96
complement of a set, 53
computer networks, models of, 160–61
computers
    and binary numbers, 17–18
    as information system, 157–62
conflict among users, 152, 154
consonance, 181
conversion of one base to another
    decimal to binary, 15–17
    Russian peasant algorithm, 109–10
cooling of computer components, 160
costs
    e-mail, 176
    information management, 155
counterintuitive information, 207–18
    counterintuitive situations, 210–14
    information both true and false, 208
    mean *vs.* median, 208
    opposite of false may not be true, 207
counting, 105–37, 215–16
counting boards, 105–7
counting methods
    casting out nines, 108–9
    chisenbop, 110–11
    Russian peasant algorithm, 109–10

crossing a room, impossibility of, 209
cryptograms, 10–11
cryptography, 76–91

D
da Vinci, Leonardo, 125
data compression, 158–60
Data Encryption Standard (DES), 81
data storage and binary numbers, 15
data *vs.* information, 2
decimal system, 12–14, 15–17
decryption methods, 78–79
Descartes, René, 141
Dewey Decimal System, 50
differential backups, 64–65
Diffie, Whitfield, 85, 86–87
digital divide, 173–74
digital signatures, 83
disaster planning, 62, 63–64
discrete logarithms, 84–86
dissonance, 181
distance and relevance, 49–50
distortion of information, 7–11
division by zero, 208–9, 217
documentation, 63
Doyle, Arthur Conan, 77
Durocher, Leo, 97
dynamic addressing, 166
Dynamic Host Control Protocol (DHCP), 166

E
effectiveness of retrieval, 41–42
eggs as hidden messages, 89
Egyptian fractions, 22
Einstein, Albert, 97, 218
Ellis, James, 86, 87
e-mail, cost of, 176
e-mail bombs, 70
encoding of information, 76–91
envy of system design, 154
equal-tempered tuning, 183–84
equidistant letter sequences as code, 89–90
Eratosthenes' sieve, 139
exabyte, definition, 158
exchange (bubble) sort, 34–35, 36

F
feedback in system design, 153
Feistel, Horst, 81
Fermat, Pierre de, 139, 141
Fermi, Enrico, 106
Fibonacci sequence, 122–25

file infector viruses, 69
finger-based math, 110–11
fingers
    counting paradox, 211
    and Fibonacci sequence, 124
fire protection, 62
first-in-first-out (FIFO) and first-in-last-out
    (FILO) ordering, 25
Fourier, Joseph, 180
fractal image compression, 159
French drop illusion, 73–74
frequency, definition, 180
frequency analysis decryption, 78–79
Friday the 13th, 125–26
full backups, 64
function, definition, 215
fuzzy information retrieval, 2, 50–54
fuzzy set theory (FST), 50–51

**G**
Galileo, 51
galley (counting method), 110
gateway, 61
gelosia, 110
Gematria, 143, 197–202
General Communications Headquarters (GCHQ),
    86–87
Germain primes, 142
ghoti, 10
gigabyte, definition, 158
Goldbach conjecture, 139
golden ratio
    and Fibonacci series, 123, 124–25
    meantone tuning, 183
grains on a chessboard
    legend of, 113
    and Tower of Hanoi, 127
graphics files, compression of, 159
groups of operations. *See* Precedence of
    operations
Gunter, Edmund, 106

**H**
happiness/sandwich paradox, 208
harmonics, 180
Hat Sort, 35
heads, shaved, as hidden message, 89
heat of computer components, 160
Hebrew Gematria, 197–202
Hellman, Martin, 85, 86–87
hexadecimal systems, 18–20
hidden messages, 89–90

hierarchy model of organization, 27–28
Hogwarts sort, 35
homonyms and change of meaning, 44–45
hubs, 59
Huffman encoding, 159
humor
    and information distortion, 9–11
    of numbers, 20–21
hypertext model of organization, 30–31

**I**
idioms, 8
illegal primes, 142
incipits in music, 194
incremental backups, 65
indexing files, 54–56
infinite sets, 51
infinity, 214–18
    definitions, 214–15
    history, 214
    levels of, 216–17
    Zeno's paradox, 210
information
    counting of, 105–37
    definitions, 3–7
    distortion of, 151–52
    encoding of, 76–91
    management of, 150–56
    measurement of, 92–104
    networking of, 57–61
    organization of, 25–38
    representations of, 12–24
    security of, 62–75
information overload, 9
information systems, characteristics of,
    150–56
infrastructure in system design, 153, 155
insertion sort, 34
intellectual property and music, 193
interesting numbers, 211–12
Internet
    as information system, 163–78
    models for, 176–77
    size of, 157
Internet access, right of, 172–74
Internet Metaphor Project, 168–72
Internet Protocol (IP) addresses,
    163–65
intersections in fuzzy set theory, 52
interval (music), 180
inverted files, 54–56
invisible ink, 89

ipconfig command, 167
irrational numbers
    and decimal numbers, 13
    phi, 124, 125
    pi, 142–47
    square root of two, 8, 220–21

**J**

Japanese abacus, 106
Jones, William, 144
Jordan curve, 2
journals, bibliometrics of, 95–96
just tuning, 182–83

**K**

Kaleidacousticon, 188
keys to codes, 77, 79–80
keywords
    and Boolean searching, 46
    in music classification, 190
    and vector-based retrieval, 48
al-Khwarizmi, 143
kilobyte, definition, 158
Korean finger-based math, 110–11
Kronecker, Leo, 138
*Kung Fu: The Legend Continues,* 89

**L**

lattice grating, 110
Le Corbusier, 125
least-effort principle, 95
Lehrer, Tom, 13
Lempel-Ziv compression scheme, 159
librarians with servers, 219
Library Bill of Rights, 172
Lindemann, Ferdinand von, 144
linear model of organization, 25–26
links in hypertext searching, 30–31
locks, security of, 62
logarithms, discrete, 84–86
logarithms and slide rules, 106
logic bombs, 70
logs, analysis of, 101
loops in computer code, 71–72
lossless and lossy data compression, 158
lost items paradox, 212
Lotka's Law, 93–94
lotteries, 127–31
Lucas numbers, 124
lucky numbers, 127–31
Lukasiewicz, Jan, 23

**M**

macro viruses, 69
"malware," 70
mapping, definition, 215
Marx, Groucho, 9–10
matching methods for retrieval, 39–41
Mayan calendar and Gematria, 200–201
mean *vs.* median in counterintuitive statements,
    208
meaning in information, 5–6
meantone systems, 183
measurement of information, 92–104, 150
megabyte, definition, 158
melodies, retrieval of, 195
melody machines, 186–88
Mendeleyev, Dmitry, 5
Merkle, Ralph, 85, 86–87
Mersenne primes, 141
mesh topology, 59
message digest value, 83
metaphors
    distortion by, 8
    for Internet, 168–72
microdots as hidden messages, 89
misdirection in computer attacks, 73–75
missing day mystery, 210–11
Möbius strips, 2
modems and data compression, 159–60
modulo functions, 84
Mondrian, Piet, 125
monoalphabetic substitution codes, 78
moving arrow paradox, 210
Mozart melody machine, 187–88
multipartite viruses, 69
multitasking, 160–61
multithreading computer processes, 160
music, 179–96
    databases, 190
    and numerology, 202
    physics of, 179–81
    queries in, 191–92
    as sets of notes, 44
music information retrieval (MIR), 188–95
music notation, machine-readable, 192–93

**N**

Native American music, 193
Navajo code talkers, 87–88
netstat command, 167
networking of information
    security of, 66
    technical aspects, 57–61

New Jersey Nightline, 6
nines, casting out, 108–9
noise in signals, 4
nonadaptive systems, 1
null set, 42
numbers, types of, 138–49
numerology
    Chinese, 202–3
    Hebrew, 197–202
    music, 202

**O**

octave, 180
office supplies, costs of, 155
one-time pad encryption, 80
one-way functions, 84–86
only-but-not-all, all-but-not-only problem. *See*
    All-and-only problem
operations, precedence of. *See* Precedence of
    operations
order of words in query, 46
ordering, definition, 33
organizational structures, 152
Oughtred, William, 106

**P**

paper folding paradox, 212
partition exchange sort (quicksort), 35, 36
Pascal's triangle, 147–49
password grabbers, 70
passwords
    security of, 66–68
    selection of, 68, 70
patronymics, 120
pattern recognition in music retrieval, 193
peer-to-peer model of computer networks, 161
Penn and Teller, 73
Penniman, W. David, 3
periodic table of elements, 5
petabyte, definition, 158
phi (golden ratio), 124, 125
pi, 13, 142–47
    in Bible, 143
    history of, 143–44
    messages in, 146–47
    mnemonics for, 144–45
    politics of, 145–46
Pick-3, Pick-4, or Pick-6 lottery, 128–31
ping command, 167
pitch (music), 180
pitching (baseball), 98
plants and Fibonacci sequence, 124

Poe, Edgar Allan, 77, 79
poker, 131–33
Polish notation, 23
polyalphabetic substitution codes, 78
postfix representation, 22–23
precedence of operations
    arithmetical, 22–23
    Boolean, 45
precision and recall, 41–42
prefix representation, 22–23
prime numbers
    characteristics of, 138–42
    in encryption, 84
    and music, 183
private/public key cryptography. *See* Asymmetric
    cryptography
privileges and rights, 172–74
probabilistic queries in music, 191–92
problem solving *vs.* matching, 39–41
productivity of authors, 94
productivity of journals, 95–96
progress reports in system design, 153
project management, need for, 154–55
pronunciation rules, 10
proper subsets, 42–43
prototypes, 152–53
proximity in searching
    and Boolean logic, 46
    in vector-based retrieval, 48–49
pseudo-raise paradox, 211
Ptolemy, 143
public library as information access model,
    174–75
punctuation and change of meaning, 6–7,
    44–45
puns (plays on words), 9–10
purpose of information systems, 150–51
Pythagorean tuning, 181–82

**Q**

Quadrille Melodist, 188
quantum cryptography, 88–89
qubit-based encryption methods, 88–89
quicksort, 35, 36
quilts as hidden messages, 89
quota system, 72–73

**R**

rabbits, counting of, 122–23
"Rain Doll" (Rijndael) standard, 81
random access model of organization, 31–33
random number generation, 80–81

rational numbers, 8
recall and precision, 41–42
red car paradox, 212
relational model of organization, 28–29
relevance
    and distance, 49–50
    in music retrieval, 190
    scoring of, 48–49
retrieval of information, 39–56
    Boolean, 42–47
    fuzzy set theory, 50–54
    goal of, 41
    matching *vs.* problem solving, 39–41
    recall *vs.* precision, 41–42
    and sorted information, 33
    vector methods, 47–50
reverse Polish notation (RPN), 23
Rhind papyrus, 143
"Rhine Doll" (Rijndael) standard, 81
rights and privileges, 172–74
Rijndael standard, 81
ring topology, 58–59
risks of system management, 156
Rivest, Ron, 85, 86–87
Roman abacus, 106
Roman fractions, 21–22
Rot-13 cipher, 78
router, network, 61
RSA method of encryption, 86–87
Ruben, Brent, 5
run-length encoding (RLE), 159
Russian abacus, 106
Russian peasant algorithm, 109–10

**S**
sabermetrics, 96–101
sabotage, 156
sandwich/happiness paradox, 208
Sargon of Assyria, 197
scale (music), 180–81, 184–85
Schickele, Peter, 192
Schninzel conjecture, 139
scores, musical, 192
scoring of search results, 48–49
searching using Boolean operators, 46–47
security, 62–75
    backup, 63–66
    of computer systems, 160
    costs of, 155
    data, 63
    of passwords, 67–68
    physical security, 62

    of private/public key cryptography, 83–84
    server, 63
selection sort, 35, 36
sequencing, 33
servers, security of, 63
sets
    in Boolean logic, 42–43
    definition, 215
    fuzzy sets, 51
Seurat, Georges, 125
Shamir, Adi, 85, 86–87
Shannon, Claude, 3–4, 7
Shannon count of chess games, 114–15
Shaw, George Bernard, 10
short-circuit evaluation, 44
shoulder surfing, 70
signal-to-noise ratio, 118
single-key encryption. *See* Symmetric
    cryptography
slide rules, 107–8
slugging average, 98
social courtesies and computer attacks, 70
social engineering and misdirection, 73–75
software support, 151
sorting algorithms, 33–36
spreadsheets as relational model, 29
staff for information systems, 150–51, 155
Stallings, William, 5
star topology, 59
star-bus hybrid topology, 60
star-ring hybrid topology, 60
static addressing, 166
steganography, 89–90
Stern, Isaac, 192
Stewart count of chess games, 115–16
Stifel, Michael, 142
"stop" words
    in inverted files, 54
    in Zipf's law, 94
stopped clock paradox, 210
storage systems
    linear models, 26
    media of, 65
    random access, 31–33
    and sorted information, 34
    tables (in relational models), 29
straight bets, 128
structure in information, 5–6
style, musical, 194
subnets, 168
substitution cipher, 78
supernets, 168

surnames, counting of, 120–22
switch, network, 61
symmetric cryptography, 77, 81
system, definition, 1–2
system analysis, 153
system design
    approaches, 151–52
    pitfalls, 154–55
    process of, 152–53

**T**
table in relational model, 28–29
Talking Stick token, 58
Talmud as hypertext, 30
TCP/IP (Transmission Control Protocol/Internet
    Protocol), 163–65
telephone service as right, 173
templates in information support, 151
terabyte, definition, 158
testing of systems, 153
theft of information, 156. *See also* Security
themes, musical, 194–95
thumbnails, music, 194
token ring topology, 58–59
topologies, network, 57–61
Tower of Hanoi, 126–27
traceroute command, 167
transfinite arithmetic, 217
translation, distortion by, 8
transposition ciphers, 78–79
trapdoor schemes, 85
Trojan horse programs, 69
Tsu Chung Chi, 143
tuning (music), 181–84
twelve-tone scale, 184–86
two, square root of, 8, 220–21
two-key cryptography. *See* Asymmetric
    cryptography

**U**
unions in fuzzy set theory, 52
UNIX operating system
    grep command, 46
    hierarchy model, 27–28
    security in, 160
upgrades to computers, 63

U.S. Electoral College, 118–20
U.S. presidential elections in years ending in
    zero, 205–6
user needs, 152

**V**
validity of measures
    baseball, 97
    citation analysis, 92–93
vector-based retrieval methods, 47–50
vendors, costs of, 155
Verne, Jules, 77
viruses, computer, 69
votes, counting of, 118–20

**W**
wavelength, definition, 180
Weaver, Warren, 3–4, 7
web metrics, 101–2
whitespace compression, 158
"Who's on First?" routine, 10, 222–27
Williams, Ted, 97
Williamson, Malcolm, 87
Wilson, Woodrow, 213
words, counting of, 117–18
World Wide Web
    and 666, 204
    and citation analysis, 93
    as hypertext, 30–31
    measures of, 101–2
worms, computer, 69

**X**
XML as music retrieval language,
    192–93

**Y**
Yanghui triangle. *See* Pascal's triangle
yottabyte, definition, 158

**Z**
Zeno, paradoxes of, 209–10
zero, division by, 208–9, 217
Zero factor in U.S. elections, 205–6
zettabyte, definition, 158
Zipf's Law, 94–95